OLDER AMERICANS ACT OF 1965

As Amended In 2006 (Public Law 109-365)

ISBN: 978-1987462142

Congress passed the Older Americans Act (OAA) in 1965 in response to concern by policymakers about a lack of community social services for older persons. The original legislation established authority for grants to States for community planning and social services, research and development projects, and personnel training in the field of aging. The law also established the Administration on Aging (AoA) to administer the newly created grant programs and to serve as the Federal focal point on matters concerning older persons.

Although older individuals may receive services under many other Federal programs, today the OAA is considered to be the major vehicle for the organization and delivery of social and nutrition services to this group and their caregivers. It authorizes a wide array of service programs through a national network of 56 State agencies on aging, 629 area agencies on aging, nearly 20,000 service providers, 244 Tribal organizations, and 2 Native Hawaiian organizations representing 400 Tribes. The OAA also includes community service employment for low-income older Americans; training, research, and demonstration activities in the field of aging; and vulnerable elder rights protection activities. This book offers an unofficial compilation of the OAA, an outline of changes made to the OAA at the most recent reauthorization (2006), a set of frequently asked questions (FAQs) about the OAA and other related sources of information/data.

This book is intended to serve as a resource for professionals working in aging services.

OLDER AMERICANS ACT OF 1965

As Amended In 2006 (Public Law 109-365)

Table of Contents

Frequently Asked Questions (FAQs)

Below is a list of frequently asked questions (FAQs) to assist the Aging Network with implementation of the 2006 Amendments to the Older Americans Act (OAA). Periodically, AoA will add new FAQs that are of general interest to the Network. We invite users to submit questions and comments regarding the Amendments that may be used in the development of future FAQs for this page.

Please note: questions/comments that are specific to an individual participant, provider, Area Agency on Aging (AAA) or State Agency on Aging will be referred to the appropriate agency for action.

- Aging and Disability Resource Centers (ADRCs)

- Civic Engagement

- Elder Justice

- Evidence-Based Health Promotion Disease Prevention Programs

- Mental health

- National Family Caregiver Support Program (NFCSP)

- Nutrition

- Payer of Last Resort

- Private Pay

- Religious Activities

- Self Directed Care

- State Plans

- Targeting

- Transportation

Aging and Disability Resource Centers (ADRCs)

The 2006 Reauthorization provides the Assistant Secretary for Aging the authority to "implement in all States Aging and Disability Resource Centers." In what ways can States begin planning and directing resources for this implementation?

The Administration on Aging continues to seek and direct resources to assist States in the development and expansion of ADRCs. In addition, many States have creatively used other Federal resources to advance ADRCs. For example, some States have utilized CMS REAL CHOICE SYSTEM CHANGE grants, including the Systems Transformation Grants, to support their efforts to create single points of entry. Many ADRC grantee States are seeking increased Federal Financial Participation (FFP) through Medicaid to support their ADRC efforts.

ADRC grantees are also utilizing State and other funding support, for example:

- Six States have passed ADRC/single point of entry legislation

- Seventeen States have received State funding to support ADRC pilot sites

- Twenty-four ADRC grantee States report pursuing, or have already received, private grants
  to support their efforts at the State or local level.

Civic Engagement

Programs administered by the Corporation for National Community Service (CNCS), e.g., Legacy Corps, now permit applicants to use other sources of Federal funding as match. Does this mean that OAA funds can be used as match?

To maximize flexibility of funding and to enhance services to older adults, Older Americans Act grantees have the option to use III E funds to meet the match requirements for certain programs administered by the National Community Service (CNCS). With this option, the Aging Network is afforded additional opportunities to better meet local home and community service and caregiver needs, and to further the goals of providing volunteer (Civic Engagement) opportunities to older adults and their caregivers.

It is imperative to note that 45 CFR Parts 74.23(a) and 92.24(b) do not allow OAA grantees to use any Federal funds (including CNCS funds) to meet the OAA non-Federal share (match) of project expenditures. It is also important to note that any proposed use of OAA funds (including funds that would be used as match for CNCS programs) must be consistent with the terms and conditions of the grant/contract award, including all applicable Older Americans Act provisions and uniform grant administration rules (45 CFR Parts 74 and 92).

A local provider may only use such funds for allowable services under Title III E, and such services must be part of the overall comprehensive system of services in the planning and service area. (Sec. 303(c)(2)). State and area agencies on aging remain fully responsible for administration and oversight of OAA funds, notwithstanding CNCS's acceptance of any OAA funds under a grant/contract as cost sharing or matching.

For clarity, the following conditions must be met if OAA funds are to be used to match CNCS funds:

- All specific terms and conditions of the OAA grant;
- The intent of the OAA;
- All applicable Federal, State and local legislation; and

The Federal agency (CNCS) has the statutory provisions necessary to allow its grantees to count other federal funds as matching contributions for their CNCS project costs.

Elder Justice

What new opportunities exist for States and Tribal organizations in the new Elder Justice provisions and how can elder justice provisions integrate with the AoA's other long-term care reforms?

New language in Title II and Title VII emphasize multi-disciplinary and collaborative approaches to addressing elder maltreatment when developing programs and long-term strategic plans for elder justice activities. AoA has funded the National Center on Elder Abuse (NCEA) to examine issues, current practices, and future directions for the enhanced coordination between elder rights and ADRC systems. In FY 2008, the NCEA will study successful collaboration between home and community-based service providers, Adult Protective Services, and Long-Term Care Ombudsman to ensure the safety and well-being of vulnerable seniors as they are diverted or transitioned from institutional settings to community based care.

States and Tribes will have the opportunity to work with AoA in developing a long-term plan to facilitate the development, implementation, and continuous improvement of a coordinated, multi-disciplinary elder justice system in the United States. New language in Title VII expands the options for States and tribal organizations to use some portion of the Title VII allotments for detection, assessment, intervention in, investigation of and response to elder abuse, neglect, and exploitation.

AoA's elder abuse prevention program is exploring best practice examples of ADRCs incorporating crisis management and risk identification and successful collaborations between elder rights providers and ADRCs. Similarly, the National Long-Term Care Ombudsman Resource Center is providing training and technical assistance to long-term care ombudsmen in diversion and transition activities including coordination with ADRC's. Additional coordination efforts include the statewide SMP Programs (formerly Senior Medicare Patrol), the National Resource and Education Center on Women and Retirement Planning , and the National Legal Resource Centers Model Approaches to Statewide Legal Assistance, and Pension Counseling.

Evidence-Based Health Promotion Disease Prevention Programs

What new opportunities does the 2006 Reauthorization offer the Aging Services Network for developing or enhancing evidence-based health promotion/disease prevention strategies?

Evidence-based disease prevention is the utilization of clinically tested and proven tools and behavioral changes to manage an individual's health and disease. Evidence-based prevention programs take place at the community level to help participants avoid hospitalizations and unnecessary physician visits.

Evidence Based Programming, regardless of funding source, is central to empowering older adults to take responsibility for their health by making informed health choices and adopting healthful behaviors. It is important to modernize programs by using the best available science and evidence and leveraging funding and expertise through community resources.

The 2006 Amendments reaffirm AoA's commitment to ensuring that all older Americans have access to programs and services that help reduce the impact of disease and chronic disabilities and encourage the promotion of preventive measures to eliminate or reduce the occurrence of new diseases and disabilities. Under Titles III and IV, States continue to have the option to design programs to advance chronic disease self-care practices, increase physical activity, prevent falls, promote proper nutrition and diet, and address depression and/or substance abuse in older persons.

Mental health

Mental health is referenced numerous times throughout the 2006 amendments to the Older Americans Act. What are these new provisions and how will they enable the Aging Services Network to more fully meet the needs of older Americans?

For the first time, the Administration on Aging and the Aging Services Network are directed to apply a greater focus on the prevention and treatment of mental disorders. To effectively carry out the new mental health references in the Act, AoA will develop objectives, priorities and a long-term plan for supporting State and local efforts pertaining to education, prevention, detection and treatment of mental disorders, including age-related dementia, depression, and Alzheimer's disease and related neurological disorders with neurological and organic brain dysfunction.

Although the 2006 Amendments include no specific requirements for States regarding the new Title II mental health provisions, there are significant opportunities for States to:

- Ensure that mental health programs and services are aware of the role ADRCs play in connecting consumers with resources to meet their needs.

- Explore the availability of evidence-based mental health programs and incorporating them where practicable.

- Strengthen partnerships between mental health programs and services and the Aging Services Network at the State and AAA/community levels.

National Family Caregiver Support Program (NFCSP)

How does the Modernization of the Older Americans Act benefit family caregivers?

AoA, in partnership with CMS, designed the Aging and Disability Resource Centers (ADRCs), now operational in 43 States and territories, to provide consumers and caregivers information on home and community-based long-term care services. ADRCs provide consumers information, options counseling, referral, assessment, educational and assistance in planning for future needs. AoA is emphasizing the importance of integration of proven evidence-based health promotion interventions, which can lessen disability related to chronic illnesses, prevent falls, and reduce the burden experienced by family caregivers of individuals who are older and/or disabled.

For individuals with a high-risk for nursing home placement, funds can be used by States to target these low and moderate income individuals and their caregivers who may be better served through home and community-based services. Through a variety of consumer-directed options, such consumers may select their own providers and direct how their services will be delivered.

What eligibility changes were made to the National Family Caregiver Support Program as a result of the Reauthorization of the Older Americans Act in 2006?

The eligibility changes in the NFCSP are:

- Family caregivers of a person with Alzheimer's disease or a related dementia may be served regardless of the age of the person with dementia.

- Grandparents and other relative caregivers providing care to children (under age 18 years) may receive services at 55 years of age and older;

- Grandparent or relative caregivers, providing care for adult children with a disability, who are between 19 and 59 years of age, can now be served under the NFCSP as follows:

  o Caregivers must be age 55 years and older;

  o Priority is given to caregivers providing care for an adult child with severe disabilities; and

  o Services provided to these caregivers are not counted against the 10% ceiling for grandparents and other caregivers providing care to children under the age of 18 years.

Can older caregivers providing care to their own adult children with disabilities be served in the NFCSP?

Older caregivers providing care to their adult children with disabilities can be served in the NFCSP if the adult children are 60 years of age and older.

How should the term "related disorders with neurological or organic brain dysfunction" be defined in the "family caregiver" definition?

Absent a comprehensive definition of "related disorders with neurological or organic brain dysfunction" States may identify such disorders based on their local experience, expertise and need.

Are funds under the National Family Caregiver Support Program "earmarked" or targeted for specific services, e.g. respite?

Funds under the National Family Caregiver Support Program (NFCSP) are not earmarked or targeted for any specific service. States have the flexibility to determine the funding allocated to provide the five categories of services authorized: 1) information about services; 2) assistance with access to services; 3) individual counseling, organization of support groups, and caregiver training; 4) respite care; and 5) supplemental services, on a limited basis.

The OAA calls for States to implement a comprehensive caregiver program which includes the five services outlined, however; a State may address one or more of the service categories with other sources of funding.

Are direct payments to family caregivers to purchase services allowed in the National Family Caregiver Support Program?

Direct payments to family caregivers are neither specifically included in, nor precluded by, the Older Americans Act. As such, direct payments to family caregivers may be possible to purchase services if so defined by the state.

Are grandchildren cared for by grandparents, required to have a disability or chronic illness (including those with mental retardation and developmental disabilities) in order to receive services?

There is no requirement that the grandchildren have a disability. Under the NFCSP, states may design services for grandparents or older individuals who are relative caregivers. In these instances, the grandparent or relative caregiver must be an older individual (55+), who lives with the child, is the primary caregiver of the child, and has a legal relationship to the child or is raising the child informally. The child must be no more than 18 years old.

Note: The 2006 amendments to the Older Americans Act included an eligibility change which allows services to be provided to grandparents and other relative caregivers (55+) who are primary caregivers of an adult between the ages of 18 to 59 years with a disability. Biological or adoptive parents were not included in this change.

Can respite and supplemental services be provided to grandparents and relative caregivers?

States have the option of using some portion of NFCSP funds (within the 10% statutory cap) to provide respite and supplemental services to grandparents and relative caregivers.

To allow grandparents a break from their daily caregiving responsibilities, funds under respite could be provided to pay expenses such as after school programs, summer/day camps, weekend programs and individual in-home respite. Supplemental funds could be provided to pay for expenses such as school supplies, legal issues associated with custody/adoption and other needs determined at the local level.

Nutrition

What nutrition quality standards have changed under the Older Americans Act?
Section 339 of the OAA indicates that a State which establishes and operates a nutrition project shall ensure that meals:

- Meet the most recent **Dietary Guidelines for Americans**, published by the Secretaries of Health and Human Services and Agriculture;

- Provide to each participating individual a minimum of one-third of the **Dietary Reference Intakes**, established by the Food and Nutrition Board of the Institute of Medicine of the National Academy of Sciences, if one meal is served, two-thirds if two meals are served, and 100 percent if 3 meals are served; and

- Comply with applicable provisions of State and local food service laws.

The OAA nutrition quality standards provide the scientific basis for State agencies on Aging (SUAs), Indian Tribal Organizations (ITOs), area agencies on aging (AAAs), and local nutrition service providers to serve meals and provide nutrition services to keep older adults healthy, reduce their risk of chronic disease and disability and help them manage chronic diseases and conditions.

The OAA places responsibility for implementing the DIETARY GUIDELINES FOR AMERICANS and the DIETARY REFERENCE INTAKES on the SUAs and ITOs with input from AAAs and/or local nutrition service providers. AoA fosters flexibility and innovation to meal program operators in meeting these requirements and discourages strictly regulatory compliance approaches.

The changes in the reauthorization provide the foundation to allow programs to modernize by using the most current available science and evidence to help keep older adults healthy and in the community through access to healthy meals, provision of healthy choices, opportunities to maintain healthy lifestyle behaviors, and referrals to other appropriate programs and resources.

What does "Sense of Congress" regarding vitamin and mineral supplements mean?
Congress recognizes a role for vitamin and mineral supplements to fill a gap in nutrient intake that may not be met by food. The "Sense of Congress" provision encourages additional local flexibility by allowing the appropriate and safe distribution of vitamin-mineral supplements to individuals in need of such supplements.

Can local nutrition service providers use OAA funds to pay for vitamin and mineral supplements?

Sections 331, 336, and 339 list nutrition services funded by the OAA and do not list the provision of vitamin-mineral supplements as a fundable OAA service.

Does each meal provided through the nutrition program have to offer every older adult the nutrition requirements contained in the Older Americans Act (Sec. 331, 336 and 339)?

The OAA requires that meals meet the nutrient and food requirements found in the Dietary Reference Intakes and the DIETARY GUIDELINES FOR AMERICANS. An older adult may be offered a particular food, but that individual may refuse the food and it does not need to be served.

Does the OAA provide options for self-directed nutrition choices?

The OAA definition of "self-directed care" (Sec. 102(46) indicates that SUAs, AAAs and ITOs have the opportunity to expand decision-making roles of consumers in the type, amount, management, and budgeting of home and community based services they receive. For an individual able to actively participate in informed decision making and able to make appropriate choices, these services may include congregate and home delivered meals.

Individuals choosing self-directed nutrition services may benefit from nutrition education and nutrition counseling. This counseling may include an appropriate nutrition care plan, instruction on appropriate food choices based on needs, and other mechanisms such as vouchers.

One example of enhanced nutrition choice is offering a soup and salad bar or soup and sandwich bar as an alternative to a hot meal. The Older Americans Act (OAA) does not prescribe and therefore offers considerable flexibility in menu format, meal pattern and method of service.

Each State will determine whether to include self-directed care options in the nutrition service, as well as how the service is to be implemented and requirements of the OAA are met.

A number of factors are increasing the cost of meals. Are there ways to work within the Dietary Reference Intakes (DRIs) and the DIETARY GUIDELINES FOR AMERICANS (DGAS) and meet these challenges?

The DGAS can be implemented by following two different meal patterns (the United State Department of Agriculture's Food Guide or My Pyramid, and the Dietary Approaches to Stop Hypertension or DASH diet) and suggested caloric levels which determine portion sizes to best meet the needs of older adults being served.

Implementation of the DRIs and DGAs do not require the production of high cost meals, however; the translation of these requirements into low-cost meals is a technical skill that may require the expertise of a registered dietician or individual with comparable education and training.

Recommendations for implementation including flexibility recommendations are found in the DIETARY GUIDELINES FOR AMERICANS2005 Nutrition Service Providers Guide found at http://nutritionandaging.fiu.edu/DRI_and_DGs/dg_resources.asp.

Payer of Last Resort

If services are being provided to an older adult under the Older Americans Act, should the OAA continue providing payment for services if the person is later determined eligible for the same services under a Medicaid waiver?

Title III of the Older Americans Act (OAA) does not create a legal requirement to finance services for any individual. Individuals age 60 and over may receive benefits under the OAA but no individual is entitled to them. An individual who is eligible for Medicaid benefits programs may also receive services under the OAA; however, the State may not require that OAA programs fund benefits that can be funded by Medicaid. Although individuals may not be entitled to specific services under the OAA, Medicaid-eligible individuals may receive such services.

Private Pay

Can the Aging Network implement private pay services?

Private pay services can create opportunities to reach a segment of the population not traditionally served by the network, however; such activities are optional for States, Area Agencies and service providers. In general, private payment for services occurs when individuals pay the full cost of the services they receive. Because there is no public funding involved, private pay services are not subject to the 'cost sharing' provisions under the Older Americans Act (OAA, Sec. 315(a)).

Note: Private pay services to individuals and caregivers are also distinct from establishing "Private Pay Relationships" with profit-making organizations and are therefore not subject to Sec. 212(a) of the OAA.

Religious Activities

Is prayer allowed at Title III funded congregate meal sites?

The Older Americans Act does not forbid older adults from praying before a meal at a senior center or some other location that provides a meal with funding from the OAA. The AoA recommends that each nutrition program adopt a policy that ensures that each individual participant has a free choice whether to pray either silently or audibly, and that the prayer is not officially sponsored, led or organized by persons administering the Nutrition Program or the meal site.

Are bible studies and other religious activities allowed at Title III funded program sites?

Title III funded programs may not use OAA funds (or local matching funds) to support inherently religious activities, such as worship, religious instruction, or proselytization. If the organization engages in such activities, it must offer them separately, in time or location, from the programs or services funded with OAA funds, and participation must be voluntary.

This restriction does not mean that an organization that sponsors the Title III program (i.e., the contractor or grantee) may not engage in inherently religious activities, but only that the organization may not use OAA funds for such purposes.

Self-Directed Care

To what extent does the OAA now encourage the Aging Services Network to implement self-directed care options in all service categories?

State agencies on aging, area agencies on aging, and Tribes have the opportunity to expand the decision-making roles of consumers in the type, amount, management and budgeting of the home and community-based services they receive. Through effective and efficient models, including cash and counseling vouchers, expanded service choices, etc., AoA encourages the implementation of self-directed care provisions through OAA services whenever possible, however; each State will determine which services include such provisions and how they will be implemented .

Can Title III service funds be used to provide fiscal management services (FMS) related to nursing home diversion and other home and community based programs designed to maintain older adults in the community?

Financial Management Services (FMS) are an essential element of self-directed care programs. FMS supports self-directed programs by assisting individuals with enrolment, payroll and employment tax issues, and by performing fiscal accounting and expenditure reporting to the individual and to the sponsoring program.

Title III-B and III-E funds may be used to provide FMS so long as the services supported by FMS are allowable under these two program parts, e.g., transportation, information, support groups, respite, etc., and are provided to adults age 60 years and over (III-B) and/or to caregivers (III-E). It is incumbent upon States and area agencies on aging (AAA) to assure Title III expenditures for FMS meet all Older Americans Act requirements.

State Plans

The AoA Program Instruction (AoA-PI-08-01) points out that a national aging services Planning Model is available to assist States. Is this Model required to complete the State Plan? The Plan Model states that the Plan Narrative is to be 20 pages. Is this an absolute limit?

The national aging services Planning Model was developed by the National Association of State Units on Aging (AoA Grant 90AM3032). It is available to assist States in the development of the State Plans. While strongly encouraged, its use is not required in law or regulation. This web based tool will provide the resources necessary to develop a comprehensive, yet concise, State Plan on Aging. It is a recommendation that the State Plan be 20 - 30 pages in length with the opportunity to attach data and other reports in appendices. Some states may need more narrative, but clarity and conciseness are the intended result.

Targeting

What implications do the new targeting provisions create for service delivery and long-term care modernization?

Targeting references are made throughout the Older Americans Act (OAA), as amended in 2006. The Amendments maintain all of the previous targeting groups but revise the group "LIMITED ENGLISH SPEAKING" to "LIMITED ENGLISH PROFICIENCY," and add a new group, "OLDER INDIVIDUALS AT RISK FOR INSTITUTIONAL PLACEMENT." A reference to OLDER INDIVIDUALS WITH LIMITED ENGLISH PROFICIENCY is added to all sections of the OAA where previously the phrase 'with particular attention to low-income minority older individuals and older individuals residing in rural areas" was used.

The revision and addition of these two groups assures that the Aging Network will prioritize the provision of services to those individuals in greatest need of long-term care services, and address the specific needs of such individuals in all aspects of planning, advocacy and resource development.

Does "greatest social need" as defined in the Older Americans allow communities to target funds to populations they identify as experiencing cultural, social or geographic isolation other than isolation caused by racial or ethnic status?

While the definition of "GREATEST SOCIAL NEED" in the Older Americans Act includes isolation caused by racial or ethnic status, the definition is not intended to exclude the targeting of other populations that experience cultural social or geographic isolation due to other factors. In some communities, such isolation may be caused by minority religious affiliation. In others, isolation due to sexual orientation or gender identity may restrict a person's ability to perform normal daily tasks or live independently. Each planning and service area must assess their particular environment to determine those populations best targeted based on "GREATEST SOCIAL NEED".

Transportation

Does the 2006 Reauthorization include specific opportunities to more fully coordinate transportation services?

In recognition of the importance of the role of the Aging Services Network, AoA entered into a memorandum of understanding with the Federal Transit Administration in January 2003. As a result of this collaboration, AoA has become a key partner at the federal level in promoting the coordination of transportation across programs and agencies.

The 2006 Reauthorization contains specific requirements for States and area agencies to develop and implement comprehensive and coordinated systems for home and community-based services, including transportation. These requirements afford the Aging Services Network with significant opportunities to strengthen coordination of transportation services and/or ensure its inclusion in the planning and delivery of transportation services. States and communities are encouraged to use the resources available on the National Center on Senior Transportation Website **http://seniortransportation.easterseals.com/site/PageServer?pagename=NCST2_homepage**, to assist in developing and enhancing coordinated transportation services.

Programs administered by the Federal Transit Administration (e.g., 5310, 5311, & 5317) now permit applicants to use other sources of Federal funding as match. Does this mean that OAA funds can be used as match?

To maximize flexibility of funding and to enhance services to older adults, Older Americans Act grantees have the option to use Title III B funds to meet the match requirements for programs administered by the Federal Transit Administration (FTA). With this option, the Aging Network is afforded additional opportunities to better meet local transportation needs and further the goals of United We Ride, including providing more rides for the same or fewer assets, facilitating access to services and increasing customer satisfaction.

It is imperative to note that 45 CFR Parts 74.23(a) and 92.24(b) do not allow OAA grantees to use any Federal funds (including FTA funds) to meet the OAA non-Federal share (match) of project expenditures. It is also important to note that any proposed use of OAA funds (including funds that would be used as match for FTA programs) must be consistent with the terms and conditions of the grant/contract award, including all applicable Older Americans Act provisions and uniform grant administration rules (45 CFR Parts 74 and 92).

A local transportation provider receiving Title III funds for transportation services may only use such funds for the transport of seniors (and caregivers who are escorting seniors). Such services must be part of the overall comprehensive system of services in the planning and service area. (Sec. 303(c)(2)). State and area agencies on aging remain fully responsible for administration and oversight of OAA funds, notwithstanding FTA's acceptance of any OAA funds under a grant/contract as cost sharing or matching.

For clarity, the following conditions must be met if OAA funds are to be used to match FTA funds:

- All specific terms and conditions of the OAA grant;

- The intent of the OAA;

- All applicable Federal, State and local legislation; and

- The Federal agency (FTA) has the statutory provisions necessary to allow its grantees to count non-FTA federal funds as matching contributions for their project costs.

OLDER AMERICANS ACT OF 2006

TITLE I — DECLARATION OF OBJECTIVES; DEFINITIONS

Section. 101. DECLARATION OF OBJECTIVES FOR OLDER AMERICANS

The Congress hereby finds and declares that, in keeping with the traditional American concept of the inherent dignity of the individual in our democratic society, the older people of our Nation are entitled to, and it is the joint and several duty and responsibility of the governments of the United States, of the several States and their political subdivisions, and of Indian tribes to assist our older people to secure equal opportunity to the full and free enjoyment of the following objectives

(1)   An adequate income in retirement in accordance with the American standard of living.

(2)   The best possible physical and mental health which science can make available and without regard to economic status.

(3)   Obtaining and maintaining suitable housing, independently selected, designed and located with reference to special needs and available at costs which older citizens can afford.

(4)   Full restorative services for those who require institutional care, and a comprehensive array of community-based, long-term care services adequate to appropriately sustain older people in their communities and in their homes, including support to family members and other persons providing voluntary care to older individuals needing long-term care services.

(5)   Opportunity for employment with no discriminatory personnel practices because of age.

(6)   Retirement in health, honor, dignity — after years of contribution to the economy.

(7)   Participating in and contributing to meaningful activity within the widest range of civic, cultural, educational and training and recreational opportunities.

(8)   Efficient community services, including access to low cost transportation, which provide a choice in supported living arrangements and social assistance in a coordinated manner and which are readily available when needed, with emphasis on maintaining a continuum of care for vulnerable older individuals.

(9)   Immediate benefit from proven research knowledge which can sustain and improve health and happiness.

(10)   Freedom, independence, and the free exercise of individual initiative in planning and managing their own lives, full participation in the planning and operation of community based services and programs provided for their benefit, and protection against abuse, neglect, and exploitation.

(42 U.S.C. 3001)

Section. 102. DEFINITIONS

(a) For the purposes of this Act —

    (1) The term "abuse" means the willful —

        (A) infliction of injury, unreasonable confinement, intimidation, or cruel punishment with resulting physical harm, pain, or mental anguish; or

(B) deprivation by a person, including a caregiver, of goods or services that are necessary to avoid physical harm, mental anguish, or mental illness.

(2) The term "Administration" means the Administration on Aging.

(3) The term "adult child with a disability" means a child who—
(A) is 18 years of age or older;
(B) is financially dependent on an older individual who is a parent of the child; and
(C) has a disability.

(4) The term 'Aging and Disability Resource Center' means an entity established by a State as part of the State system of long-term care, to provide a coordinated system for providing –
(A) comprehensive information on the full range of available public and private long-term care programs, options, service providers, and resources within a community, including information on the availability of integrated long-term care;
(B) personal counseling to assist individuals in assessing their existing or anticipated long-term care needs, and developing and implementing a plan for long-term care designed to meet their specific needs and circumstances; and
(C) consumers access to the range of publicly-supported long-term care programs for which consumers may be eligible, by serving as a convenient point of entry for such programs.

(5) The term "aging network" means the network of—
(A) State agencies, area agencies on aging, title VI grantees, and the Administration; and
(B) organizations that—
(I) are providers of direct services to older individuals; or
(II) are institutions of higher education; and
(III) receive funding under this Act.

(6) The term "area agency on aging" means an area agency on aging designated under section 305(a)(2)(A) or a State agency performing the functions of an area agency on aging under section 305(b)(5).

(7) The term "Assistant Secretary" means the Assistant Secretary for Aging.

(8) (A) The term 'assistive device' includes an assistive technology device.
(B) The terms 'assistive technology', "assistive technology device', and 'assistive technology service' have the meanings given such terms in section 3 of the Assistive Technology Act of 1998 (29 U.S.C. 3002).

(9) The term 'at risk for institutional placement' means, with respect to an older individual, that such individual is unable to perform at least 2 activities of daily living without substantial assistance (including verbal reminding, physical cuing, or supervision) and is determined by the State involved to be in need of placement in a long-term care facility.

(10) The term "board and care facility" means an institution regulated by a State pursuant to section 1616(e) of the Social Security Act (42 U.S.C. 1382e(e)).

(11) The term "case management service"—
(A) means a service provided to an older individual, at the direction of the older individual or a family member of the individual—
(i) by an individual who is trained or experienced in the case management skills that are required to deliver the services and coordination described in subparagraph (B); and
(ii) to assess the needs, and to arrange, coordinate, and monitor an optimum package of services to meet the needs, of the older individual; and
(B) includes services and coordination such as—

     (i)   comprehensive assessment of the older individual (including the physical, psychological, and social needs of the individual);

     (ii) development and implementation of a service plan with the older individual to mobilize the formal and informal resources and services identified in the assessment to meet the needs of the older individual, including coordination of the resources and services—

          (I)   with any other plans that exist for various formal services, such as hospital discharge plans; and

          (II) with the information and assistance services provided under this Act;

     (iii) coordination and monitoring of formal and informal service delivery, including coordination and monitoring to ensure that services specified in the plan are being provided;

     (iv) periodic reassessment and revision of the status of the older individual with—

          (I)   the older individual; or

          (II) if necessary, a primary caregiver or family member of the older individual; and

     (v)   in accordance with the wishes of the older individual, advocacy on behalf of the older individual for needed services or resources.

(12) The term 'civic engagement' means an individual or collective action designed to address a public concern or an unmet human, educational, health care, environmental, or public safety need.

(13) The term "disability" means (except when such term is used in the phrase "severe disability", "developmental disability- "physical or mental disability", "physical and mental disabilities", or "physical disabilities") a disability attributable to mental or physical impairment, or a combination of mental and physical impairments, that results in substantial functional limitations in 1 or more of the following areas of major life activity:

   (A) self-care,

   (B) receptive and expressive language,

   (C) learning,

   (D) mobility,

   (E) self-direction,

   (F) capacity for independent living,

   (G) economic self-sufficiency,

   (H) cognitive functioning, and

   (I) emotional adjustment.

(14) The term "disease prevention and health promotion services" means—

   (A) health risk assessments;

   (B) routine health screening, which may include hypertension, glaucoma, cholesterol, cancer, vision, hearing, diabetes, bone density, and nutrition screening;

   (C) nutritional counseling and educational services for individuals and their primary caregivers;

   (D) evidence-based health promotion programs, including programs related to the prevention and mitigation of the effects of chronic disease (including osteoporosis, hypertension, obesity, diabetes, and cardiovascular disease), alcohol and substance abuse reduction, smoking cessation, weight loss and control, stress management, falls prevention, physical activity and improved nutrition;

(E) programs regarding physical fitness, group exercise, and music therapy, art therapy, and dance-movement therapy, including programs for multigenerational participation that are provided by—
    (i) an institution of higher education;
    (ii) a local educational agency, as defined in section 14101 of the Elementary and Secondary Education Act of 1965 (20 U.S.C. 8801); or
    (iii) a community-based organization;
(F) home injury control services, including screening of high-risk home environments and provision of educational programs on injury prevention (including fall and fracture prevention) in the home environment;
(G) screening for the prevention of depression, coordination of community mental health services, provision of educational activities, and referral to psychiatric and psychological services;
(H) educational programs on the availability, benefits, and appropriate use of preventive health services covered under title XVIII of the Social Security Act (42 U.S.C. 1395 et seq.);
(I) medication management screening and education to prevent incorrect medication and adverse drug reactions;
(J) information concerning diagnosis, prevention, treatment, and rehabilitation concerning age-related diseases and chronic disabling conditions, including osteoporosis, cardiovascular diseases, diabetes, and Alzheimer's disease and related disorders with neurological and organic brain dysfunction;
(K) gerontological counseling; and
(L) counseling regarding social services and follow up health services based on any of the services described in subparagraphs (A) through (K). The term shall not include services for which payment may be made under titles XVIII and XIX of the Social Security Act (42 U.S.C. 1395 et seq., 1396 et seq.).

(15) The term "elder abuse" means abuse of an older individual.

(16) The term "elder abuse, neglect, and exploitation" means abuse, neglect, and exploitation, of an older individual.

(17) The term 'elder justice' –
    (A) used with respect to older individuals, collectively, means efforts to prevent, detect, treat, intervene in, and respond to elder abuse, neglect, and exploitation and to protect older individuals with diminished capacity while maximizing their autonomy; and
    (B) used with respect to an individual who is an older individual, means the recognition of the individual's rights, including the right to be free of abuse, neglect, and exploitation.

(18) (A) The term 'exploitation' means the fraudulent or otherwise illegal, unauthorized, or improper act or process of an individual, including a caregiver or fiduciary, that uses the resources of an older individual for monetary or personal benefit, profit, or gain, or that results in depriving an older individual of rightful access to, or use of, benefits, resources, belongings, or assets.

(B) In subparagraph (A), the term 'caregiver' means an individual who has the responsibility for the care of an older individual, either voluntarily, by contract, by receipt of payment for care, or as a result of the operation of law and means a family member or other individual who provides (on behalf of such individual or of a public or private agency, organization, or institution) compensated or uncompensated care to an older individual.

(19) The term "family violence" has the same meaning given the term in the Family Violence Prevention and Services Act (42 U.S.C. 10408).

(20) The term 'fiduciary'-

    (A) means a person or entity with the legal responsibility –

        (i) to make decisions on behalf of and for the benefit of another person; and

        (ii) to act in good faith and with fairness; and

    (B) includes a trustee, a guardian, a conservator, an executor, an agent under a financial power of attorney or health care power of attorney, or a representative payee.

(21) The term "focal point" means a facility established to encourage the maximum collocation and coordination of services for older individuals.

(22) The term "frail" means, with respect to an older individual in a State, that the older individual is determined to be functionally impaired because the individual —

    (A) (i) is unable to perform at least two activities of daily living without substantial human assistance, including verbal reminding, physical cueing, or supervision; or

        (ii) at the option of the State, is unable to perform at least three such activities without such assistance; or

    (B) due to a cognitive or other mental impairment, requires substantial supervision because the individual behaves in a manner that poses a serious health or safety hazard to the individual or to another individual.

(23) The term "greatest economic need" means the need resulting from an income level at or below the poverty line.

(24) The term "greatest social need" means the need caused by non-economic factors, which include—

    (A) physical and mental disabilities;

    (B) language barriers; and

    (C) cultural, social, or geographical isolation, including isolation caused by racial or ethnic status, that—

        (i) restricts the ability of an individual to perform normal daily tasks; or

        (ii) threatens the capacity of the individual to live independently.

(25) The term 'Hispanic-serving institution' has the meaning given the term in section 502 of the Higher Education Act of 1965 (20 U.S.C. 1101a).

(26) The term "Indian" means a person who is a member of an Indian tribe.

(27) Except for the purposes of title VI of this Act, the term "Indian tribe" means any tribe, band, nation, or other organized group or community of Indians (including any Alaska Native village or regional or village corporation as defined in or established pursuant to the Alaska Native Claims Settlement Act (Public Law 92–203; 85 Stat. 688) which (A) is recognized as eligible for the special programs and services provided by the United States to Indians because of their status as Indians; or (B) is located on, or in proximity to, a Federal or State reservation or rancheria.

(28) The term "information and assistance service" means a service for older individuals that—

(A) provides the individuals with current information on opportunities and services available to the individuals within their communities, including information relating to assistive technology;

(B) assesses the problems and capacities of the individuals;

(C) links the individuals to the opportunities and services that are available;

(D) to the maximum extent practicable, ensures that the individuals receive the services needed by the individuals, and are aware of the opportunities available to the individuals, by establishing adequate follow-up procedures; and

(E) serves the entire community of older individuals, particularly —
    (i)   older individuals with greatest social need;
    (ii) older individuals with greatest economic need; and
    (iii) older individuals at risk for institutional placement.

(29) The term "information and referral" includes information relating to assistive technology.

(30) The term "in-home services" includes —

(A) services of homemakers and home health aides;

(B) visiting and telephone reassurance;

(C) chore maintenance;

(D) in-home respite care for families, and adult day care as a respite service for families;

(E) minor modification of homes that is necessary to facilitate the ability of older individuals to remain at home and that is not available under another program (other than a program carried out under this Act);

(F) personal care services; and

(G) other in-home services as defined —
    (i)   by the State agency in the State plan submitted in accordance with section 307; and
    (ii) by the area agency on aging in the area plan submitted in accordance with section 306.

(31) The term "institution of higher education" has the meaning given the term in section 101 of the Higher Education Act of 1965.

(32) The term 'integrated long-term care'-

(A) means items and services that consist of –
    (i)   with respect to long-term care –
        (I)   long-term care items or services provided under a State plan for medical assistance under the Medicaid program established under Title XIX of the Social Security Act (42 U.S.C. 1396 et seq.), including nursing facility services, home and community-based services, personal care services, and case management services provided under the plan; and
        (II) any other supports, items, or services that are available under any federally funded long-term care program; and
    (ii) with respect to other health care, items and services covered under –
        (I)   the Medicare program established under title XVIII of the Social Security Act (42 U.S.C. 1395 et seq.);
        (II) the State plan for medical assistance under the Medicaid program; or
        (III) any other federally funded health care program; and

(B) includes items or services described in subparagraph (A) that are provided under a public or private managed care plan or through any other service provider.

(33) The term "legal assistance" —

(A) means legal advice and representation provided by an attorney to older individuals with economic or social needs; and

(B) includes—

  (i) to the extent feasible, counseling or other appropriate assistance by a paralegal or law student under the direct supervision of an attorney; and

  (ii) counseling or representation by a non-lawyer where permitted by law.

(34) The term 'long-term care' means any service, care, or item (including an assistive device), including a disease prevention and health promotion service, an in-home service, and a case management service –

(A) intended to assist individuals in coping with, and to the extent practicable compensate for, a functional impairment in carrying out activities of daily living;

(B) furnished at home, in a community care setting (including a small community care setting as defined in subsection (g)(1), and a large community care setting as defined in subsection (h)(1), of section 1929 of the Social Security Act (42 U.S.C. 1396t)), or in a long-term care facility; and

(C) not furnished to prevent, diagnose, treat, or cure a medical disease or condition.

(35) The term "long-term care facility" means—

(A) any skilled nursing facility, as defined in section 1819(a) of the Social Security Act (42 U.S.C. 1395i–3(a));

(B) any nursing facility, as defined in section 1919(a) of the Social Security Act (42 U.S.C. 1396r(a));

(C) for purposes of sections 307(a)(12)[1] and 712, a board and care facility; and

(D) any other adult care home, including an assisted living facility, similar to a facility or institution described in subparagraphs (A) through (C).

(36) The term "multipurpose senior center" means a community facility for the organization and provision of a broad spectrum of services, which shall include provision of health (including mental health), social, nutritional, and educational services and the provision of facilities for recreational activities for older individuals.

(37) The term "Native American" means—

(A) an Indian as defined in paragraph (5); and

(B) a Native Hawaiian, as defined in section 625.

(38) The term 'neglect' means-

(A) the failure of a caregiver (as defined in paragraph (18)(B) or fiduciary to provide the goods or services that are necessary to maintain the health or safety of an older individual; or

(B) self-neglect.

(39) The term "nonprofit" as applied to any agency, institution, or organization means an agency, institution, or organization which is, or is owned and operated by, one or more corporations or associations no part of the net earnings of which inures, or may lawfully inure, to the benefit of any private shareholder or individual.

(40) The term "older individual" means an individual who is 60 years of age or older.

(41) The term "physical harm" means bodily injury, impairment, or disease.

(42) The term "planning and service area" means an area designated by a State agency under section 305(a)(1)(E), including a single planning and service area described in section 305(b)(5)(A).

---

(43) The term "poverty line" means the official poverty line (as defined by the Office of Management and Budget, and adjusted by the Secretary in accordance with section 673(2) of the Community Services Block Grant Act (42 U.S.C. 9902(2)).

(44) The term "representative payee" means a person who is appointed by a governmental entity to receive, on behalf of an older individual who is unable to manage funds by reason of a physical or mental incapacity, any funds owed to such individual by such entity.

(45) The term "Secretary" means the Secretary of Health and Human Services, expect that for purposes of title V such term means the Secretary of Labor.

(46) The term 'self-directed care' means an approach to providing services (including programs, benefits, supports, and technology) under this Act intended to assist an individual with activities of daily living, in which –

(A) such services (including the amount, duration, scope, provider, and location of such services) are planned, budgeted, and purchased under the direction and control of such individual;

(B) such individual is provided with such information and assistance as are necessary and appropriate to enable such individual to make informed decisions about the individual's care options;

(C) the needs, capabilities, and preferences of such individual with respect to such services, and such individual's ability to direct and control the individual's receipt of such services, are assessed by the area agency on aging (or other agency designated by the area a agency on aging) involved;

(D) based on the assessment made under subparagraph (C), the area agency on aging (or other agency designated by the area agency on aging) develops together with such individual and the individual's family, caregiver (as defined in paragraph (18)(B)), or legal representative –

(i) a plan of services for such individual that specifies which services such individual will be responsible for directing;

(ii) a determination of the role of family members (and others whose participation is sought by such individual) in providing services under such plan; and

(iii) a budget for such services; and

(E) the area agency on aging or State agency provides for oversight of such individual's self-directed receipt of services, including steps to ensure the quality of services provided and the appropriate use of funds under this Act.

(47) The term 'self-neglect' means an adult's inability, due to physical or mental impairment or diminished capacity, to perform essential self-care tasks including –

(A) obtaining essential food, clothing, shelter, and medical care;

(B) obtaining goods and services necessary to maintain physical health, mental health, or general safety; or

(C) managing one's own financial affairs.

(48) The term "severe disability" means a severe, chronic disability attributable to mental or physical impairment, or a combination of mental and physical impairments, that—

(A) is likely to continue indefinitely; and

(B) results in substantial functional limitation in 3 or more of the major life activities specified in subparagraphs (A) through (G) of paragraph (8).

(49) The term "sexual assault" has the meaning given the term in section 2003 of the Omnibus Crime Control and Safe Streets Act of 1968 (42 U.S.C. 3796gg–2).

(50) The term "State" means any of the several States, the District of Columbia, the Virgin Islands of the United States, the Commonwealth of Puerto Rico, Guam, American Samoa, and the Commonwealth of the Northern Mariana Islands.

(51) The term "State agency" means the agency designated under section 305(a)(1).

(52) The term 'State system of long-term care' means the Federal, State, and local programs and activities administered by a State that provide, support, or facilitate access to long-term care for individuals in such State.

(53) The term "supportive service" means a service described in section 321(a).

(54) Except for the purposes of title VI of this Act, the term "tribal organization" means the recognized governing body of any Indian tribe, or any legally established organization of Indians which is controlled, sanctioned, or chartered by such governing body. In any case in which a contract is let or grant made to an organization to perform services benefiting more than one Indian tribe, the approval of each such Indian tribe shall be a prerequisite to the letting or making of such contract or grant.

(42 U.S.C. 3002)

TITLE II — ADMINISTRATION ON AGING

Section. 201. ESTABLISHMENT OF ADMINISTRATION ON AGING

(a) There is established in the Office of the Secretary an Administration on Aging which shall be headed by an Assistant Secretary for Aging. Except for title V, the Administration shall be the agency for carrying out this Act. There shall be a direct reporting relationship between the Assistant Secretary and the Secretary. In the performance of the functions of the Assistant Secretary, the Assistant Secretary shall be directly responsible to the Secretary. The Secretary shall not approve or require any delegation of the functions of the Assistant Secretary (including the functions of the Assistant Secretary carried out through regional offices) to any other officer not directly responsible to the Assistant Secretary.

(b) The Assistant Secretary shall be appointed by the President by and with the advice and consent of the Senate.

(c) (1) There is established in the Administration an Office for American Indian, Alaskan Native, and Native Hawaiian Programs.

    (2) The Office shall be headed by a Director of the Office for American Indian, Alaskan Native, and Native Hawaiian Aging appointed by the Assistant Secretary.

    (3) The Director of the Office for American Indian, Alaskan Native, and Native Hawaiian Aging shall—

        (A) (i) evaluate the adequacy of outreach under title III and title VI for older individuals who are Native Americans and recommend to the Assistant Secretary necessary action to improve service delivery, outreach, coordination between title III and title VI services, and particular problems faced by older Indians and Native Hawaiians; and

            (ii) include a description of the results of such evaluation and recommendations in the annual report required by section 207(a) to be submitted by the Assistant Secretary;

        (B) serve as the effective and visible advocate in behalf of older individuals who are Native Americans within the Department of Health and Human Services and with other departments and agencies of the Federal Government regarding all Federal policies affecting such individuals, with particular attention to services provided to Native Americans by the Indian Health Service;

        (C) coordinate activities between other Federal departments and agencies to assure a continuum of improved services through memoranda of agreements or through other appropriate means of coordination;

        (D) administer and evaluate the grants provided under this Act to Indian tribes, public agencies and nonprofit private organizations serving Native Hawaiians;

        (E) recommend to the Assistant Secretary policies and priorities with respect to the development and operation of programs and activities conducted under this Act relating to older individuals who are Native Americans;

(F) collect and disseminate information related to problems experienced by older Native Americans, including information (compiled with assistance from public or nonprofit private entities, including institutions of higher education, with experience in assessing the characteristics and health status of older individuals who are Native Americans) on elder abuse, in-home care, health problems, and other problems unique to Native Americans;

(G) develop research plans, and conduct and arrange for research, in the field of American Native aging with a special emphasis on the gathering of statistics on the status of older individuals who are Native Americans;

(H) develop and provide technical assistance and training programs to grantees under title VI;

(I) promote coordination—

    (i) between the administration of title III and the administration of title VI; and

    (ii) between programs established under title III by the Assistant Secretary and programs established under title VI by the Assistant Secretary; including sharing among grantees information on programs funded, and on training and technical assistance provided, under such titles; and

(J) serve as the effective and visible advocate on behalf of older individuals who are Indians, Alaskan Natives, and Native Hawaiians, in the States to promote the enhanced delivery of services and implementation of programs, under this Act and other Federal Acts, for the benefit of such individuals.

(d) (1) There is established in the Administration the Office of Long-Term Care Ombudsman Programs (in this subsection referred to as the "Office").

(2) (A) The Office shall be headed by a Director of the Office of Long-Term Care Ombudsman Programs (in this subsection referred to as the "Director") who shall be appointed by the Assistant Secretary from among individuals who have expertise and background in the fields of long-term care advocacy and management. The Director shall report directly to the Assistant Secretary.

(B) No individual shall be appointed Director if—

    (i) the individual has been employed within the previous 2 years by—

        (I) a long-term care facility;

        (II) a corporation that then owned or operated a long-term care facility; or

        (III) an association of long-term care facilities;

    (ii) the individual—

        (I) has an ownership or investment interest (represented by equity, debt, or other financial relationship) in a long-term care facility or long-term care service, or

        (II) receives, or has the right to receive, directly or indirectly remuneration (in cash or in kind) under a compensation arrangement with an owner or operator of a long-term care facility; or

    (iii) the individual, or any member of the immediate family of the individual, is subject to a conflict of interest.

(3) The Director shall—

(A) serve as an effective and visible advocate on behalf of older individuals who reside in long-term care facilities, within the Department of Health and Human Services and with other departments, agencies, and instrumentalities of the Federal Government regarding all Federal policies affecting such individuals;

(B) review and make recommendations to the Assistant Secretary regarding—
  (i) the approval of the provisions in State plans submitted under section 307(a) that relate to State Long-Term Care Ombudsman programs; and
  (ii) the adequacy of State budgets and policies relating to the programs;
(C) after consultation with State Long-Term Care Ombudsmen and the State agencies, make recommendations to the Assistant Secretary regarding—
  (i) policies designed to assist State Long-Term Care Ombudsmen; and
  (ii) methods to periodically monitor and evaluate the operation of State Long-Term Care Ombudsman programs, to ensure that the programs satisfy the requirements of section 307(a)(9) and section 712, including provision of service to residents of board and care facilities and of similar adult care facilities;
(D) keep the Assistant Secretary and the Secretary fully and currently informed about—
  (i) problems relating to State Long-Term Care Ombudsman programs; and
  (ii) the necessity for, and the progress toward, solving the problems;
(E) review, and make recommendations to the Secretary and the Assistant Secretary regarding, existing and proposed Federal legislation, regulations, and policies regarding the operation of State Long-Term Care Ombudsman programs;
(F) make recommendations to the Assistant Secretary and the Secretary regarding the policies of the Administration, and coordinate the activities of the Administration with the activities of other Federal entities, State and local entities, and nongovernmental entities, relating to State Long-Term Care Ombudsman programs;
(G) supervise the activities carried out under the authority of the Administration that relate to State Long-Term Care Ombudsman programs;
(H) administer the National Ombudsman Resource Center established under section 202(a)(21) and make recommendations to the Assistant Secretary regarding the operation of the National Ombudsman Resource Center;
(I) advocate, monitor, and coordinate Federal and State activities of Long-Term Care Ombudsmen under this Act;
(J) submit to the Speaker of the House of Representatives and the President pro tempore of the Senate an annual report on the effectiveness of services provided under section 307(a)(9) and section 712;
(K) have authority to investigate the operation or violation of any Federal law administered by the Department of Health and Human Services that may adversely affect the health, safety, welfare, or rights of older individuals; and
(L) not later than 180 days after the date of the enactment of the Older Americans Act Amendments of 1992, establish standards applicable to the training required by section 712(h)(4).
(e) (1) The Assistant Secretary is authorized to designate within the Administration a person to have responsibility for elder abuse prevention and services.
(2) It shall be the duty of the Assistant Secretary, acting through the person designated to have responsibility for elder abuse prevention and services-
  (A) to develop objectives, priorities, policy, and a long-term plan for-
    (i) facilitating the development, implementation, and continuous improvement of a coordinated, multidisciplinary elder justice system in the United States;
    (ii) providing Federal leadership to support State efforts in carrying out elder justice programs and activities relating to-

(I)   elder abuse prevention, detection, treatment, intervention, and response;

(II)   training of individuals regarding the matters described in subclause (I); and

(III) the development of a State comprehensive elder justice system, as defined in section 752(b);

(iii)   establishing Federal guidelines and disseminating best practices for uniform data collection and reporting by States;

(iv)   working with States, the Department of Justice, and other Federal entities to annually collect, maintain, and disseminate data relating to elder abuse, neglect, and exploitation, to the extent practicable;

(v)   establishing an information clearinghouse to collect, maintain, and disseminate information concerning best practices and resources for training, technical assistance, and other activities to assist States and communities to carry out evidence-based programs to prevent and address elder abuse, neglect, and exploitation;

(vi)   conducting research related to elder abuse, neglect, and exploitation;

(vii) providing technical assistance to States and other eligible entities that provide or fund the provision of the services described in title VII;

(viii) carrying out a study to determine the national incidence and prevalence of elder abuse, neglect, and exploitation in all settings; and

(ix)   promoting collaborative efforts and diminishing duplicative efforts in the development and carrying out of elder justice programs at the Federal, State and local levels; and

(B)   to assist States and other eligible entities under title VII to develop strategic plans to better coordinate elder justice activities, research, and training.

(4)   The Secretary, acting through the Assistant Secretary, may issue such regulations as may be necessary to carry out this subsection and section 752.

(f)   (1) The Assistant Secretary may designate an officer or employee who shall be responsible for the administration of mental health services authorized under this Act.

(A)   It shall be the duty of the Assistant Secretary, acting through the individual designated under paragraph (1), to develop objectives, priorities, and a long-term plan for supporting State and local efforts involving education about and prevention, detection, and treatment of mental disorders, including age-related dementia, depression, and Alzheimer's disease and related neurological disorders with neurological and organic brain dysfunction.

(42 U.S.C. 3011)

Section. 202. FUNCTIONS OF ASSISTANT SECRETARY

(a)   It shall be the duty and function of the Administration to—

(1)   serve as the effective and visible advocate for older individuals within the Department of Health and Human Services and with other departments, agencies, and instrumentalities of the Federal Government by maintaining active review and commenting responsibilities over all Federal policies affecting older individuals;

(2)   collect and disseminate information related to problems of the aged and aging;

(3)   directly assist the Secretary in all matters pertaining to problems of the aged and aging;

(4)   administer the grants provided by this Act;

(5) develop plans, conduct and arrange for research in the field of aging, and assist in the establishment and implementation of programs designed to meet the needs of older individuals for supportive services, including nutrition, hospitalization, education and training services (including pre-retirement training, and continuing education), low-cost transportation and housing, **assistive technology**, and health (including mental health) services;

(6) provide technical assistance and consultation to States and political subdivisions thereof with respect to programs for the aged and aging;

(7) prepare, publish, and disseminate educational materials dealing with the welfare of older individuals;

(8) gather statistics in the field of aging which other Federal agencies are not collecting, and take whatever action is necessary to achieve coordination of activities carried out or assisted by all departments, agencies, and instrumentalities of the Federal Government with respect to the collection, preparation, and dissemination of information relevant to older individuals;

(9) develop basic policies and set priorities with respect to the development and operation of programs and activities conducted under authority of this Act;

(10) coordinate Federal programs and activities related to such purposes;

(11) coordinate, and assist in, the planning and development by public (including Federal, State, and local agencies) and private organizations or programs for older individuals with a view to the establishment of a nationwide network of comprehensive, coordinated services and opportunities for such individuals;

(12) (A) consult and coordinate activities with the Administrator of the Centers for Medicare and Medicaid Services and the heads of other Federal entities to implement and build awareness of programs providing benefits affecting older individuals; and

(B) carry on a continuing evaluation of the programs and activities related to the objectives of this Act, with particular attention to the impact of the programs and activities carried out under –

(i) titles XVIII and XIX of the Social Security Act (42 U.S.C. 1395 et seq., 1396 et seq.);

(ii) the Age Discrimination in Employment Act of 1967 (29 U.S.C. 621 et seq.); and

(iii) the National Housing Act (12 U.S.C. 1701 et seq.) relating to housing for older individuals and the setting of standards for the licensing of nursing homes, intermediate care homes, and other facilities providing care for such individuals;

(13) provide information and assistance to private organizations for the establishment and operation by them of programs and activities related to the objectives of this Act;

(14) develop, in coordination with other agencies, a national plan for meeting the needs for trained personnel in the field of aging, and for training persons for carrying out programs related to the objectives of this Act, and conduct and provide for the conducting of such training;

(15) consult with national organizations representing minority individuals to develop and disseminate training packages and to provide technical assistance efforts designed to assist State and area agencies on aging, and service providers, in providing services to older individuals with greatest economic need or individuals with greatest social need, with particular attention to and specific objectives for providing services to low-income minority individuals and older individuals residing in rural areas;

(16) collect for each fiscal year, for fiscal years beginning after September 30, 1988, directly or by contract, statistical data regarding programs and activities carried out with funds provided under this Act, including—
  (A) with respect to each type of service or activity provided with such funds—
  (i)   the aggregate amount of such funds expended to provide such service or activity;
  (ii) the number of individuals who received such service or activity; and
  (iii) the number of units of such service or activity provided;
  (B) the number of senior centers which received such funds; and
  (C) the extent to which each area agency on aging designated under section 305(a) satisfied the requirements of paragraphs (2) and (5)(A) of section 306(a)[2];
(17) obtain from—
  (A) the Department of Agriculture information explaining the requirements for eligibility to receive benefits under the Food Stamp Act of 1977; and
  (B) the Social Security Administration information explaining the requirements for eligibility to receive supplemental security income benefits under title XVI of the Social Security Act (or assistance under a State plan program under title XVI of that Act); and distribute such information, in written form, to State agencies, for redistribution to area agencies on aging, to carry out outreach activities and application assistance;
  (C) (18)(A) establish and operate the National Ombudsman Resource Center (in this paragraph referred to as the "Center"), under the administration of the Director of the Office of Long-Term Care Ombudsman Programs, that will—
    (i) by grant or contract—
      (I)   conduct research;
      (II) provide training, technical assistance, and information to State Long-Term Care Ombudsmen;
      (III) analyze laws, regulations, programs, and practices; and
      (IV) provide assistance in recruiting and retaining volunteers for State Long-Term Care Ombudsman programs by establishing a national program for recruitment efforts that utilizes the organizations that have established a successful record in recruiting and retaining volunteers for ombudsman or other programs; relating to Federal, State, and local long-term care ombudsman policies; and
    (ii) assist State Long-Term Care Ombudsmen in the implementation of State Long-Term Care Ombudsman programs; and
  (B) make available to the Center not less than the amount of resources made available to the Long-Term Care Ombudsman National Resource Center for fiscal year 2000,
(18) conduct strict monitoring of State compliance with the requirements in effect, under this Act to prohibit conflicts of interest and to maintain the integrity and public purpose of services provided and service providers, under this Act in all contractual and commercial relationships;
(19) (A) encourage, and provide technical assistance to, States, area agencies on aging, and service providers to carry out outreach and benefits enrollment assistance to inform and enroll older individuals with greatest economic need, who may be eligible to participate, but who are not participating, in Federal and State programs providing benefits for which the individuals are eligible, including –

    (i)   supplemental security income benefits under title XVI of the Social Security Act (42 U.S.C. 1381 et seq.), or assistance under a State plan program under such title;

    (ii) medical assistance under title XIX of such Act (42 U.S.C. 1396 et seq.);

    (iii) benefits under the Food Stamp Act of 1977 (7 U.S.C. 2011 et seq.); or

    (iv) benefits under any other applicable program; and

(C) at the election of the Assistant Secretary and in cooperation with related Federal agency partners administering the Federal programs, make a grant to or enter into a contract with a qualified, experienced entity to establish a National Center on Senior Benefits Outreach and Enrollment, which shall-

    (i)   maintain and update web-based decision support and enrollment tools, and integrated, person-centered systems, designed to inform older individuals about the full range of benefits for which the individuals may be eligible under Federal and State programs;

    (ii) utilize cost-effective strategies to find older individuals with greatest economic need and enroll the individuals in the programs;

    (iii) create and support efforts for Aging and Disability Resource Centers, and other public and private State and community-based organizations, including faith-based organizations and coalitions, to serve as benefits enrollment centers for the programs;

    (iv) develop and maintain an information clearinghouse on best practices and cost-effective methods for finding and enrolling older individuals with greatest economic need in the programs for which the individuals are eligible; and

    (v)   provide, in collaboration with related Federal agency partners administering the Federal programs, training and technical assistance on effective outreach, screening, enrollment, and follow-up strategies;

(21) establish information and assistance services as priority services for older individuals, and develop and operate, either directly or through contracts, grants, or cooperative agreements, a National Eldercare Locator Service, providing information and assistance services through a nationwide toll free number to identify community resources for older individuals;

(22) develop guidelines for area agencies on aging to follow in choosing and evaluating providers of legal assistance;

(23) develop guidelines and a model job description for choosing and evaluating legal assistance developers referred to in sections 307(a)(18) and 731(b)(2)[3];

(24) establish and carry out pension counseling and information programs described in section 215;

(25) provide technical assistance, training, and other means of assistance to State agencies, area agencies on aging, and service providers regarding State and local data collection and analysis;

(26) design and implement, for purposes of compliance with paragraph (19), uniform data collection procedures for use by State agencies, including—

    (A) uniform definitions and nomenclature;

    (B) standardized data collection procedures;

    (C) a participant identification and description system;

    (D) procedures for collecting information on services needed by older individuals including services that would permit such individuals to receive long-term care in home and community-based settings) as identified by service providers in assisting clients through the provision of the supportive services; and

    (E) procedures for the assessment of unmet needs for services under this Act;

(27) improve the delivery of services to older individuals living in rural areas through—
    (A) synthesizing results of research on how best to meet the service needs of older individuals in rural areas;
    (B) developing a resource guide on best practices for States, area agencies on aging, and service providers; **and**
    (C) providing training and technical assistance to States to implement these best practices of service delivery; and
(28) make available to States, area agencies on aging, and service providers information and technical assistance to support the provision of evidence-based disease prevention and health promotion services.

(b) To promote the development and implementation of comprehensive, coordinated systems at Federal, State, and local levels that enable older individuals to receive long-term care in home and community-based settings, in a manner responsive to the needs and preferences of older individuals and their family caregivers, the Assistant Secretary shall, consistent with the applicable provisions of this title –

(1) collaborate, coordinate, and consult with other Federal entities responsible for formulating and implementing programs, benefits, and services related to providing long-term care, and may make grants, contracts, and cooperative agreements with funds received from other Federal entities;

(2) conduct research and demonstration projects to identify innovative, cost-effective strategies for modifying State systems of long-term care to –
    (A) respond to the needs and preferences of older individuals and family caregivers; and
    (B) target services to individuals at risk for institutional placement, to permit such individuals to remain in home and community-based settings;

(3) establish criteria for and promote the implementation (through area agencies on aging, service providers, and such other entities as the Assistant Secretary determines to be appropriate) of evidence-based programs to assist older individuals and their family caregivers in learning about and making behavioral changes intended to reduce the risk of injury, disease, and disability among older individuals;

(4) facilitate, in coordination with the Administrator of the Centers for Medicare and Medicaid Services, and other heads of Federal entities as appropriate, the provision of long-term care in home and community-based settings, including the provision of such care through self-directed care models that-
    (I) provide for the assessment of the needs and preferences of an individual at risk for institutional placement to help such individual avoid unnecessary institutional placement and depletion of income and assets to qualify for benefits under the Medicaid program under title XIX of the Social Security Act (42 U.S.C. 1396 et seq.);
    (II) respond to the needs and preferences of such individual and provide the option –
        (i) for the individual to direct and control the receipt of supportive services provided; or

(ii) as appropriate, for a person who was appointed by the individual, or is legally acting on the individual's behalf, in order to represent or advise the individual in financial or service coordination matters (referred to in this paragraph as a "representative" of the individual), to direct and control the receipt of those services; and

(C) assist an older individual (or, as appropriate, a representative of the individual) to develop a plan for long-term support, including selecting, budgeting for, and purchasing home and community-based long-term care and supportive services;

(5) provide for the Administration to play a lead role with respect to issues concerning home and community-based long-term care, including-

(A) directing (as the Secretary or the President determines to be appropriate) or otherwise participating in departmental and interdepartmental activities concerning long-term care;

(B) reviewing and commenting on departmental rules, regulations, and policies related to providing long-term care; and

(C) making recommendations to the Secretary with respect to home and community-based long-term care, including recommendations based on findings made through projects conducted under paragraph (2);

(6) promote, in coordination with other appropriate Federal agencies –

(A) enhanced awareness by the public of the importance of planning in advance for long-term care; and

(B) the availability of information and resources to assist in such planning;

(7) ensure access to, and the dissemination of, information about all long-term care options and service providers, including the availability of integrated long-term care;

(8) implement in all States Aging and Disability Resource Centers-

(A) to serve as visible and trusted sources of information on the full range of long-term care options, including both institutional and home and community-based care, which are available in the community;

(B) to provide personalized and consumer-friendly assistance to empower individuals to make informed decisions about their care options;

(C) to provide coordinated and streamlined access to all publicly supported long-term care options so that consumers can obtain the care they need through a single intake, assessment, and eligibility determination process;

(D) to help individuals to plan ahead for their future long-term care needs; and

(E) to assist (in coordination with the entities carrying out the health insurance information, counseling, and assistance program (receiving funding under section 4360 of the Omnibus Budget Reconciliation Act of 1990 (42 U.S.C. 1395b-4)) in the States) beneficiaries, and prospective beneficiaries, under the Medicare program established under title XVIII of the Social Security Act (42 U.S.C. 1395 et seq.) in understanding and accessing prescription drug and preventative health benefits under the provisions of, and amendments made by, the Medicare Prescription Drug, Improvement, and Modernization Act of 2003;

(9) establish, either directly or through grants or contracts, national technical assistance programs to assist State agencies, area agencies on aging, and community-based service providers funded under this Act in implementing –

(A) home and community-based long-term care systems, including evidence-based programs; and

(B) evidence-based disease prevention and health promotion services programs;

(10) develop, in collaboration with the Administrator of the Centers for Medicare & Medicaid Services, performance standards and measures for use by States to determine the extent to which their State systems of long-term care fulfill the objectives described in this subsection; and

(11) conduct such other activities as the Assistant Secretary determines to be appropriate.

(c) The Assistant Secretary, in consultation with the Chief Executive Officer of the Corporation for National and Community Service, shall-

(1) encourage and permit volunteer groups (including organizations carrying out national service programs and including organizations of youth in secondary or postsecondary school) that are active in supportive services and civic engagement to participate and be involved individually or through representative groups in supportive service and civic engagement programs or activities to the maximum extent feasible;

(2) develop a comprehensive strategy for utilizing older individuals to address critical local needs of national concern, including the engagement of older individuals in the activities of public and nonprofit organizations such as community-based organizations, including faith-based organizations; and

(3) encourage other community capacity-building initiatives involving older individuals, with particular attention to initiatives that demonstrate effectiveness and cost savings in meeting critical needs.

(d) (1) The Assistant Secretary shall establish and operate the National Center on Elder Abuse (in this subsection referred to as the "Center").

(2) In operating the Center, the Assistant Secretary shall —

(A) annually compile, publish, and disseminate a summary of recently conducted research on elder abuse, neglect, and exploitation;

(B) develop and maintain an information clearinghouse on all programs (including private programs) showing promise of success, for the prevention, identification, and treatment of elder abuse, neglect, and exploitation;

(C) compile, publish, and disseminate training materials for personnel who are engaged or intend to engage in the prevention, identification, and treatment of elder abuse, neglect, and exploitation;

(D) provide technical assistance to State agencies and to other public and nonprofit private agencies and organizations to assist the agencies and organizations in planning, improving, developing, and carrying out programs and activities relating to the special problems of elder abuse, neglect, and exploitation, and

(E) conduct research and demonstration projects regarding the causes, prevention, identification, and treatment of elder abuse, neglect, and exploitation.

(3) (A) The Assistant Secretary shall carry out paragraph (2) through grants or contracts.

(B) The Assistant Secretary shall issue criteria applicable to the recipients of funds under this subsection. To be eligible to receive a grant or enter into a contract under subparagraph (A), an entity shall submit an application to the Assistant Secretary at such time, in such manner, and containing such information as the Assistant Secretary may require.

(C) The Assistant Secretary shall—

(i)   establish research priorities for making grants or contracts to carry out paragraph (2)(E); and

(ii)   not later than 60 days before the date on which the Assistant Secretary establishes such priorities, publish in the Federal Register for public comment a statement of such proposed priorities.

(4)   The Assistant Secretary shall make available to the Center such resources as are necessary for the Center to carry out effectively the functions of the Center under this Act and not less than the amount of resources made available to the Resource Center on Elder Abuse for fiscal year 2000.

(e) (1) (A) The Assistant Secretary shall make grants or enter into contracts with eligible entities to establish the National Aging Information Center (in this subsection referred to as the "Center") to—

(i)   [4] provide information about grants and projects under title IV;

(ii)   annually compile, analyze, publish, and disseminate—

(I)   statistical data collected under subsection (a)(19);

(II) census data on aging demographics; and

(III) data from other Federal agencies on the health, social, and economic status of older individuals and on the services provided to older individuals;

(iii) biennially compile, analyze, publish, and disseminate statistical data collected on the functions, staffing patterns, and funding sources of State agencies and area agencies on aging;

(iv) analyze the information collected under section 201(c)(3)(F) by the Director of the Office for American Indian, Alaskan Native, and Native Hawaiian Aging;

(v) provide technical assistance, training, and other means of assistance to State agencies, area agencies on aging, and service providers, regarding State and local data collection and analysis; and

(vi) be a national resource on statistical data regarding Aging.

(B)   To be eligible to receive a grant or enter into a contract under subparagraph (A), an entity shall submit an application to the Assistant Secretary at such time, in such manner, and containing such information as the Assistant Secretary may require.

(C)   Entities eligible to receive a grant or enter into a contract under subparagraph (A) shall be organizations with a demonstrated record of experience in education and information dissemination.

(2) (A) The Assistant Secretary shall establish procedures specifying the length of time that the Center shall provide the information described in paragraph (1) with respect to a particular project or activity. The procedures shall require the Center to maintain the information beyond the term of the grant awarded, or contract entered into, to carry out the project or activity.

(B)   The Assistant Secretary shall establish the procedures described in subparagraph (A) after consultation with—

(i)   practitioners in the field of aging;

(ii)   older individuals;

(iii) representatives of institutions of higher education;

(iv) national aging organizations;

(v) State agencies;

      (vi) area agencies on aging;
      (vii) legal assistance providers;
      (viii)   service providers; and
      (ix) other persons with an interest in the field of aging.

(f) (1) The Assistant Secretary, in accordance with the process described in paragraph (2), and in collaboration with a representative group of State agencies, tribal organizations, area agencies on aging, and providers of services involved in the performance outcome measures shall develop and publish by December 31, 2001, a set of performance outcome measures for planning, managing, and evaluating activities performed and services provided under this Act. To the maximum extent possible, the Assistant Secretary shall use data currently collected (as of the date of development of the measures) by State agencies, area agencies on aging, and service providers through the National Aging Program Information System and other applicable sources of information in developing such measures.

     (2) The process for developing the performance outcome measures described in paragraph (1) shall include—

      (A) a review of such measures currently in use by State agencies and area agencies on aging (as of the date of the review);

      (B) development of a proposed set of such measures that provides information about the major activities performed and services provided under this Act;

      (C) pilot testing of the proposed set of such measures, including an identification of resource, infrastructure, and data collection issues at the State and local levels; and

      (D) evaluation of the pilot test and recommendations for modification of the proposed set of such measures.

(42 U.S.C. 3012)

Section. 203. FEDERAL AGENCY CONSULTATION

(a) (1) The Assistant Secretary, in carrying out the objectives and provisions of this Act, shall coordinate, advise, consult with, and cooperate with the head of each department, agency, or instrumentality of the Federal Government proposing or administering programs or services substantially related to the objectives of this Act, with respect to such programs or services. In particular, the Assistant Secretary shall coordinate, advise, consult, and cooperate with the Secretary of Labor in carrying out title V and with the Corporation for National and Community Service in carrying out this Act.

     (2) The head of each department, agency, or instrumentality of the Federal Government proposing to establish programs and services substantially related to the objectives of this Act shall consult with the Assistant Secretary prior to the establishment of such programs and services. To achieve appropriate coordination, the head of each department, agency, or instrumentality of the Federal Government administering any program substantially related to the objectives of this Act, particularly administering any program referred to in subsection (b), shall consult and cooperate with the Assistant Secretary in carrying out such program. In particular, the Secretary of Labor shall consult and cooperate with the Assistant Secretary in carrying out the Job Training Partnership Act and[5] title I of the Workforce Investment Act of 1998.

(3) The head of each department, agency, or instrumentality of the Federal Government administering programs and services substantially related to the objectives of this Act shall collaborate with the Assistant Secretary in carrying out this Act, and shall develop a written analysis, for review and comment by the Assistant Secretary, of the impact of such programs and services on—

    (A) older individuals (with particular attention to low-income older individuals, including low-income minority older individuals, older individuals with limited English proficiency, and older individuals residing in rural areas) and eligible individuals (as defined in section 518); and

    (B) the functions and responsibilities of State agencies and area agencies on aging.

(b) For the purposes of subsection (a), programs related to the objectives of this Act shall include—

    (1) the Job Training Partnership Act or title I of the Workforce Investment Act of 1998,[6]

    (2) title II of the Domestic Volunteer Service Act of 1973,

    (3) titles XVI, XVIII, XIX, and XX of the Social Security Act,

    (4) sections 231 and 232 of the National Housing Act,

    (5) the United States Housing Act of 1937,

    (6) section 202 of the Housing Act of 1959,

    (7) title I of the Housing and Community Development Act of 1974,

    (8) title I of the Higher Education Act of 1965 and the Adult Education and Family Literacy Act,

    (9) sections 3, 9, and 16 of the Urban Mass Transportation Act of 1964,

    (10) the Public Health Service Act, including block grants under title XIX of such Act,

    (11) the Low-Income Home Energy Assistance Act of 1981,

    (12) part A of the Energy Conservation in Existing Buildings Act of 1976, relating to weatherization assistance for low income persons,

    (13) the Community Services Block Grant Act,

    (14) demographic statistics and analysis programs conducted by the Bureau of the Census under title 13, United States Code,

    (15) parts II and III of title 38, United States Code,

    (16) the Rehabilitation Act of 1973,

    (17) the Developmental Disabilities Assistance and Bill of Rights Act of 2000,

    (18) the Edward Byrne Memorial State and Local Law Enforcement Assistance Programs, established under part E of title I of the Omnibus Crime Control and Safe Streets Act of 1968 (42 U.S.C. 3750–3766b)),and

    (19) sections 4 and 5 of the Assistive Technology Act of 1998 (29 U.S.C. 3003, 3004).

(c) (1) The Secretary, in collaboration with the Federal officials specified in paragraph (2), shall establish an Interagency Coordinating Committee on Aging (referred to in this subsection as the "Committee") focusing on the coordination of agencies with respect to aging issues.

    (2) The officials referred to in paragraph (1) shall include the Secretary of Labor and the Secretary of Housing and Urban Development, and may include, at the direction of the President, the Attorney General, the Secretary of Transportation, the Secretary of the Treasury, the Secretary of Agriculture, the Secretary of Homeland Security, the Commissioner of Social Security, and such other Federal officials as the President may direct. An official described in this paragraph may appoint a designee to carry out the official's duties under paragraph (1).

(3) The Secretary of Health and Human Services shall serve as the first chairperson of the Committee, for 1 term, and the Secretary of Housing and Urban Development shall serve as the chairperson for the following term. After that following term, the Committee shall select a chairperson from among the members of the Committee, and any member may serve as the chairperson. No member may serve as the chairperson for more than 1 consecutive term.

(4) For purposes of this subsection, a term shall be a period of 2 calendar years.

(5) The Committee shall meet not less often than once each year.

(6) The Committee shall-

(A) share information with and establish an ongoing system to improve coordination among Federal agencies with responsibility for programs and services for older individuals and recommend improvements to such system with an emphasis on –

    (i) improving access to programs and services for older individuals;

    (ii) maximizing the impact of federally funded programs and services for older individuals by increasing the efficiency, effectiveness, and delivery of such programs and services;

    (iii) planning and preparing for the impact of demographic changes on programs and services for older individuals; and

    (iv) reducing or eliminating areas of overlap and duplication by Federal agencies in the provision and accessibility of such programs and services;

(B) identify, promote, and implement (as appropriate), best practices and evidence-based program and service models to assist older individuals in meeting their housing, health care, and other supportive service needs, including –

    (i) consumer-directed care models for home and community-based care and supportive services that link housing, health care, and other supportive services and that facilitate aging in place, enabling older individuals to remain in their homes and communities as the individuals age; and

    (ii) innovations in technology applications (including assistive technology devices and assistive technology services) that give older individuals access to information on available services or that help in providing services to older individuals;

(C) collect and disseminate information about older individuals and the programs and services available to the individuals to ensure that the individuals can access comprehensive information;

(D) work with the Federal Interagency Forum on Aging-Related Statistics, the Bureau of the Census, and member agencies to ensure the continued collection of data relating to the housing, health care, and other supportive service needs of older individuals and to support efforts to identify and address unmet data needs;

(E) actively seek input from and consult with nongovernmental experts and organizations, including public health interest and research groups and foundations about the activities described in subparagraphs (A) through (F);

(F) identify any barriers and impediments, including barriers and impediments in statutory and regulatory law, to the access and use by older individuals of federally funded programs and services; and

(G) work with States to better provide housing, health care, and other supportive services to older individuals by –

    (i) holding meetings with State agencies;

(ii) providing ongoing technical assistance to States about better meeting the needs of older individuals; and

(iii) working with States to designate liaisons, from the State agencies to the Committee.

(7) Not later than 90 days following the end of each term, the Committee shall prepare and submit to the Committee on Financial Services of the House of Representatives, the Committee on Education and the Workforce of the House of Representatives, the Committee on Energy and Commerce of the House of Representatives, the Committee on Ways and Means of the House of Representatives, the Committee on Banking, Housing, and Urban Affairs of the Senate, the Committee on Health, Education, Labor, and Pensions of the Senate, and the Special Committee on Aging of the Senate, a report that-

(A) describes the activities and accomplishments of the Committee in –

(i) enhancing the overall coordination of federally funded programs and services for older individuals; and

(ii) meeting the requirements of paragraph (6);

(B) incorporates an analysis from the head of each agency that is a member of the interagency coordinating committee established under paragraph (1) that describes the barriers and impediments, including barriers and impediments in statutory and regulatory law (as the chairperson of the Committee determines to be appropriate), to the access and use by older individuals of programs and services administered by such agency; and

(C) makes such recommendations as the chairman determines to be appropriate for actions to meet the needs described in paragraph (6) and for coordinating programs and services designed to meet those needs.

(8) On the request of the Committee, any Federal Government employee may be detailed to the Committee without reimbursement, and such detail shall be without interruption or loss of civil service status or privilege.

(42 U.S.C. 3013)

Section. 203A. CONSULTATION WITH STATE AGENCIES, AREA AGENCIES ON AGING, AND NATIVE AMERICAN GRANT RECIPIENTS.

The Assistant Secretary shall consult and coordinate with State agencies, area agencies on aging, and recipients of grants under title VI in the development of Federal goals, regulations, program instructions, and policies under this Act.

(42 U.S.C. 3013a)

Section. 204. GIFTS AND DONATIONS.

(a) GIFTS AND DONATIONS.—The Assistant Secretary may accept, use, and dispose of, on behalf of the United States, gifts or donations (in cash or in kind, including voluntary and uncompensated services or property), which shall be available until expended for the purposes specified in subsection (b). Gifts of cash and proceeds of the sale of property shall be available in addition to amounts appropriated to carry out this Act.

(b) USE OF GIFTS AND DONATIONS.—Gifts and donations accepted pursuant to subsection (a) may be used either directly, or for grants to or contracts with public or nonprofit private entities, for the following activities:

(1) The design and implementation of demonstrations of innovative ideas and best practices in programs and services for older individuals.

(2) The planning and conduct of conferences for the purpose of exchanging information, among concerned individuals and public and private entities and organizations, relating to programs and services provided under this Act and other programs and services for older individuals.

(3) The development, publication, and dissemination of informational materials (in print, visual, electronic, or other media) relating to the programs and services provided under this Act and other matters of concern to older individuals.

(c) ETHICS GUIDELINES.—The Assistant Secretary shall establish written guidelines setting forth the criteria to be used in determining whether a gift or donation should be declined under this section because the acceptance of the gift or donation would—

(1) reflect unfavorably upon the ability of the Administration, the Department of Health and Human Services, or any employee of the Administration or Department, to carry out responsibilities or official duties under this Act in a fair and objective manner; or

(2) compromise the integrity or the appearance of integrity of programs or services provided under this Act or of any official involved in those programs or services.

(42 U.S.C. 3015)

Section. 205. ADMINISTRATION OF THE ACT

(a) (1) In carrying out the objectives of this Act, the Assistant Secretary is authorized to—

(A) provide consultative services and technical assistance to public or nonprofit private agencies and organizations;

(B) provide short-term training and technical instruction;

(C) conduct research and demonstrations; **and**

(D) collect, prepare, publish, and disseminate special educational or informational materials, including reports of the projects for which funds are provided under this Act.

(2) (A) The Assistant Secretary shall designate an officer or employee who shall serve on a full-time basis and who shall be responsible for the administration of the nutrition services described in subparts 1 and 2 of part C of title III and shall have duties that include—

(i) designing, implementing, and evaluating evidence-based programs to support improved nutrition and regular physical activity for older individuals;

(ii) developing guidelines for nutrition providers concerning safety, sanitary handling of food, equipment, preparation, and food storage;

(iii) conducting outreach and disseminating evidence-based information to nutrition service providers about the benefits of healthful diets and regular physical activity, including information about the most current Dietary Guidelines for Americans published under section 301 of the National Nutrition Monitoring and Related Research Act of 1990 (7 U.S.C. 5341), the Food Guidance System of the Department of Agriculture, and advances in nutrition science;

(iv) promoting coordination between nutrition service providers and community-based organizations serving older individuals;

(v) developing guidelines on cost containment;

(vi)   defining a long range role for the nutrition services in community-based care systems;

(vii)   developing model menus and other appropriate materials for serving special needs populations and meeting cultural meal preferences;

(viii)   disseminating guidance that describes strategies for improving the nutritional quality of meals provided under title III, including strategies for increasing the consumption of whole grains, low fat dairy products, fruits, and vegetables;

(ix)   developing and disseminating guidelines for conducting nutrient analyses of meals provided under subparts 1 and 2 of part C of title III, including guidelines for averaging key nutrients over an appropriate period of time; and

(x)   providing technical assistance to the regional offices of the Administration with respect to each duty described in clauses (i) through (ix).

(A)   The regional offices of the Administration shall be responsible for disseminating, and providing technical assistance regarding, the guidelines and information described in clauses (ii), (iii), and (v) of subparagraph (A) to State agencies, area agencies on aging, and persons that provide nutrition services under part C of title III.

(B)   The officer or employee designated under subparagraph (A) shall—

(i)   have expertise in nutrition, energy balance, and meal planning; and

(ii)   (I)   be a registered dietitian;

(II)   be a credentialed nutrition professional; or

(III) have education and training that is substantially equivalent to the education and training for a registered dietitian or a credentialed nutrition professional.

(b)   In administering the functions of the Administration under this Act, the Assistant Secretary may utilize the services and facilities of any agency of the Federal Government and of any other public or nonprofit agency or organization, in accordance with agreements between the Assistant Secretary and the head thereof, and is authorized to pay therefore, in advance or by way of reimbursement, as may be provided in the agreement.

(c)   For the purpose of carrying out this section, there are authorized to be appropriated such sums as may be necessary.

(42 U.S.C. 3016)

Section. 206. EVALUATION

(a)   The Secretary shall measure and evaluate the impact of all programs authorized by this Act, their effectiveness in achieving stated goals in general, and in relation to their cost, their impact on related programs, their effectiveness in targeting for services under this Act unserved older individuals with greatest economic need (including low-income minority individuals and older individuals residing in rural areas) and unserved older individuals with greatest social need (including low-income minority individuals and older individuals residing in rural areas), and their structure and mechanisms for delivery of services, including, where appropriate, comparisons with appropriate control groups composed of persons who have not participated in such programs. Evaluations shall be conducted by persons not immediately involved in the administration of the program or project evaluated.

(b) The Secretary may not make grants or contracts under title IV of this Act until the Secretary develops and publishes general standards to be used by the Secretary in evaluating the programs and projects assisted under such title. Results of evaluations conducted pursuant to such standards shall be included in the reports required by section 207.

(c) In carrying out evaluations under this section, the Secretary shall, whenever possible, arrange to obtain the opinions of program and project participants about the strengths and weaknesses of the programs and projects, and conduct, where appropriate, evaluations which compare the effectiveness of related programs in achieving common objectives. In carrying out such evaluations, the Secretary shall consult with organizations concerned with older individuals, including those representing minority individuals, older individuals residing in rural areas and older individuals with disabilities.

(d) The Secretary shall annually publish summaries and analyses of the results of evaluative research and evaluation of program and project impact and effectiveness, including, as appropriate, health and nutrition education demonstration projects conducted under section 307(f) the full contents of which shall be transmitted to Congress, be disseminated to Federal, State, and local agencies and private organizations with an interest in aging, and be accessible to the public.

(e) The Secretary shall take the necessary action to assure that all studies, evaluations, proposals, and data produced or developed with Federal funds shall become the property of the United States.

(f) Such information as the Secretary may deem necessary for purposes of the evaluations conducted under this section shall be made available to him, upon request, by the departments and agencies of the executive branch.

(g) From the total amount appropriated for each fiscal year to carry out title III, the Secretary may use such sums as may be necessary, but not to exceed 1/2 of 1 percent of such amount, for purposes of conducting evaluations under this section, either directly or through grants or contracts.

No part of such sums may be reprogrammed, transferred, or used for any other purpose. Funds expended under this subsection shall be justified and accounted for by the Secretary.

(42 U.S.C. 3017(g))

Section. 207. REPORTS

(a) Not later than one hundred and twenty days after the close of each fiscal year, the Assistant Secretary shall prepare and submit to the President and to the Congress a full and complete report on the activities carried out under this Act. Such annual reports shall include—
   (1) statistical data reflecting services and activities provided to individuals during the preceding fiscal year;
   (2) statistical data collected under section 202(a)(19);
   (3) statistical data and an analysis of information regarding the effectiveness of the State agency and area agencies on aging in targeting services to older individuals with greatest economic need and older individuals with greatest social need, with particular attention to low-income minority individuals, older individuals residing in rural areas, low-income individuals, and frail individuals (including individuals with any physical or mental functional impairment); and
   (4) a description of the implementation of the plan required by section 202(a)(17).

(b) (1) Not later than March 1 of each year, the Assistant Secretary shall compile a report—
      (A) summarizing and analyzing the data collected under titles III and VII in accordance with section 712(c) for the then most recently concluded fiscal year;

(B) identifying significant problems and issues revealed by such data (with special emphasis on problems relating to quality of care and residents' rights);

(C) discussing current issues concerning the long-term care ombudsman programs of the States; and

(D) making recommendations regarding legislation and administrative actions to resolve such problems.

(2) The Assistant Secretary shall submit the report required by paragraph (1) to—

(A) the Special Committee on Aging of the Senate;

(B) the Committee on Education and the Workforce of the House of Representatives; and

(C) the Committee on **Health, Education, Labor, and Pensions** of the Senate.

(3) The Assistant Secretary shall provide the report required by paragraph (1), and make the State reports required under titles III and VII in accordance with section 712(h)(1) available, to—

(A) the Administrator of the Health Care Finance[7] Administration;

(B) the Office of the Inspector General of the Department of Health and Human Services;

(C) the Office of Civil Rights of the Department of Health and Human Services;

(D) the Secretary of Veterans Affairs; and

(E) each public agency or private organization designated as an Office of the State Long-Term Care Ombudsman under title III or VII in accordance with section 712(a)(4)(A).

(c) The Assistant Secretary shall, as part of the annual report submitted under subsection (a), prepare and submit a report on the outreach activities supported under this Act, together with such recommendations as the Assistant Secretary deems appropriate. In carrying out this subsection, the Assistant Secretary shall consider—

(1) the number of older individuals reached through the activities;

(2) the dollar amount of the assistance and benefits received by older individuals as a result of such activities;

(3) the cost of such activities in terms of the number of individuals reached and the dollar amount described in paragraph (2);

(4) the effect of such activities on supportive services and nutrition services furnished under title III of this Act; and

(5) the effectiveness of State and local efforts to target older individuals with greatest economic need (including low-income minority individuals and older individuals residing in rural areas) and older individuals with greatest social need (including low-income minority individuals and older individuals residing in rural areas) to receive services under this Act.

(42 U.S.C. 3018)

Section. 208. JOINT FUNDING OF PROJECTS

Pursuant to regulations prescribed by the President and to the extent consistent with the other provisions of this Act, where funds are provided for a single project by more than one Federal agency to any agency or organization assisted under this Act, the Federal agency principally involved may be designated to act for all in administering the funds provided. In such cases, a single non-Federal share requirement may be established according to the proportion of funds advanced by each Federal agency, and any such agency may waive any technical grant or contract requirement (as defined by such regulations) which is inconsistent with the similar requirements of the administering agency or which the administering agency does not impose.

(42 U.S.C. 3019)

Section. 209. ADVANCE FUNDING

(a) For the purpose of affording adequate notice of funding available under this Act, appropriations under this Act are authorized to be included in the appropriation Act for the fiscal year preceding the fiscal year for which they are available for obligation.
(b) In order to effect a transition to the advance funding method of timing appropriation action, subsection (a) shall apply notwithstanding that its initial application will result in the enactment in the same year (whether in the same appropriation Act or otherwise) of two separate appropriations, one for the then current fiscal year and one for the succeeding fiscal year.

(42 U.S.C. 3020)

Section. 210. APPLICATION OF OTHER LAWS

(a) The provisions and requirements of the Act of December 5, 1974 (Public Law 93–510; 88 Stat. 1604) shall not apply to the administration of the provisions of this Act or to the administration of any program or activity under this Act.
(b) No part of the costs of any project under any title of this Act may be treated as income or benefits to any eligible individual (other than any wage or salary to such individual) for the purpose of any other program or provision of Federal or State law.

(42 U.S.C. 3020a)

Section. 211. REDUCTION OF PAPERWORK

In order to reduce unnecessary, duplicative, or disruptive demands for information, the Assistant Secretary, in consultation with State agencies and other appropriate agencies and organizations, shall continually review and evaluate all requests by the Administration for information under this Act and take such action as may be necessary to reduce the paperwork required under this Act. The Assistant Secretary shall request only such information as the Assistant Secretary deems essential to carry out the objectives and provisions of this Act and, in gathering such information, shall make use of uniform service definitions to the extent that such definitions are available.

(42 U.S.C. 3020b)

Section. 212. CONTRACTING AND GRANT AUTHORITY; PRIVATE PAY RELATIONSHIPS; APPROPRIATE USE OF FUNDS.

(a) IN GENERAL. —Subject to subsection (b), this Act shall not be construed to prevent a recipient of a grant or a contract under this Act (other than title V) from entering into an agreement with a profit-making organization for the recipient to provide services to individuals or entities not otherwise receiving services under this Act, provided that—
    (1) if funds provided under this Act to such recipient are initially used by the recipient to pay part or all of a cost incurred by the recipient in developing and carrying out such agreement, such agreement guarantees that the cost is reimbursed to the recipient;

(2) if such agreement provides for the provision of 1 or more services, of the type provided under this Act by or on behalf of such recipient, to an individual or entity seeking to receive such services—

(A) the individuals and entities may only purchase such services at their fair market rate;

(B) all costs incurred by the recipient in providing such services (and not otherwise reimbursed under paragraph (1)), are reimbursed to such recipient; and

(C) the recipient reports the rates for providing such services under such agreement in accordance with subsection (c) and the rates are consistent with the prevailing market rate for provision of such services in the relevant geographic area as determined by the State agency or area agency on aging (as applicable); and

(3) any amount of payment to the recipient under the agreement that exceeds reimbursement under this subsection of the recipient's costs is used to provide, or support the provision of, services under this Act.

(b) ENSURING APPROPRIATE USE OF FUNDS.—An agreement described in subsection (a) may not—

(1) be made without the prior approval of the State agency (or, in the case of a grantee under title VI, without the prior recommendation of the Director of the Office for American Indian, Alaska Native, and Native Hawaiian Aging and the prior approval of the Assistant Secretary), after timely submission of all relevant documents related to the agreement including information on all costs incurred;

(2) directly or indirectly provide for, or have the effect of, paying, reimbursing, subsidizing, or otherwise compensating an individual or entity in an amount that exceeds the fair market value of the services subject to such agreement;

(3) result in the displacement of services otherwise available to an older individual with greatest social need, an older individual with greatest economic need, or an older individual who is at risk for institutional placement; or

(4) in any other way compromise, undermine, or be inconsistent with the objective of serving the needs of older individuals, as determined by the Assistant Secretary.

(c) MONITORING AND REPORTING.—To ensure that any agreement described in subsection (a) complies with the requirements of this section and other applicable provisions of this Act, the Assistant Secretary shall develop and implement uniform monitoring procedures and reporting requirements consistent with the provisions of subparagraphs (A) through (E) of section 306(a)(13) in consultation with the State agencies and area agencies on aging. The Assistant Secretary shall annually prepare and submit to the chairpersons and ranking members of the appropriate committees of Congress a report analyzing all such agreements, and the costs incurred and services provided under the agreements. This report shall contain information on the number of the agreements per State, summaries of all the agreements, and information on the type of organizations participating in the agreements, types of services provided under the agreements, and the net proceeds from, and documentation of funds spent and reimbursed, under the agreements.

(d) TIMELY REIMBURSEMENT.—All reimbursements made under this section shall be made in a timely manner, according to standards specified by the Assistant Secretary.

(e) Cost.—In this section, the term 'cost' means an expense, including an administrative expense, incurred by a recipient in developing or carrying out an agreement described in subsection (a), whether the recipient contributed funds, staff time, or other plant, equipment, or services to meet the expense.

(42 U.S.C. 3020c)

Section. 213. SURPLUS PROPERTY ELIGIBILITY

Any State or local government agency, and any nonprofit organization or institution, which receives funds appropriated for programs for older individuals under this Act, under title IV or title XX of the Social Security Act, or under titles VIII and X of the Economic Opportunity Act of 1964 and the Community Services Block Grant Act, shall be deemed eligible to receive for such programs, property which is declared surplus to the needs of the Federal Government in accordance with laws applicable to surplus property.

(42 U.S.C. 3020d)

Section. 214. NUTRITION EDUCATION.

The Assistant Secretary, in consultation with the Secretary of Agriculture, shall conduct outreach and provide technical assistance to agencies and organizations that serve older individuals to assist such agencies and organizations to carry out integrated health promotion and disease prevention programs that—

    (1)   are designed for older individuals; and

    (2)   include—

        (A)   nutrition education;

        (B)   physical activity; and

        (C)   other activities to modify behavior and to improve health literacy, including providing information on optimal nutrient intake, through nutrition education and nutrition assessment and counseling, in accordance with section 339(2)(J).

Section. 215. PENSION COUNSELING AND INFORMATION PROGRAMS.

(a)   DEFINITIONS.—In this section:

(1) PENSION AND OTHER RETIREMENT BENEFITS.—The term "pension and other retirement benefits" means private, civil service, and other public pensions and retirement benefits, including benefits provided under—

        (A)   the Social Security program under title II of the Social Security Act (42 U.S.C. 401 et seq.);

        (B)   the railroad retirement program under the Railroad Retirement Act of 1974 (45 U.S.C. 231 et seq.);

        (C)   the government retirement benefits programs under the Civil Service Retirement System set forth in chapter 83 of title 5, United States Code, the Federal Employees Retirement System set forth in chapter 84 of title 5, United States Code, or other Federal retirement systems; or

        (D)   employee pension benefit plans as defined in section 3(2) of the Employee Retirement Income Security Act of 1974 (29 U.S.C. 1002(2)).

    (2)   PENSION COUNSELING AND INFORMATION PROGRAM.— The term "pension counseling and information program" means a program described in subsection (b).

(b) PROGRAM AUTHORIZED.—The Assistant Secretary shall award grants to eligible entities to establish and carry out pension counseling and information programs that create or continue a sufficient number of pension assistance and counseling programs to provide outreach, information, counseling, referral, and other assistance regarding pension and other retirement benefits, and rights related to such benefits, to individuals in the United States.

(c) ELIGIBLE ENTITIES.—The Assistant Secretary shall award grants under this section to—

(1) State agencies or area agencies on aging; and

(2) nonprofit organizations with a proven record of providing—

    (A) services related to retirement of older individuals;

    (B) services to Native Americans; or

    (C) specific pension counseling.

(d) CITIZEN ADVISORY PANEL.—The Assistant Secretary shall establish a citizen advisory panel to advise the Assistant Secretary regarding which entities should receive grant awards under this section. Such panel shall include representatives of business, labor, national senior advocates, and national pension rights advocates. The Assistant Secretary shall consult such panel prior to awarding grants under this section.

(e) APPLICATION.—To be eligible to receive a grant under this section, an entity shall submit an application to the Assistant Secretary at such time, in such manner, and containing such information as the Assistant Secretary may require, including—

(1) a plan to establish a pension counseling and information program that—

    (A) establishes or continues a State or area pension counseling and information program;

    (B) serves a specific geographic area;

    (C) provides counseling (including direct counseling and assistance to individuals who need information regarding pension and other retirement benefits) and information that may assist individuals in obtaining, or establishing rights to, and filing claims or complaints regarding, pension and other retirement benefits;

    (D) provides information on sources of pension and other retirement benefits;

    (E) establishes a system to make referrals for legal services and other advocacy programs;

    (F) establishes a system of referral to Federal, State, and local departments or agencies related to pension and other retirement benefits;

    (G) provides a sufficient number of staff positions (including volunteer positions) to ensure information, counseling, referral, and assistance regarding pension and other retirement benefits;

    (H) provides training programs for staff members, including volunteer staff members, of pension and other retirement benefits programs;

    (I) makes recommendations to the Administration, the Department of Labor and other Federal, State, and local agencies concerning issues for older individuals related to pension and other retirement benefits; and

    (J) establishes or continues an outreach program to provide information, counseling, referral and assistance regarding pension and other retirement benefits, with particular emphasis on outreach to women, minorities, older individuals residing in rural areas, low-income retirees, and older individuals with limited English proficiency.

(2) an assurance that staff members (including volunteer staff members) have no conflict of interest in providing the services described in the plan described in paragraph (1).

(f) CRITERIA.—The Assistant Secretary shall consider the following criteria in awarding grants under this section:

(1) Evidence of a commitment by the entity to carry out a proposed pension counseling and information program.

(2) The ability of the entity to perform effective outreach to affected populations, particularly populations with limited English proficiency and other populations that are identified as in need of special outreach.

(3) Reliable information that the population to be served by the entity has a demonstrable need for the services proposed to be provided under the program.

(4) The ability of the entity to provide services under the program on a statewide or regional basis.

(g) TRAINING AND TECHNICAL ASSISTANCE PROGRAM.—

(1) IN GENERAL.—The Assistant Secretary shall award grants to eligible entities to establish training and technical assistance programs that shall provide information and technical assistance to the staffs of entities operating pension counseling and information programs described in subsection (b), and general assistance to such entities, including assistance in the design of program evaluation tools.

(2) ELIGIBLE ENTITIES.—Entities that are eligible to receive a grant under this subsection include nonprofit private organizations with a record of providing national information, referral, and advocacy in matters related to pension and other retirement benefits.

(3) APPLICATION.—To be eligible to receive a grant under this subsection, an entity shall submit an application to the Assistant Secretary at such time, in such manner, and containing such information as the Assistant Secretary may require.

(h) PENSION ASSISTANCE HOTLINE AND INTRAGENCY COORDINATION.—

(1) HOTLINE.—The Assistant Secretary shall enter into agreements with other Federal agencies to establish and administer a national telephone hotline that shall provide information regarding pension and other retirement benefits, and rights related to such benefits.

(2) CONTENT.—Such hotline described in paragraph (1) shall provide information for individuals (including individuals with limited English proficiency) seeking outreach, information, counseling, referral, and assistance regarding pension and other retirement benefits, and rights related to such benefits.

(3) AGREEMENTS.—The Assistant Secretary may enter into agreements with the Secretary of Labor and the heads of other Federal agencies that regulate the provision of pension and other retirement benefits in order to carry out this subsection.

(i) REPORT TO CONGRESS.—Not later than 30 months after the date of the enactment of this section, the Assistant Secretary shall submit to the Committee on Education and the Workforce of the House of Representatives and the Committee on Health, Education, Labor and Pensions of the Senate a report that—

(1) summarizes the distribution of funds authorized for grants under this section and the expenditure of such funds;

(2) summarizes the scope and content of training and assistance provided under a program carried out under this section and the degree to which the training and assistance can be replicated;

(3) outlines the problems that individuals participating in programs funded under this section encountered concerning rights related to pension and other retirement benefits; and

(4) makes recommendations regarding the manner in which services provided in programs funded under this section can be incorporated into the ongoing programs of State agencies, area agencies on aging, multipurpose senior centers and other similar entities.

(j) ADMINISTRATIVE EXPENSES.—Of the funds appropriated under section 216 to carry out this section for a fiscal year, not more than $100,000 may be used by the Administration for administrative expenses.

(42 U.S.C. 3020e–1)

Section. 216. AUTHORIZATION OF APPROPRIATIONS.

(a) IN GENERAL.—For purposes of carrying out this Act, there are authorized to be appropriated for administration, salaries, and expenses of the Administration such sums as may be necessary for fiscal years 2007, 2008, 2009, 2010, and 2011.

(b) ELDERCARE LOCATOR SERVICE.—There are authorized to be appropriated to carry out section 202(a)(24) (relating to the National Eldercare Locator Service) such sums as may be necessary for fiscal years 2007, 2008, 2009, 2010, and 2011.

(c) PENSION COUNSELING AND INFORMATION PROGRAMS.—There are authorized to be appropriated to carry out section 215, such sums as may be necessary for fiscal years 2007, 2008, 2009, 2010, and 2011.

TITLE III – GRANTS FOR STATE AND COMMUNITY PROGRAMS ON AGING

PART A – GENERAL PROVISIONS

Section. 301. PURPOSE; ADMINISTRATION

(a) (1) It is the purpose of this title to encourage and assist State agencies and area agencies on aging to concentrate resources in order to develop greater capacity and foster the development and implementation of comprehensive and coordinated systems to serve older individuals by entering into new cooperative arrangements in each State with the persons described in paragraph (2), for the planning, and for the provision of, supportive services, and multipurpose senior centers, in order to —

    (A) secure and maintain maximum independence and dignity in a home environment for older individuals capable of self-care with appropriate supportive services;

    (B) remove individual and social barriers to economic and personal independence for older individuals;

    (C) provide a continuum of care for vulnerable older individuals; and

    (D) secure the opportunity for older individuals to receive managed in-home and community-based long-term care services.

  (2) The persons referred to in paragraph (1) include —

    (A) State agencies and area agencies on aging;

    (B) other State agencies, including agencies that administer home and community care programs;

    (C) Indian tribes, tribal organizations, and Native Hawaiian organizations;

    (D) the providers, including voluntary organizations or other private sector organizations, of supportive services, nutrition services, and multipurpose senior centers;

    (E) organizations representing or employing older individuals or their families; and

    (F) organizations that have experience in providing training, placement, and stipends for volunteers or participants who are older individuals (such as organizations carrying out Federal service programs administered by the Corporation for National and Community Service), in community service settings.

(b) (1) In order to effectively carry out the purpose of this title, the Assistant Secretary shall administer programs under this title through the Administration.

  (2) In carrying out the provisions of this title, the Assistant Secretary may request the technical assistance and cooperation of the Department of Education, the Department of Labor, the Department of Housing and Urban Development, the Department of Transportation, the Office of Community Services, the Department of Veterans Affairs, the Substance Abuse and Mental Health Services Administration, and such other agencies and departments of the Federal Government as may be appropriate.

(c) The Assistant Secretary shall provide technical assistance and training (by contract, grant, or otherwise) to State long-term care ombudsman programs established under section 307(a)(9) in accordance with section 712, and to individuals within such programs designated under section 712 to be representatives of a long-term care ombudsman, in order to enable such ombudsmen and such representatives to carry out the ombudsman program effectively.

(d) (1) Any funds received under an allotment as described in section 304(a), or funds contributed toward the non-Federal share under section 304(d), shall be used only for activities and services to benefit older individuals and other individuals as specifically provided for in this title.

   (2) No provision of this title shall be construed as prohibiting a State agency or area agency on aging from providing services by using funds from sources not described in paragraph (1).

(42 U.S.C. 3021)

Section. 302. DEFINITIONS

For the purpose of this title —

   (1) The term "comprehensive and coordinated system" means a system for providing all necessary supportive services, including nutrition services, in a manner designed to —
   (A) facilitate accessibility to, and utilization of, all supportive services and nutrition services provided within the geographic area served by such system by any public or private agency or organization;
   (B) develop and make the most efficient use of supportive services and nutrition services in meeting the needs of older individuals;
   (C) use available resources efficiently and with a minimum of duplication; and
   (D) encourage and assist public and private entities that have unrealized potential for meeting the service needs of older individuals to assist the older individuals on a voluntary basis.

   (2) The term "education and training service" means a supportive service designed to assist older individuals to better cope with their economic, health, and personal needs through services such as consumer education, continuing education, health education, pre-retirement education, financial planning, and other education and training services which will advance the objectives of this Act.

   (3) The term 'family caregiver' means an adult family member, or another individual, who is an informal provider of in-home and community care to an older individual or to an individual with Alzheimer's disease or a related disorder with neurological and organic brain dysfunction.

   (4) The term "unit of general purpose local government" means —
   (A) a political subdivision of the State whose authority is general and not limited to only one function or combination of related functions; or
   (B) an Indian tribal organization.

(42 U.S.C. 3022)

Section. 303. AUTHORIZATION OF APPROPRIATIONS; USES OF FUNDS

(a) (1) There are authorized to be appropriated to carry out part B (relating to supportive services) such sums as may be necessary for fiscal years 2007, 2008, 2009, 2010, and 2011.

   (2) Funds appropriated under paragraph (1) shall be available to carry out section 712.'

(b) (1) There are authorized to be appropriated to carry out subpart 1 of part C (relating to congregate nutrition services) such sums as may be necessary for fiscal years 2007, 2008, 2009, 2010, and 2011.

(2) There are authorized to be appropriated to carry out subpart 2 of part C (relating to home delivered nutrition services) such sums as may be necessary for fiscal years 2007, 2008, 2009, 2010, and 2011.

(c) Grants made under part B, and subparts 1 and 2 of part C, of this title may be used for paying part of the cost of—

(1) the administration of area plans by area agencies on aging designated under section 305(a)(2)(A), including the preparation of area plans on aging consistent with section 306 and the evaluation of activities carried out under such plans; and

(2) the development of comprehensive and coordinated systems for supportive services, congregate and home delivered nutrition services under subparts 1 and 2 of part C, the development and operation of multipurpose senior centers, and the delivery of legal assistance.

(d) There are authorized to be appropriated to carry out part D (relating to disease prevention and health promotion services) such sums as may be necessary for fiscal years 2007, 2008, 2009, 2010, and 2011.

(e) (1) There are authorized to be appropriated to carry out part E (relating to family caregiver support) $160,000,000 for fiscal year 2007.

(2) There are authorized to be appropriated to carry out part E (relating to family caregiver support) $166,500,000 for fiscal year 2008, $173,000,000 for fiscal year 2009, $180,000,000 for fiscal year 2010, and $187,000,000 for fiscal year 2011.

(3) Of the funds appropriated under paragraphs (1) and (2), not more than 1 percent of such funds may be reserved to carry out activities described in section 411(a)(11)(42 U.S.C. 3023)

Section. 304. ALLOTMENT; FEDERAL SHARE

(a) (1) From the sums appropriated under subsections (a) through (d) of section 303 for each fiscal year, each State shall be allotted an amount which bears the same ratio to such sums as the population of older individuals in such State bears to the population of older individuals in all States.

(2) In determining the amounts allotted to States from the sums appropriated under section 303 for a fiscal year, the Assistant Secretary shall first determine the amount allotted to each State under paragraph (1) and then proportionately adjust such amounts, if necessary, to meet the requirements of paragraph (3).

(3) (A) No State shall be allotted less than 1/2 of 1 percent of the sum appropriated for the fiscal year for which the determination is made.

(B) Guam and the United States Virgin Islands shall each be allotted not less than 1/4 of 1 percent of the sum appropriated for the fiscal year for which the determination is made.

(C) American Samoa and the Commonwealth of the Northern Mariana Islands shall each be allotted not less than 1/16 of 1 percent of the sum appropriated for the fiscal year for which the determination is made. For the purposes of the exception contained in subparagraph (A) only, the term "State" [8]does not include Guam, American Samoa, the United States Virgin Islands, and the Commonwealth of the Northern Mariana Islands.

(D) (i) No State shall be allotted less than the total amount allotted to the State for fiscal year 2006.

    (ii) No State shall receive a percentage increase in an allotment, above the State's fiscal year 2006 allotment, that is less than—

        (I) for fiscal year 2007, 20 percent of the percentage increase above the fiscal year 2006 allotments for all of the States;

        (II) for fiscal year 2008, 15 percent of the percentage increase above the fiscal year 2006 allotments for all of the States;

        (III) for fiscal year 2009, 10 percent of the percentage increase above the fiscal year 2006 allotments for all of the States; and

        (IV) For fiscal year 2010, 5 percent of the percentage increase above the fiscal year 2006 allotments for all of the States.

(4) The number of individuals aged 60 or older in any State and in all States shall be determined by the Assistant Secretary on the basis of the most recent data available from the Bureau of the Census, and other reliable demographic data satisfactory to the Assistant Secretary.

(5) State allotments for a fiscal year under this section shall be proportionally reduced to the extent that appropriations may be insufficient to provide the full allotments of the prior year.

(b) Whenever the Assistant Secretary determines that any amount allotted to a State under part B or C, or subpart 1 of part E, for a fiscal year under this section will not be used by such State for carrying out the purpose for which the allotment was made, the Assistant Secretary shall make such allotment available for carrying out such purpose to one or more other States to the extent the Assistant Secretary determines that such other State will be able to use such additional amount for carrying out such purpose. Any amount made available to a State from an appropriation for a fiscal year in accordance with the preceding sentence shall, for purposes of this title, be regarded as part of such State's allotment (as determined under subsection (a)) for such year, but shall remain available until the end of the succeeding fiscal year.

(c) If the Assistant Secretary finds that any State has failed to qualify under the State plan requirements of section 307 or the Assistant Secretary does not approve the funding formula required under section 305(a)(2)(C), the Assistant Secretary shall withhold the allotment of funds to such State referred to in subsection (a). The Assistant Secretary shall disburse the funds so withheld directly to any public or private nonprofit institution or organization, agency, or political subdivision of such State submitting an approved plan under section 307, which includes an agreement that any such payment shall be matched in the proportion determined under subsection (d)(1)(D) for such State, by funds or in-kind resources from non-Federal sources.

(d) (1) From any State's allotment, after the application of section 308(b), under this section for any fiscal year—

    (A) such amount as the State agency determines, but not more than 10 percent thereof, shall be available for paying such percentage as the agency determines, but not more than 75 percent, of the cost of administration of area plans;

    (B) such amount (excluding any amount attributable to funds appropriated under section 303(a)(3)) as the State agency determines to be adequate for conducting an effective ombudsman program under section 307(a)(9) shall be available for conducting such program;

    (C) not less than $150,000 and not more than 4 percent of the amount allotted to the State for carrying out part B, shall be available for conducting outreach demonstration projects under section 706; and

(D) the remainder of such allotment shall be available to such State only for paying such percentage as the State agency determines, but not more than 85 percent of the cost of supportive services, senior centers, and nutrition services under this title provided in the State as part of a comprehensive and coordinated system in planning and service areas for which there is an area plan approved by the State agency.

(2) The non-Federal share shall be in cash or in kind. In determining the amount of the non-Federal share, the Assistant Secretary may attribute fair market value to services and facilities contributed from non-Federal sources.

(42 U.S.C. 3024)

Section. 305. ORGANIZATION

i. In order for a State to be eligible to participate in programs of grants to States from allotments under this title—

(1) the State shall, in accordance with regulations of the Assistant Secretary, designate a State agency as the sole State agency to—

(A) develop a State plan to be submitted to the Assistant Secretary for approval under section 307;

(B) administer the State plan within such State;

(C) be primarily responsible for the planning, policy development, administration, coordination, priority setting, and evaluation of all State activities related to the objectives of this Act;

(D) serve as an effective and visible advocate for older individuals by reviewing and commenting upon all State plans, budgets, and policies which affect older individuals and providing technical assistance to any agency, organization, association, or individual representing the needs of older individuals; and

(E) divide the State into distinct planning and service areas (or in the case of a State specified in subsection (b)(5)(A), designate the entire State as a single planning and service area), in accordance with guidelines issued by the Assistant Secretary, after considering the geographical distribution of older individuals in the State, the incidence of the need for supportive services, nutrition services, multipurpose senior centers, and legal assistance, the distribution of older individuals who have greatest economic need (with particular attention to low-income older individuals, including low-income minority older individuals, older individuals with limited English proficiency, and older individuals residing in rural areas) residing in such areas, the distribution of older individuals who have greatest social need (with particular attention to low-income older individuals, including low-income minority older individuals, older individuals with limited English proficiency, and older individuals residing in rural areas) residing in such areas, the distribution of older individuals who are Indians residing in such areas, the distribution of resources available to provide such services or centers, the boundaries of existing areas within the State which were drawn for the planning or administration of supportive services programs, the location of units of general purpose local government within the State, and any other relevant factors;

(2) the State agency shall—

(A) except as provided in subsection (b)(5), designate for each such area after consideration of the views offered by the unit or units of general purpose local government in such area, a public or private nonprofit agency or organization as the area agency on aging for such area;

(B) provide assurances, satisfactory to the Assistant Secretary, that the State agency will take into account, in connection with matters of general policy arising in the development and administration of the State plan for any fiscal year, the views of recipients of supportive services or nutrition services, or individuals using multipurpose senior centers provided under such plan;

(C) in consultation with area agencies, in accordance with guidelines issued by the Assistant Secretary, and using the best available data, develop and publish for review and comment a formula for distribution within the State of funds received under this title that takes into account—

    (i) the geographical distribution of older individuals in the State; and

    (ii) the distribution among planning and service areas of older individuals with greatest economic need and older individuals with greatest social need, with particular attention to low-income minority older individuals;

(D) submit its formula developed under subparagraph (C) to the Assistant Secretary for approval;

(E) provide assurance that preference will be given to providing services to older individuals with greatest economic need and older individuals with greatest social need (with particular attention to low-income older individuals, including low-income minority older individuals, older individuals with limited English proficiency, and older individuals residing in rural areas) and include proposed methods of carrying out the preference in the State plan;

(F) provide assurances that the State agency will require use of outreach efforts described in section 307(a)(16); and

(G) (i) set specific objectives, in consultation with area agencies on aging, for each planning and service area for providing services funded under this title to low-income minority older individuals and older individuals residing in rural areas;

    (ii) provide an assurance that the State agency will undertake specific program development, advocacy, and outreach efforts focused on the needs of low-income minority older individuals[9]; and

    (iii) provide a description of the efforts described in clause (ii) that will be undertaken by the State agency; and

(3) the State agency shall, consistent with this section, promote the development and implementation of a State system of long-term care that is a comprehensive, coordinated system that enables older individuals to receive long-term care in home and community-based settings, in a manner responsive to the needs and preferences of the older individuals and their family caregivers, by—

(A) collaborating, coordinating, and consulting with other agencies in such State responsible for formulating, implementing, and administering programs, benefits, and services related to providing long-term care;

(B) participating in any State government activities concerning long-term care, including reviewing and commenting on any State rules, regulations, and policies related to long-term care;

(C) conducting analyses and making recommendations with respect to strategies for modifying the State system of long-term care to better —
  (i) respond to the needs and preferences of older individuals and family caregivers;
  (ii) facilitate the provision, by service providers, of long-term care in home and community-based settings; and
  (iii) target services to individuals at risk for institutional placement, to permit such individuals to remain in home and community-based settings;
(D) implementing (through area agencies on aging, service providers, and such other entities as the State determines to be appropriate) evidence-based programs to assist older individuals and their family caregivers in learning about and making behavioral changes intended to reduce the risk of injury, disease, and disability among older individuals; and
(E) providing for the availability and distribution (through public education campaigns, Aging and Disability Resource Centers, area agencies on aging, and other appropriate means) of information relating to—
  (i) the need to plan in advance for long-term care; and
  (ii) the full range of available public and private long-term care (including integrated long-term care) programs, options, service providers, and resources.

(b) (1) In carrying out the requirement of subsection (a)(1), the State may designate as a planning and service area any unit of general purpose local government which has a population of 100,000 or more. In any case in which a unit of general purpose local government makes application to the State agency under the preceding sentence to be designated as a planning and service area, the State agency shall, upon request, provide an opportunity for a hearing to such unit of general purpose local government. A State may designate as a planning and service area under subsection (a)(1) any region within the State recognized for purposes of area wide planning which includes one or more such units of general purpose local government when the State determines that the designation of such a regional planning and service area is necessary for, and will enhance, the effective administration of the programs authorized by this title. The State may include in any planning and service area designated under subsection (a)(1) such additional areas adjacent to the unit of general purpose local government or regions so designated as the State determines to be necessary for, and will enhance the effective administration of the programs authorized by this title.

(2) The State is encouraged in carrying out the requirement of subsection (a)(1) to include the area covered by the appropriate economic development district involved in any planning and service area designated under subsection (a)(1), and to include all portions of an Indian reservation within a single planning and service area, if feasible.

(3) The chief executive officer of each State in which a planning and service area crosses State boundaries, or in which an interstate Indian reservation is located, may apply to the Assistant Secretary to request re-designation as an interstate planning and service area comprising the entire metropolitan area or Indian reservation. If the Assistant Secretary approves such an application, the Assistant Secretary shall adjust the State allotments of the areas within the planning and service area in which the interstate planning and service area is established to reflect the number of older individuals within the area who will be served by an interstate planning and service area not within the State.

(4)	Whenever a unit of general purpose local government, a region, a metropolitan area or an Indian reservation is denied designation under the provisions of subsection (a)(1), such unit of general purpose local government, region, metropolitan area, or Indian reservation may appeal the decision of the State agency to the Assistant Secretary. The Assistant Secretary shall afford such unit, region, metropolitan area, or Indian reservation an opportunity for a hearing. In carrying out the provisions of this paragraph, the Assistant Secretary may approve the decision of the State agency, disapprove the decision of the State agency and require the State agency to designate the unit, region, area, or Indian reservation appealing the decision as a planning and service area, or take such other action as the Assistant Secretary deems appropriate.

(5)	(A) A State which on or before October 1, 1980, had designated, with the approval of the Assistant Secretary, a single planning and service area covering all of the older individuals in the State, in which the State agency was administering the area plan, may after that date designate one or more additional planning and service areas within the State to be administered by public or private nonprofit agencies or organizations as area agencies on aging, after considering the factors specified in subsection (a)(1)(E). The State agency shall continue to perform the functions of an area agency on aging for any area of the State not included in a planning and service area for which an area agency on aging has been designated.

(B)	Whenever a State agency designates a new area agency on aging after the date of enactment of the Older Americans Act Amendments of 1984, the State agency shall give the right to first refusal to a unit of general purpose local government if

(i)	such unit can meet the requirements of subsection (c), and

(ii)	the boundaries of such a unit and the boundaries of the area are reasonably contiguous.

(C)	(i)	A State agency shall establish and follow appropriate procedures to provide due process to affected parties, if the State agency initiates an action or proceeding to —

(I)	revoke the designation of the area agency on aging under subsection (a);

(II)	designate an additional planning and service area in a State;

(III)	divide the State into different planning and services[10] areas; or

(IV)	otherwise affect the boundaries of the planning and service areas in the State.

(ii)	The procedures described in clause (i) shall include procedures for —

(I)	providing notice of an action or proceeding described in clause (i);

(II)	documenting the need for the action or proceeding;

(III)	conducting a public hearing for the action or proceeding;

(IV)	involving area agencies on aging, service providers, and older individuals in the action or proceeding; and

(V)	allowing an appeal of the decision of the State agency in the action or proceeding to the Assistant Secretary.

(iii)	An adversely affected party involved in an action or proceeding described in clause (i) may bring an appeal described in clause (ii)(V) on the basis of —

(I)	the facts and merits of the matter that is the subject of the action or proceeding; or

(II)	procedural grounds.

(iv) In deciding an appeal described in clause (ii)(V), the Assistant Secretary may affirm or set aside the decision of the State agency. If the Assistant Secretary sets aside the decision, and the State agency has taken an action described in sub-clauses (I) through (III) of clause (i), the State agency shall nullify the action.

(c) An area agency on aging designated under subsection (a) shall be—

(1) an established office of aging which is operating within a planning and service area designated under subsection (a);

(2) any office or agency of a unit of general purpose local government, which is designated to function only for the purpose of serving as an area agency on aging by the chief elected official of such unit;

(3) any office or agency designated by the appropriate chief elected officials of any combination of units of general purpose local government to act only on behalf of such combination for such purpose;

(4) any public or nonprofit private agency in a planning and service area, or any separate organizational unit within such agency, which is under the supervision or direction for this purpose of the designated State agency and which can and will engage only in the planning or provision of a broad range of supportive services, or nutrition services within such planning and service area; or

(5) in the case of a State specified in subsection (b)(5), the State agency; and shall provide assurance, determined adequate by the State agency, that the area agency on aging will have the ability to develop an area plan and to carry out, directly or through contractual or other arrangements, a program in accordance with the plan within the planning and service area. In designating an area agency on aging within the planning and service area or within any unit of general purpose local government designated as a planning and service area the State shall give preference to an established office on aging, unless the State agency finds that no such office within the planning and service area will have the capacity to carry out the area plan.

(d) The publication for review and comment required by paragraph (2)(C) of subsection (a) shall include—

(1) a descriptive statement of the formula's assumptions and goals, and the application of the definitions of greatest economic or social need,

(2) a numerical statement of the actual funding formula to be used,

(3) a listing of the population, economic, and social data to be used for each planning and service area in the State, and

(4) a demonstration of the allocation of funds, pursuant to the funding formula, to each planning and service area in the State.

(42 U.S.C. 3025)

Section. 306. AREA PLANS

(a) Each area agency on aging designated under section 305(a)(2)(A) shall, in order to be approved by the State agency, prepare and develop an area plan for a planning and service area for a two-, three-, or four-year period determined by the State agency, with such annual adjustments as may be necessary. Each such plan shall be based upon a uniform format for area plans within the State prepared in accordance with section 307(a)(1). Each such plan shall—

(1) provide, through a comprehensive and coordinated system, for supportive services, nutrition services, and, where appropriate, for the establishment, maintenance, or construction of multipurpose senior centers, within the planning and service area covered by the plan, including determining the extent of need for supportive services, nutrition services, and multipurpose senior centers in such area (taking into consideration, among other things, the number of older individuals with low incomes residing in such area, the number of older individuals who have greatest economic need (with particular attention to low-income older individuals, including low-income minority older individuals, older individuals with limited English proficiency, and older individuals residing in rural areas) residing in such area, the number of older individuals who have greatest social need (with particular attention to low-income older individuals, including low-income minority older individuals, older individuals with limited English proficiency, and older individuals residing in rural areas) residing in such area, the number of older individuals at risk for institutional placement residing in such area, and the number of older individuals who are Indians residing in such area, and the efforts of voluntary organizations in the community, evaluating the effectiveness of the use of resources in meeting such need, and entering into agreements with providers of supportive services, nutrition services, or multipurpose senior centers in such area, for the provision of such services or centers to meet such need;

(2) provide assurances that an adequate proportion, as required under section 307(a)(2), of the amount allotted for part B to the planning and service area will be expended for the delivery of each of the following categories of services—

    (A) services associated with access to services (transportation, health services (including mental health services) outreach, information and assistance, (which may include information and assistance to consumers on availability of services under part B and how to receive benefits under and participate in publicly supported programs for which the consumer may be eligible) and case management services);

    (B) in-home services, including supportive services for families of older individuals who are victims of Alzheimer's disease and related disorders with neurological and organic brain dysfunction; and

    (C) legal assistance; and assurances that the area agency on aging will report annually to the State agency in detail the amount of funds expended for each such category during the fiscal year most recently concluded;

(3) (A) designate, where feasible, a focal point for comprehensive service delivery in each community, giving special consideration to designating multipurpose senior centers (including multipurpose senior centers operated by organizations referred to in paragraph (6)(C)) as such focal point; and

    (1) specify, in grants, contracts, and agreements implementing the plan, the identity of each focal point so designated;

(4) (A)(i)   (I) provide assurances that the area agency on aging will—

        (aa) set specific objectives, consistent with State policy, for providing services to older individuals with greatest economic need, older individuals with greatest social need, and older individuals at risk for institutional placement;

        (bb) include specific objectives for providing services to low-income minority older individuals, older individuals with limited English proficiency, and older individuals residing in rural areas; and

(II) include proposed methods to achieve the objectives described in items (aa) and (bb) of subclause (I);

(ii) provide assurances that the area agency on aging will include in each agreement made with a provider of any service under this title, a requirement that such provider will—

(I) specify how the provider intends to satisfy the service needs of low-income minority individuals, older individuals with limited English proficiency, and older individuals residing in rural areas in the area served by the provider;

(II) to the maximum extent feasible, provide services to low-income minority individuals, older individuals with limited English proficiency, and older individuals residing in rural areas in accordance with their need for such services; and

(III) meet specific objectives established by the area agency on aging, for providing services to low-income minority individuals, older individuals with limited English proficiency, and older individuals residing in rural areas within the planning and service area; and

(iii) with respect to the fiscal year preceding the fiscal year for which such plan is prepared—

(I) identify the number of low-income minority older individuals in the planning and service area;

(II) describe the methods used to satisfy the service needs of such minority older individuals; and

(III) provide information on the extent to which the area agency on aging met the objectives described in clause (i);

(B) provide assurances that the area agency on aging will use outreach efforts that will—

(i) identify individuals eligible for assistance under this Act, with special emphasis on—

(I) older individuals residing in rural areas;

(II) older individuals with greatest economic need (with particular attention to low-income minority individuals and older individuals residing in rural areas);

(III) older individuals with greatest social need (with particular attention to low-income minority individuals and older individuals residing in rural areas);

(IV) older individuals with severe disabilities;

(V) older individuals with limited English proficiency;

(VI) older individuals with Alzheimer's disease and related disorders with neurological and organic brain dysfunction (and the caretakers of such individuals); and

(VII) older individuals at risk for institutional placement; and

(ii) inform the older individuals referred to in sub-clauses (I) through (VII) of clause (i), and the caretakers of such individuals, of the availability of such assistance; and

(C) contain an assurance that the area agency on aging will ensure that each activity undertaken by the agency, including planning, advocacy, and systems development, will include a focus on the needs of low-income minority older individuals and older individuals residing in rural areas;

(5) provide assurances that the area agency on aging will coordinate planning, identification, assessment of needs, and provision of services for older individuals with disabilities, with particular attention to individuals with severe disabilities, and individuals at risk for institutional placement with agencies that develop or provide services for individuals with disabilities;

(6) provide that the area agency on aging will—

(A) take into account in connection with matters of general policy arising in the development and administration of the area plan, the views of recipients of services under such plan;

(B) serve as the advocate and focal point for older individuals within the community by (in cooperation with agencies, organizations, and individuals participating in activities under the plan) monitoring, evaluating, and commenting upon all policies, programs, hearings, levies, and community actions which will affect older individuals;

(C) (i) where possible, enter into arrangements with organizations providing day care services for children, assistance to older individuals caring for relatives who are children, and respite for families, so as to provide opportunities for older individuals to aid or assist on a voluntary basis in the delivery of such services to children, adults, and families;

(ii) if possible regarding the provision of services under this title, enter into arrangements and coordinate with organizations that have a proven record of providing services to older individuals, that-

(I) were officially designated as community action agencies or community action programs under section 210 of the Economic Opportunity Act of 1964 (42 U.S.C. 2790) for fiscal year 1981, and did not lose the designation as a result of failure to comply with such Act; or

(II) came into existence during fiscal year 1982 as direct successors in interest to such community action agencies or community action programs; and that meet the requirements under section 676B of the Community Services Block Grant Act; and

(iii) make use of trained volunteers in providing direct services delivered to older individuals and individuals with disabilities needing such services and, if possible, work in coordination with organizations that have experience in providing training, placement, and stipends for volunteers or participants (such as organizations carrying out Federal service programs administered by the Corporation for National and Community Service), in community service settings;

(D) establish an advisory council consisting of older individuals (including minority individuals and older individuals residing in rural areas) who are participants or who are eligible to participate in programs assisted under this Act, family caregivers of such individuals, representatives of older individuals, service providers, representatives of the business community, local elected officials, providers of veterans' health care (if appropriate), and the general public, to advise continuously the area agency on aging on all matters relating to the development of the area plan, the administration of the plan and operations conducted under the plan;

(E) establish effective and efficient procedures for coordination of—

(i) entities conducting programs that receive assistance under this Act within the planning and service area served by the agency; and

(ii) entities conducting other Federal programs for older individuals at the local level, with particular emphasis on entities conducting programs described in section 203(b), within the area;

(F) in coordination with the State agency and with the State agency responsible for mental health services, increase public awareness of mental health disorders, remove barriers to diagnosis and treatment, and coordinate mental health services (including mental health screenings) provided with funds expended by the area agency on aging with mental health services provided by community health centers and by other public agencies and nonprofit private organizations;

(G) if there is a significant population of older individuals who are Indians in the planning and service area of the area agency on aging, the area agency on aging shall conduct outreach activities to identify such individuals in such area and shall inform such individuals of the availability of assistance under this Act;

(7) provide that the area agency on aging shall, consistent with this section, facilitate the area-wide development and implementation of a comprehensive, coordinated system for providing long-term care in home and community-based settings, in a manner responsive to the needs and preferences of older individuals and their family caregivers, by —

(A) collaborating, coordinating activities, and consulting with other local public and private agencies and organizations responsible for administering programs, benefits, and services related to providing long-term care;

(B) conducting analyses and making recommendations with respect to strategies for modifying the local system of long-term care to better —

(i) respond to the needs and preferences of older individuals and family caregivers;

(ii) facilitate the provision, by service providers, of long-term care in home and community-based settings; and

(iii) target services to older individuals at risk for institutional placement, to permit such individuals to remain in home and community-based settings;

(C) implementing, through the agency or service providers, evidence-based programs to assist older individuals and their family caregivers in learning about and making behavioral changes intended to reduce the risk of injury, disease, and disability among older individuals; and

(D) providing for the availability and distribution (through public education campaigns, Aging and Disability Resource Centers, the area agency on aging itself, and other appropriate means) of information relating to —

(i) the need to plan in advance for long-term care; and

(ii) the full range of available public and private long-term care (including integrated long-term care) programs, options, service providers, and resources;

(8) provide that case management services provided under this title through the area agency on aging will —

(A) not duplicate case management services provided through other Federal and State programs;

(B) be coordinated with services described in subparagraph (A); and

(C) be provided by a public agency or a nonprofit private agency that —

(i) gives each older individual seeking services under this title a list of agencies that provide similar services within the jurisdiction of the area agency on aging;

     (ii) gives each individual described in clause (i) a statement specifying that the individual has a right to make an independent choice of service providers and documents receipt by such individual of such statement;

     (iii) has case managers acting as agents for the individuals receiving the services and not as promoters for the agency providing such services; or

     (iv) is located in a rural area and obtains a waiver of the requirements described in clauses (i) through (iii);

(9) provide assurances that the area agency on aging, in carrying out the State Long-Term Care Ombudsman program under section 307(a)(9), will expend not less than the total amount of funds appropriated under this Act and expended by the agency in fiscal year 2000 in carrying out such a program under this title;

(10) provide a grievance procedure for older individuals who are dissatisfied with or denied services under this title;

(11) provide information and assurances concerning services to older individuals who are Native Americans (referred to in this paragraph as "older Native Americans"), including—

    (A) information concerning whether there is a significant population of older Native Americans in the planning and service area and if so, an assurance that the area agency on aging will pursue activities, including outreach, to increase access of those older Native Americans to programs and benefits provided under this title;

    (B) an assurance that the area agency on aging will, to the maximum extent practicable, coordinate the services the agency provides under this title with services provided under title VI; and

    (C) an assurance that the area agency on aging will make services under the area plan available, to the same extent as such services are available to older individuals within the planning and service area, to older Native Americans; and

(12) provide that the area agency on aging will establish procedures for coordination of services with entities conducting other Federal or federally assisted programs for older individuals at the local level, with particular emphasis on entities conducting programs described in section 203(b) within the planning and service area.

(13) provide assurances that the area agency on aging will—

    (A) maintain the integrity and public purpose of services provided, and service providers, under this title in all contractual and commercial relationships;

    (B) disclose to the Assistant Secretary and the State agency—

     (i) the identity of each nongovernmental entity with which such agency has a contract or commercial relationship relating to providing any service to older individuals; and

     (ii) the nature of such contract or such relationship;

    (C) demonstrate that a loss or diminution in the quantity or quality of the services provided, or to be provided, under this title by such agency has not resulted and will not result from such contract or such relationship;

    (D) demonstrate that the quantity or quality of the services to be provided under this title by such agency will be enhanced as a result of such contract or such relationship; and

    (E) on the request of the Assistant Secretary or the State, for the purpose of monitoring compliance with this Act (including conducting an audit), disclose all sources and expenditures of funds such agency receives or expends to provide services to older individuals;

(14) provide assurances that preference in receiving services under this title will not be given by the area agency on aging to particular older individuals as a result of a contract or commercial relationship that is not carried out to implement this title;

(15) provide assurances that funds received under this title will be used —

    (A) to provide benefits and services to older individuals, giving priority to older individuals identified in paragraph (4)(A)(i); and

    (B) in compliance with the assurances specified in paragraph (13) and the limitations specified in section 212;

(16) provide, to the extent feasible, for the furnishing of services under this Act, consistent with self-directed care; and

(17) include information detailing how the area agency on aging will coordinate activities, and develop long-range emergency preparedness plans, with local and State emergency response agencies, relief organizations, local and State governments, and any other institutions that have responsibility for disaster relief service delivery.

(b) (1) An area agency on aging may include in the area plan an assessment of how prepared the area agency on aging and service providers in the planning and service area are for any anticipated change in the number of older individuals during the 10-year period following the fiscal year for which the plan is submitted.

(2) Such assessment may include —

    (A) the projected change in the number of older individuals in the planning and service area;

    (B) an analysis of how such change may affect such individuals, including individuals with low incomes, individuals with greatest economic need, minority older individuals, older individuals residing in rural areas, and older individuals with limited English proficiency;

    (C) an analysis of how the programs, policies, and services provided by such area agency can be improved, and how resource levels can be adjusted to meet the needs of the changing population of older individuals in the planning and service area; and

    (D) an analysis of how the change in the number of individuals age 85 and older in the planning and service area is expected to affect the need for supportive services.

(3) An area agency on aging, in cooperation with government officials, State agencies, tribal organizations, or local entities, may make recommendations to government officials in the planning and service area and the State, on actions determined by the area agency to build the capacity in the planning and service area to meet the needs of older individuals for —

    (A) health and human services;

    (B) land use;

    (C) housing;

    (D) transportation;

    (E) public safety;

    (F) workforce and economic development;

    (G) recreation;

    (H) education;

    (I) civic engagement;

    (J) emergency preparedness; and

    (K) any other service as determined by such agency.

(c) Each State, in approving area agency on aging plans under this section, shall waive the requirement described in paragraph (2) of subsection (a) for any category of services described in such paragraph if the area agency on aging demonstrates to the State agency that services being furnished for such category in the area are sufficient to meet the need for such services in such area and had conducted a timely public hearing upon request.

(d) (1) Subject to regulations prescribed by the Assistant Secretary, an area agency on aging designated under section 305(a)(2)(A) or, in areas of a State where no such agency has been designated, the State agency, may enter into agreement with agencies administering programs under the Rehabilitation Act of 1973, and titles XIX and XX of the Social Security Act for the purpose of developing and implementing plans for meeting the common need for transportation services of individuals receiving benefits under such Acts and older individuals participating in programs authorized by this title.

(2) In accordance with an agreement entered into under paragraph (1), funds appropriated under this title may be used to purchase transportation services for older individuals and may be pooled with funds made available for the provision of transportation services under the Rehabilitation Act of 1973, and titles XIX and XX of the Social Security Act.

(e) An area agency on aging may not require any provider of legal assistance under this title to reveal any information that is protected by the attorney-client privilege.

(f) (1) If the head of a State agency finds that an area agency on aging has failed to comply with Federal or State laws, including the area plan requirements of this section, regulations, or policies, the State may withhold a portion of the funds to the area agency on aging available under this title.

(2) (A) The head of a State agency shall not make a final determination withholding funds under paragraph (1) without first affording the area agency on aging due process in accordance with procedures established by the State agency.

(B) At a minimum, such procedures shall include procedures for —
   (i) providing notice of an action to withhold funds;
   (ii) providing documentation of the need for such action; and
   (iii) at the request of the area agency on aging, conducting a public hearing concerning the action.

(3) (A) If a State agency withholds the funds, the State agency may use the funds withheld to directly administer programs under this title in the planning and service area served by the area agency on aging for a period not to exceed 180 days, except as provided in subparagraph (B).

(B) If the State agency determines that the area agency on aging has not taken corrective action, or if the State agency does not approve the corrective action, during the 180-day period described in subparagraph (A), the State agency may extend the period for not more than 90 days.

(42 U.S.C. 3026)

Section. 307. STATE PLANS

(a) Except as provided in the succeeding sentence and section 309(a), each State, in order to be eligible for grants from its allotment under this title for any fiscal year, shall submit to the Assistant Secretary a State plan for a two-, three-, or four year period determined by the State agency, with such annual revisions as are necessary, which meets such criteria as the Assistant Secretary may by regulation prescribe. If the Assistant Secretary determines, in the discretion of the Assistant Secretary, that a State failed in 2 successive years to comply with the requirements under this title, then the State shall submit to the Assistant Secretary a State plan for a 1-year period that meets such criteria, for subsequent years until the Assistant Secretary determines that the State is in compliance with such requirements. Each such plan shall comply with all of the following requirements:

(1) The plan shall —

   (A) require each area agency on aging designated under section 305(a)(2)(A) to develop and submit to the State agency for approval, in accordance with a uniform format developed by the State agency, an area plan meeting the requirements of section 306; and (B) be based on such area plans.

(2) The plan shall provide that the State agency will —

   (A) evaluate, using uniform procedures described in section 202(a)(29), the need for supportive services (including legal assistance pursuant to 307(a)(11), information and assistance, and transportation services), nutrition services, and multipurpose senior centers within the State;

   (B) develop a standardized process to determine the extent to which public or private programs and resources (including volunteers and programs and services of voluntary organizations) that have the capacity and actually meet such need; and

   (C) specify a minimum proportion of the funds received by each area agency on aging in the State to carry out part B that will be expended (in the absence of a waiver under section 306(c) or 316) by such area agency on aging to provide each of the categories of services specified in section 306(a)(2).

(3) The plan shall —

   (A) include (and may not be approved unless the Assistant Secretary approves) the statement and demonstration required by paragraphs (2) and (4) of section 305(d) (concerning intrastate distribution of funds); and

   (B) with respect to services for older individuals residing in rural areas —

      (i) provide assurances that the State agency will spend for each fiscal year, not less than the amount expended for such services for fiscal year 2000;

      (ii) identify, for each fiscal year to which the plan applies, the projected costs of providing such services (including the cost of providing access to such services); and

      (iii) describe the methods used to meet the needs for such services in the fiscal year preceding the first year to which such plan applies.

(4) The plan shall provide that the State agency will conduct periodic evaluations of, and public hearings on, activities and projects carried out in the State under this title and title VII, including evaluations of the effectiveness of services provided to individuals with greatest economic need, greatest social need, or disabilities (with particular attention to low-income minority older individuals, older individuals with limited English proficiency, and older individuals residing in rural areas).

(5) The plan shall provide that the State agency will—

    (A) afford an opportunity for a hearing upon request, in accordance with published procedures, to any area agency on aging submitting a plan under this title, to any provider of (or applicant to provide) services;

    (B) issue guidelines applicable to grievance procedures required by section 306(a)(10); and

    (C) afford an opportunity for a public hearing, upon request, by any area agency on aging, by any provider of (or applicant to provide) services, or by any recipient of services under this title regarding any waiver request, including those under section 316.

(6) The plan shall provide that the State agency will make such reports, in such form, and containing such information, as the Assistant Secretary may require, and comply with such requirements as the Assistant Secretary may impose to insure the correctness of such reports.

(7) (A) The plan shall provide satisfactory assurance that such fiscal control and fund accounting procedures will be adopted as may be necessary to assure proper disbursement of, and accounting for, Federal funds paid under this title to the State, including any such funds paid to the recipients of a grant or contract.

    (B) The plan shall provide assurances that—

        (i) no individual (appointed or otherwise) involved in the designation of the State agency or an area agency on aging, or in the designation of the head of any subdivision of the State agency or of an area agency on aging, is subject to a conflict of interest prohibited under this Act;

        (ii) no officer, employee, or other representative of the State agency or an area agency on aging is subject to a conflict of interest prohibited under this Act; and

        (iii) mechanisms are in place to identify and remove conflicts of interest prohibited under this Act.

(8) (A) The plan shall provide that no supportive services, nutrition services, or in-home services will be directly provided by the State agency or an area agency on aging in the State, unless, in the judgment of the State agency—

        (i) provision of such services by the State agency or the area agency on aging is necessary to assure an adequate supply of such services;

        (ii) such services are directly related to such State agency's or area agency on aging's administrative functions; or

        (iii) such services can be provided more economically, and with comparable quality, by such State agency or area agency on aging.

    (B) Regarding case management services, if the State agency or area agency on aging is already providing case management services (as of the date of submission of the plan) under a State program, the plan may specify that such agency is allowed to continue to provide case management services.

    (C) The plan may specify that an area agency on aging is allowed to directly provide information and assistance services and outreach.

(9) The plan shall provide assurances that the State agency will carry out, through the Office of the State Long-Term Care Ombudsman, a State Long-Term Care Ombudsman program in accordance with section 712 and this title, and will expend for such purpose an amount that is not less than an amount expended by the State agency with funds received under this title for fiscal year 2000, and an amount that is not less than the amount expended by the State agency with funds received under title VII for fiscal year 2000.

(10) The plan shall provide assurances that the special needs of older individuals residing in rural areas will be taken into consideration and shall describe how those needs have been met and describe how funds have been allocated to meet those needs.

(11) The plan shall provide that with respect to legal assistance—

   (B) the plan contains assurances that area agencies on aging will

      (i) enter into contracts with providers of legal assistance which can demonstrate the experience or capacity to deliver legal assistance;

      (ii) include in any such contract provisions to assure that any recipient of funds under division (i) will be subject to specific restrictions and regulations promulgated under the Legal Services Corporation Act (other than restrictions and regulations governing eligibility for legal assistance under such Act and governing membership of local governing boards) as determined appropriate by the Assistant Secretary; and

      (iii) attempt to involve the private bar in legal assistance activities authorized under this title, including groups within the private bar furnishing services to older individuals on a pro bono and reduced fee basis;

   (B) the plan contains assurances that no legal assistance will be furnished unless the grantee administers a program designed to provide legal assistance to older individuals with social or economic need and has agreed, if the grantee is not a Legal Services Corporation project grantee, to coordinate its services with existing Legal Services Corporation projects in the planning and service area in order to concentrate the use of funds provided under this title on individuals with the greatest such need; and the area agency on aging makes a finding, after assessment, pursuant to standards for service promulgated by the Assistant Secretary, that any grantee selected is the entity best able to provide the particular services;

   (C) the State agency will provide for the coordination of the furnishing of legal assistance to older individuals within the State, and provide advice and technical assistance in the provision of legal assistance to older individuals within the State and support the furnishing of training and technical assistance for legal assistance for older individuals;

   (D) the plan contains assurances, to the extent practicable, that legal assistance furnished under the plan will be in addition to any legal assistance for older individuals being furnished with funds from sources other than this Act and that reasonable efforts will be made to maintain existing levels of legal assistance for older individuals; and

   (E) the plan contains assurances that area agencies on aging will give priority to legal assistance related to income, health care, long-term care, nutrition, housing, utilities, protective services, defense of guardianship, abuse, neglect, and age discrimination.

(12) The plan shall provide, whenever the State desires to provide for a fiscal year for services for the prevention of abuse of older individuals—

(A) the plan contains assurances that any area agency on aging carrying out such services will conduct a program consistent with relevant State law and coordinated with existing State adult protective service activities for —

    (i)   public education to identify and prevent abuse of older individuals;

    (ii) receipt of reports of abuse of older individuals;

    (iii) active participation of older individuals participating in programs under this Act through outreach, conferences, and referral of such individuals to other social service agencies or sources of assistance where appropriate and consented to by the parties to be referred; and

    (iv) referral of complaints to law enforcement or public protective service agencies where appropriate;

  (B) the State will not permit involuntary or coerced participation in the program of services described in this paragraph by alleged victims, abusers, or their households; and

  (C) all information gathered in the course of receiving reports and making referrals shall remain confidential unless all parties to the complaint consent in writing to the release of such information, except that such information may be released to a law enforcement or public protective service agency.

(13) The plan shall provide assurances that each State will assign personnel (one of whom shall be known as a legal assistance developer) to provide State leadership in developing legal assistance programs for older individuals throughout the State.

(14) The plan shall, with respect to the fiscal year preceding the fiscal year for which such plan is prepared —

  (A) identify the number of low-income minority older individuals in the State, including the number of low income minority older individuals with limited English proficiency; and

  (B) describe the methods used to satisfy the service needs of the low-income minority older individuals described in subparagraph (A), including the plan to meet the needs of low-income minority older individuals with limited English proficiency.

(15) The plan shall provide assurances that, if a substantial number of the older individuals residing in any planning and service area in the State are of limited English-speaking ability, then the State will require the area agency on aging for each such planning and service area —

  (A) to utilize in the delivery of outreach services under section 306(a)(2)(A), the services of workers who are fluent in the language spoken by a predominant number of such older individuals who are of limited English-speaking ability; and

  (B) to designate an individual employed by the area agency on aging, or available to such area agency on aging on a full-time basis, whose responsibilities will include —

    (i)   taking such action as may be appropriate to assure that counseling assistance is made available to such older individuals who are of limited English speaking ability in order to assist such older individuals in participating in programs and receiving assistance under this Act; and

    (ii) providing guidance to individuals engaged in the delivery of supportive services under the area plan involved to enable such individuals to be aware of cultural sensitivities and to take into account effectively linguistic and cultural differences.

(16) The plan shall provide assurances that the State agency will require outreach efforts that will —

  (A) identify individuals eligible for assistance under this Act, with special emphasis on —

(i) older individuals residing in rural areas;

(ii) older individuals with greatest economic need (with particular attention to low-income older individuals, including low-income minority older individuals, older individuals with limited English proficiency, and older individuals residing in rural areas;

(iii) older individuals with greatest social need (with particular attention to low-income older individuals, including low-income minority older individuals, older individuals with limited English proficiency, and older individuals residing in rural areas;

(iv) older individuals with severe disabilities;

(v) older individuals with limited English-speaking ability; and

(vi) older individuals with Alzheimer's disease **and related** disorders with neurological and organic brain dysfunction (and the caretakers of such individuals); and

(B) inform the older individuals referred to in clauses (i) through (vi) of subparagraph (A), and the caretakers of such individuals, of the availability of such assistance.

(17) The plan shall provide, with respect to the needs of older individuals with severe disabilities, assurances that the State will coordinate planning, identification, assessment of needs, and service for older individuals with disabilities with particular attention to individuals with severe disabilities with the State agencies with primary responsibility for individuals with disabilities, including severe disabilities, to enhance services and develop collaborative programs, where appropriate, to meet the needs of older individuals with disabilities.

(18) The plan shall provide assurances that area agencies on aging will conduct efforts to facilitate the coordination of community-based, long-term care services, pursuant to section 306(a)(7), for older individuals who—

(A) reside at home and are at risk of institutionalization because of limitations on their ability to function independently;

(B) are patients in hospitals and are at risk of prolonged institutionalization; or

(C) are patients in long-term care facilities, but who can return to their homes if community-based services are provided to them.

(19) The plan shall include the assurances and description required by section 705(a).

(20) The plan shall provide assurances that special efforts will be made to provide technical assistance to minority providers of services.

(21) The plan shall—

(A) provide an assurance that the State agency will coordinate programs under this title and programs under title VI, if applicable; and

(B) provide an assurance that the State agency will pursue activities to increase access by older individuals who are Native Americans to all aging programs and benefits provided by the agency, including programs and benefits provided under this title, if applicable, and specify the ways in which the State agency intends to implement the activities.

(22) If case management services are offered to provide access to supportive services, the plan shall provide that the State agency shall ensure compliance with the requirements specified in section 306(a)(8).

(23) The plan shall provide assurances that demonstrable efforts will be made—

(A) to coordinate services provided under this Act with other State services that benefit older individuals; and

(B) to provide multigenerational activities, such as opportunities for older individuals to serve as mentors or advisers in child care, youth day care, educational assistance, at-risk youth intervention, juvenile delinquency treatment, and family support programs.

(24) The plan shall provide assurances that the State will coordinate public services within the State to assist older individuals to obtain transportation services associated with access to services provided under this title, to services under title VI, to comprehensive counseling services, and to legal assistance.

(25) The plan shall include assurances that the State has in effect a mechanism to provide for quality in the provision of in-home services under this title.

(26) The plan shall provide assurances that funds received under this title will not be used to pay any part of a cost (including an administrative cost) incurred by the State agency or an area agency on aging to carry out a contract or commercial relationship that is not carried out to implement this title.

(27) The plan shall provide assurances that area agencies on aging will provide, to the extent feasible, for the furnishing of services under this Act, consistent with self-directed care.

(28) (A) The plan shall include, at the election of the State, an assessment of how prepared the State is, under the State's statewide service delivery model, for any anticipated change in the number of older individuals during the 10-year period following the fiscal year for which the plan is submitted.

(B) Such assessment may include—
   (i) the projected change in the number of older individuals in the State;
   (ii) an analysis of how such change may affect such individuals, including individuals with low incomes, individuals with greatest economic need, minority older individuals, older individuals residing in rural areas, and older individuals with limited English proficiency;
   (iii) an analysis of how the programs, policies, and services provided by the State can be improved, including coordinating with area agencies on aging, and how resource levels can be adjusted to meet the needs of the changing population of older individuals in the State; and
   (iv) an analysis of how the change in the number of individuals age 85 and older in the State is expected to affect the need for supportive services.

(29) The plan shall include information detailing how the State will coordinate activities, and develop long-range emergency preparedness plans, with area agencies on aging, local emergency response agencies, relief organizations, local governments, State agencies responsible for emergency preparedness, and any other institutions that have responsibility for disaster relief service delivery.

(30) The plan shall include information describing the involvement of the head of the State agency in the development, revision, and implementation of emergency preparedness plans, including the State Public Health Emergency Preparedness and Response Plan.

(b) (1) The Assistant Secretary shall approve any State plan which the Assistant Secretary finds fulfills the requirements of subsection (a), except the Assistant Secretary may not approve such plan unless the Assistant Secretary determines that the formula submitted under section 305(a)(2)(D) complies with the guidelines in effect under section 305(a)(2)(C).

(2)   The Assistant Secretary, in approving any State plan under this section, may waive the requirement described in paragraph (3)(B) of subsection (a) if the State agency demonstrates to the Assistant Secretary that the service needs of older individuals residing in rural areas in the State are being met, or that the number of older individuals residing in such rural areas is not sufficient to require the State agency to comply with such requirement.

(c) (1)   The Assistant Secretary shall not make a final determination disapproving any State plan, or any modification thereof, or make a final determination that a State is ineligible under section 305, without first affording the State reasonable notice and opportunity for a hearing.

(2)   Not later than 30 days after such final determination, a State dissatisfied with such final determination may appeal such final determination to the Secretary for review. If the State timely appeals such final determination in accordance with subsection (e)(1), the Secretary shall dismiss the appeal filed under this paragraph.

(3)   If the State is dissatisfied with the decision of the Secretary after review under paragraph (2), the State may appeal such decision not later than 30 days after such decision and in the manner described in subsection (e). For purposes of appellate review under the preceding sentence, a reference in subsection (e) to the Assistant Secretary shall be deemed to be a reference to the Secretary.

(d) Whenever the Assistant Secretary, after reasonable notice and opportunity for a hearing to the State agency, finds that—

(1)   the State is not eligible under section 305,

(2)   the State plan has been so changed that it no longer complies substantially with the provisions of subsection (a), or

(3)   in the administration of the plan there is a failure to comply substantially with any such provision of subsection (a), the Assistant Secretary shall notify such State agency that no further payments from its allotments under section 304 and section 308 will be made to the State (or, in the Assistant Secretary's discretion, that further payments to the State will be limited to projects under or portions of the State plan not affected by such failure), until the Assistant Secretary is satisfied that there will no longer be any failure to comply. Until the Assistant Secretary is so satisfied, no further payments shall be made to such State from its allotments under section 304 and section 308 (or payments shall be limited to projects under or portions of the State plan not affected by such failure). The Assistant Secretary shall, in accordance with regulations the Assistant Secretary shall prescribe, disburse the funds so withheld directly to any public or nonprofit private organization or agency or political subdivision of such State submitting an approved plan in accordance with the provisions of this section. Any such payment shall be matched in the proportions specified in section 304.

(e) (1)   A State which is dissatisfied with a final action of the Assistant Secretary under subsection (b), (c), or (d) may appeal to the United States court of appeals for the circuit in which the State is located, by filing a petition with such court within 30 days after such final action. A copy of the petition shall be forthwith transmitted by the clerk of the court to the Assistant Secretary, or any officer designated by the Assistant Secretary for such purpose. The Assistant Secretary thereupon shall file in the court the record of the proceedings on which the Assistant Secretary's action is based, as provided in section 2112 of title 28, United States Code.

(2) Upon the filing of such petition, the court shall have jurisdiction to affirm the action of the Assistant Secretary or to set it aside, in whole or in part, temporarily or permanently, but until the filing of the record, the Assistant Secretary may modify or set aside the Assistant Secretary's order. The findings of the Assistant Secretary as to the facts, if supported by substantial evidence, shall be conclusive, but the court, for good cause shown may remand the case to the Assistant Secretary to take further evidence, and the Assistant Secretary shall, within 30 days, file in the court the record of those further proceedings. Such new or modified findings of fact shall likewise be conclusive if supported by substantial evidence. The judgment of the court affirming or setting aside, in whole or in part, any action of the Assistant Secretary shall be final, subject to review by the Supreme Court of the United States upon certiorari or certification as provided in section 1254 of title 28, United States Code.

(3) The commencement of proceedings under this subsection shall not, unless so specifically ordered by the court, operate as a stay of the Assistant Secretary's action.

(f) Neither a State, nor a State agency, may require any provider of legal assistance under this title to reveal any information that is protected by the attorney-client privilege.

(42 U.S.C. 3027)

Section. 308. PLANNING, COORDINATION, EVALUATION, AND ADMINISTRATION OF STATE PLANS

(a) (1) Amounts available to States under subsection (b)(1) may be used to make grants to States for paying such percentages as each State agency determines, but not more than 75 percent, of the cost of the administration of its State plan, including the preparation of the State plan, the evaluation of activities carried out under such plan, the collection of data and the carrying out of analyses related to the need for supportive services, nutrition services, and multipurpose senior centers within the State, and dissemination of information so obtained, the provision of short-term training to personnel of public or nonprofit private agencies and organizations engaged in the operation of programs authorized by this Act, and the carrying out of demonstration projects of statewide significance relating to the initiation, expansion, or improvement of services assisted under this title.

(2) Any sums available to a State under subsection (b)(1) for part of the cost of the administration of its State plan which the State determines is not needed for such purposes may be used by the State to supplement the amount available under section 304(d)(1)(A) to cover part of the cost of the administration of area plans.

(3) Any State which has been designated a single planning and service area under section 305(a)(1)(E) covering all, or substantially all, of the older individuals in such State, as determined by the Assistant Secretary, may elect to pay part of the costs of the administration of State and area plans either out of sums received under this section or out of sums made available for the administration of area plans under section 304(d)(1)(A), but shall not pay such costs out of sums received or allotted under both such sections.

(b) (1) If for any fiscal year the aggregate amount appropriated under section 303 does not exceed $800,000,000, then—

(A) except as provided in clause (ii), the greater of 5 percent of the allotment to a State under section 304(a)(1) or $300,000; and

(B) in the case of Guam, American Samoa, the United States Virgin Islands, the Trust Territory of the Pacific Islands, and the Commonwealth of the Northern Mariana Islands, the greater of 5 percent of such allotment or $75,000; shall be available to such State to carry out the purposes of this section.

(2) If for any fiscal year the aggregate amount appropriated under section 303 exceeds $800,000,000, then—

    (A) except as provided in clause (ii), the greater of 5 percent of the allotment to a State under section 304(a)(1) or $500,000; and

    (B) in the case of Guam, American Samoa, the United States Virgin Islands, the Trust Territory of the Pacific Islands, and the Commonwealth of the Northern Mariana Islands, the greater of 5 percent of such allotment or $100,000; shall be available to such State to carry out the purposes of this section.

(3) (A) If the aggregate amount appropriated under section 303 for a fiscal year does not exceed $800,000,000, then any State which desires to receive amounts, in addition to amounts allotted to such State under paragraph (1), to be used in the administration of its State plan in accordance with subsection (a) may transmit an application to the Assistant Secretary in accordance with this paragraph. Any such application shall be transmitted in such form, and according to such procedures, as the Assistant Secretary may require, except that such application may not be made as part of, or as an amendment to, the State plan.

    (B) The Assistant Secretary may approve any application transmitted by a State under subparagraph (A) if the Assistant Secretary determines, based upon a particularized showing of need that—

        (i) the State will be unable to fully and effectively administer its State plan and to carry out programs and projects authorized by this title unless such additional amounts are made available by the Assistant Secretary;

        (ii) the State is making full and effective use of its allotment under paragraph (1) and of the personnel of the State agency and area agencies designated under section 305(a)(2)(A) in the administration of its State plan in accordance with subsection (a); and

        (iii) the State agency and area agencies on aging of such State are carrying out, on a full-time basis, programs and activities which are in furtherance of the objectives of this Act.

    (C) The Assistant Secretary may approve that portion of the amount requested by a State in its application under subparagraph (A) which the Assistant Secretary determines has been justified in such application.

    (D) Amounts which any State may receive in any fiscal year under this paragraph may not exceed three-fourths of 1 percent of the sum of the amounts allotted under section 304(a) to such State to carry out the State plan for such fiscal year.

    (E) No application by a State under subparagraph (A) shall be approved unless it contains assurances that no amounts received by the State under this paragraph will be used to hire any individual to fill a job opening created by the action of the State in laying off or terminating the employment of any regular employee not supported under this Act in anticipation of filling the vacancy so created by hiring an employee to be supported through use of amounts received under this paragraph.

(4) (A) Notwithstanding any other provision of this title and except as provided in subparagraph (B), with respect to funds received by a State and attributable to funds appropriated under paragraph (1) or (2) of section 303(b), the State may elect in its plan under section 307(a)(13) regarding part C of this title,[111] to transfer not more than 40 percent of the funds so received between subpart 1 and subpart 2 of part C, for use as the State considers appropriate to meet the needs of the area served. The Assistant Secretary shall approve any such transfer unless the Assistant Secretary determines that such transfer is not consistent with the objectives of this Act.

(B) If a State demonstrates, to the satisfaction of the Assistant Secretary, that funds received by the State and attributable to funds appropriated under paragraph (1) or (2) of section 303(b), including funds transferred under subparagraph (A) without regard to this subparagraph, for any fiscal year are insufficient to satisfy the need for services under subpart 1 or subpart 2 of part C, then the Assistant Secretary may grant a waiver that permits the State to transfer under subparagraph (A) to satisfy such need an additional 10 percent of the funds so received by a State and attributable to funds appropriated under paragraph (1) or (2) of section 303(b).

(C) A State's request for a waiver under subparagraph (B) shall—

    (i) be not more than one page in length;

    (ii) include a request that the waiver be granted;

    (iii) specify the amount of the funds received by a State and attributable to funds appropriated under paragraph (1) or (2) of section 303(b), over the permissible 40 percent referred to in subparagraph (A), that the State requires to satisfy the need for services under subpart 1 or 2 of part C; and

    (iv) not include a request for a waiver with respect to an amount if the transfer of the amount would jeopardize the appropriate provision of services under subpart 1 or 2 of part C.

(5) (A) Notwithstanding any other provision of this title, of the funds received by a State attributable to funds appropriated under subsection (a)(1), and paragraphs (1) and (2) of subsection (b), of section 303, the State may elect to transfer not more than 30 percent for any fiscal year between programs under part B and part C, for use as the State considers appropriate. The State shall notify the Assistant Secretary of any such election.

(B) At a minimum, the notification described in subparagraph (A) shall include a description of the amount to be transferred, the purposes of the transfer, the need for the transfer, and the impact of the transfer on the provision of services from which the funding will be transferred.

(6) A State agency may not delegate to an area agency on aging or any other entity the authority to make a transfer under paragraph (4)(A) or (5)(A)

(7) The Assistant Secretary shall annually collect, and include in the report required by section 207(a), data regarding the transfers described in paragraphs (4)(A) and (5)(A), including—

(A) the amount of funds involved in the transfers, analyzed by State;

(B) the rationales for the transfers;

(C) in the case of transfers described in paragraphs (4)(A) and (5)(A), the effect of the transfers of the provision of services, including the effect on the number of meals served, under—

    (i) subpart 1 of part C; and

    (ii) subpart 2 of part C; and

(D) in the case of transfers described in paragraph (5)(A)—

    (i)   in the case of transfers to part B, information on the supportive services, or services provided through senior centers, for which the transfers were used; and

    (ii) the effect of the transfers on the provision of services provided under—

        (I)   part B; and

        (II) part C, including the effect on the number of meals served.

(c)   The amounts of any State's allotment under subsection (b) for any fiscal year which the Assistant Secretary determines will not be required for that year for the purposes described in subsection (a)(1) shall be available to provide services under part B or part C, or both, in the State.

(42 U.S.C. 3028)

Section. 309. PAYMENTS

(a)   Payments of grants or contracts under this title may be made (after necessary adjustments resulting from previously made overpayments or underpayments) in advance or by way of reimbursement, and in such installments, as the Assistant Secretary may determine. From a State's allotment for a fiscal year which is available under section 308 the Assistant Secretary may pay to a State which does not have a State plan approved under section 307 such amounts as the Assistant Secretary deems appropriate for the purpose of assisting such State in developing a State plan.

(b)   (1)   For each fiscal year, not less than 25 percent of the non-Federal share of the total expenditures under the State plan which is required by section 304(d) shall be met from funds from State or local public sources.

      (2)   Funds required to meet the non-Federal share required by section 304(d)(1)(D), in amounts exceeding 10 percent of the cost of the services specified in such section 304(d)(1)(D) shall be from State sources.

(c)   A State's allotment under section 304 for a fiscal year shall be reduced by the percentage (if any) by which its expenditures for such year from State sources under its State plan approved under section 307 are less than its average annual expenditures from such sources for the period of 3 fiscal years preceding such year.

(42 U.S.C. 3029)

Section. 310. DISASTER RELIEF REIMBURSEMENTS

(a)   (1)   The Assistant Secretary may provide reimbursements to any State (or to any tribal organization receiving a grant under title VI), upon application for such reimbursement, for funds such State makes available to area agencies on aging in such State (or funds used by such tribal organization) for the delivery of supportive services (and related supplies) during any major disaster declared by the President in accordance with the Robert T. Stafford Relief and Emergency Assistance Act.

      (2)   Total payments to all States and such tribal organizations under paragraph (1) in any fiscal year shall not exceed 2 percent of the total amount appropriated and available to carry out title IV.

(3) If the Assistant Secretary decides, in the 5-day period beginning on the date such disaster is declared by the President, to provide an amount of reimbursement under paragraph (1) to a State or such tribal organization, then the Assistant Secretary shall provide not less than 75 percent of such amount to such State or such tribal organization not later than 5 days after the date of such decision.

(b) (1) At the beginning of each fiscal year the Assistant Secretary shall set aside, for payment to States and such tribal organizations under subsection (a), an amount equal to 2 percent of the total amount appropriated and available to carry out title IV.

(2) Amounts set aside under paragraph (1) which are not obligated by the end of the third quarter of any fiscal year shall be made available to carry out title IV.

(c) Nothing in this section shall be construed to prohibit expenditures by States and such tribal organizations for disaster relief for older individuals in excess of amounts reimbursable under this section, by using funds made available to them under other sections of this Act or under other provisions of Federal or State law, or from private sources.

(42 U.S.C. 3030)

Section. 311. NUTRITION SERVICES INCENTIVE PROGRAM

(a) The purpose of this section is to provide incentives to encourage and reward effective performance by States and tribal organizations in the efficient delivery of nutritious meals to older individuals.

(d) (b) (1) The Secretary shall allot and provide, in accordance with this section, to or on behalf of each State agency with a plan approved under this title for a fiscal year, and to or on behalf of each grantee with an application approved under title VI for such fiscal year, an amount bearing the same ratio to the total amount appropriated for such fiscal year under subsection (e) as the number of meals served in the State under such plan approved for the preceding fiscal year (or the number of meals served by the title VI grantee, under such application approved for such preceding fiscal year), bears to the total number of such meals served in all States and by all title VI grantees under all such plans and applications approved for such preceding fiscal year.

(2) For purposes of paragraph (1), in the case of a grantee that has an application approved under title VI for a fiscal year but that did not receive assistance under this section for the preceding fiscal year, the number of meals served by the title VI grantee for the preceding fiscal year shall be deemed to equal the number of meals that the Assistant Secretary estimates will be served by the title VI grantee in the fiscal year for which the application was approved.

(c) (1) Agricultural commodities (including bonus commodities) and products purchased by the Secretary of Agriculture under section 32 of the Act of August 24, 1935 (7 U.S.C. 612c), shall be donated to a recipient of a grant or contract to be used for providing nutrition services in accordance with the provisions of this title.

(2) The Commodities Credit Corporation shall dispose of food commodities (including bonus commodities) under section 416 of the Agricultural Act of 1949 (7 U.S.C. 1431) by donating them to a recipient of a grant or contract to be used for providing nutrition services in accordance with the provisions of this title.

(3) Dairy products (including bonus commodities) purchased by the Secretary of Agriculture under section 709 of the Food and Agriculture Act of 1965 (7 U.S.C. 1446a–1) shall be used to meet the requirements of programs providing nutrition services in accordance with the provisions of this title.

(4) Among the commodities provided under this subsection, the Secretary of Agriculture shall give special emphasis to foods of high nutritional value to support the health of older individuals. The Secretary of Agriculture, in consultation with the Assistant Secretary, is authorized to prescribe the terms and conditions respecting the provision of commodities under this subsection.

(d) (1) Each State agency and each title VI grantee shall be entitled to use all or any part of amounts allotted under subsection (b) to obtain, subject to paragraphs (2) and (3), from the Secretary of Agriculture commodities available through any food program of the Department of Agriculture at the rates at which such commodities are valued for purposes of such program.

(2) The Secretary of Agriculture shall determine and report to the Secretary, by such date as the Secretary may require, the amount (if any) of its allotment under subsection (b) which each State agency and title VI grantee has elected to receive in the form of commodities. Such amount shall include an amount bearing the same ratio to the costs to the Secretary of Agriculture of providing such commodities under this subsection as the value of commodities received by such State agency or title VI grantee under this subsection bears to the total value of commodities so received.

(3) From the allotment under subsection (b) for each State agency and title VI grantee, the Secretary shall transfer funds to the Secretary of Agriculture for the costs of commodities received by such State agency or grantee, and expenses related to the procurement of the commodities on behalf of such State agency or grantee, under this subsection, and shall then pay the balance (if any) to such State agency or grantee. The amount of funds transferred for the expenses related to the procurement of the commodities shall be mutually agreed on by the Secretary and the Secretary of Agriculture. The transfer of funds for the costs of the commodities and the related expenses shall occur in a timely manner after the Secretary of Agriculture submits the corresponding report described in paragraph (2), and shall be subject to the availability of appropriations. Amounts received by the Secretary of Agriculture pursuant to this section to make commodity purchases for a fiscal year for a State agency or title VI grantee shall remain available, only for the next fiscal year, to make commodity purchases for that State agency or grantee pursuant to this section.

(4) Each State agency and title VI grantee shall promptly and equitably disburse amounts received under this subsection to recipients of grants and contracts. Such disbursements shall only be used by such recipients of grants or contracts to purchase domestically produced foods for their nutrition projects.

(5) Nothing in this subsection shall be construed to require any State agency or title VI grantee to elect to receive cash payments under this subsection.

(e) There are authorized to be appropriated to carry out this section (other than subsection (c)(1)) such sums as may be necessary for fiscal year 2007 and such sums as may be necessary for each of the 4 succeeding fiscal years.

(f) In each fiscal year, the Secretary and the Secretary of Agriculture shall jointly disseminate to State agencies, title VI grantees, area agencies on aging, and providers of nutrition services assisted under this title, information concerning the foods available to such State agencies, title VI grantees, area agencies on aging, and providers under subsection (c).

(42 U.S.C. 3030a)

Section. 312. MULTIPURPOSE SENIOR CENTERS: RECAPTURE OF PAYMENTS

If, within 10 years after acquisition, or within 20 years after the completion of construction, of any facility for which funds have been paid under this title—
  (1) the owner of the facility ceases to be a public or nonprofit private agency or organization; or
  (2) the facility ceases to be used for the purposes for which it was acquired (unless the Assistant Secretary determines, in accordance with regulations, that there is good cause for releasing the applicant or other owner from the obligation to do so); the United States shall be entitled to recover from the applicant or other owner of the facility an amount which bears to the then value of the facility (or so much thereof as constituted an approved project or projects) the same ratio as the amount of such Federal funds bore to the cost of the facility financed with the aid of such funds. Such value shall be determined by agreement of the parties or by action brought in the United States district court for the district in which such facility is situated.

(42 U.S.C. 3030b)

Section. 313. AUDIT

(a) The Assistant Secretary and the Comptroller General of the United States or any of their duly authorized representatives shall have access for the purpose of audit and examination to any books, documents, papers, and records that are pertinent to a grant or contract received under this title.
(b) State agencies and area agencies on aging shall not request information or data from providers which is not pertinent to services furnished pursuant to this Act or a payment made for such services.

(42 U.S.C. 3030c)

Section. 314. RIGHTS RELATING TO IN-HOME SERVICES FOR FRAIL OLDER INDIVIDUALS.

The Assistant Secretary shall require entities that provide inhome services under this title to promote the rights of each older individual who receives such services. Such rights include the following:
  (1) The right—
      (A) to be fully informed in advance about each in-home service provided by such entity under this title and about any change in such service that may affect the well-being of such individual; and
      (B) to participate in planning and changing an inhome service provided under this title by such entity unless such individual is judicially adjudged incompetent.
  (2) The right to voice a grievance with respect to such service that is or fails to be so provided, without discrimination or reprisal as a result of voicing such grievance.
  (3) The right to confidentiality of records relating to such individual.
  (4) The right to have the property of such individual treated with respect.
  (5) The right to be fully informed (orally and in writing), in advance of receiving an in-home service under this title, of such individual's rights and obligations under this title.

(42 U.S.C. 3030c–1)

Section. 315. CONSUMER CONTRIBUTIONS.

(a) COST SHARING. –

    (1) IN GENERAL. – Except as provided in paragraphs (2) and (3), a State is permitted to implement cost sharing for all services funded by this Act by recipients of the services.

    (2) EXCEPTION. – The State is not permitted to implement the cost sharing described in paragraph (1) for the following services:

        (C) Information and assistance, outreach, benefits counseling, or case management services.

        (D) Ombudsman, elder abuse prevention, legal assistance, or other consumer protection services.

        (E) Congregate and home delivered meals.

        (F) Any services delivered through tribal organizations.

    (3) PROHIBITIONS. – A State or tribal organization shall not permit the cost sharing described in paragraph (1) for any services delivered through tribal organizations. A State shall not permit cost sharing by a low-income older individual if the income of such individual is at or below the Federal poverty line. A State may exclude from cost sharing low-income individuals whose incomes are above the Federal poverty line. A State shall not consider any assets, savings, or other property owned by older individuals when defining low-income individuals who are exempt from cost sharing, when creating a sliding scale for the cost sharing, or when seeking contributions from any older individual.

    (4) PAYMENT RATES. – If a State permits the cost sharing described in paragraph (1), such State shall establish a sliding scale, based solely on individual income and the cost of delivering services.

    (5) REQUIREMENTS. – If a State permits the cost sharing described in paragraph (1), such State shall require each area agency on aging in the State to ensure that each service provider involved, and the area agency on aging, will –

        (A) protect the privacy and confidentiality of each older individual with respect to the declaration or nondeclaration of individual income and to any share of costs paid or unpaid by an individual;

        (B) establish appropriate procedures to safeguard and account for cost share payments;

        (C) use each collected cost share payment to expand the service for which such payment was given;

        (D) not consider assets, savings, or other property owned by an older individual in determining whether cost sharing is permitted;

        (E) not deny any service for which funds are received under this Act for an older individual due to the income of such individual or such individual's failure to make a cost sharing payment;

        (F) determine the eligibility of older individuals to cost share solely by a confidential declaration of income and with no requirement for verification; and

        (G) widely distribute State created written materials in languages reflecting the reading abilities of older individuals that describe the criteria for cost sharing, the State's sliding scale, and the mandate described under subparagraph (E).

(6) WAIVER.—An area agency on aging may request a waiver to the State's cost sharing policies, and the State shall approve such a waiver if the area agency on aging can adequately demonstrate that—

    (A) a significant proportion of persons receiving services under this Act subject to cost sharing in the planning and service area have incomes below the threshold established in State policy; or

    (B) cost sharing would be an unreasonable administrative or financial burden upon the area agency on aging.

(b) VOLUNTARY CONTRIBUTIONS.—

(1) IN GENERAL.—Voluntary contributions shall be allowed and may be solicited for all services for which funds are received under this Act if the method of solicitation is non-coercive. Such contributions shall be encouraged for individuals whose self-declared income is at or above 185 percent of the poverty line, at contribution levels based on the actual cost of services.

(2) LOCAL DECISION.—The area agency on aging shall consult with the relevant service providers and older individuals in agency's planning and service area in a State to determine the best method for accepting voluntary contributions under this subsection.

(3) PROHIBITED ACTS.—The area agency on aging and service providers shall not means test for any service for which contributions are accepted or deny services to any individual who does not contribute to the cost of the service.

(4) REQUIRED ACTS.—The area agency on aging shall ensure that each service provider will—

    (A) provide each recipient with an opportunity to voluntarily contribute to the cost of the service;

    (B) clearly inform each recipient that there is no obligation to contribute and that the contribution is purely voluntary;

    (C) protect the privacy and confidentiality of each recipient with respect to the recipient's contribution or lack of contribution;

    (D) establish appropriate procedures to safeguard and account for all contributions; and

    (E) use all collected contributions to expand the service for which the contributions were given and to supplement (not supplant) funds received under this Act.

(c) PARTICIPATION.—

(1) IN GENERAL.—The State and area agencies on aging, in conducting public hearings on State and area plans, shall solicit the views of older individuals, providers, and other stakeholders on implementation of cost-sharing in the service area or the State.

(2) PLANS.—Prior to the implementation of cost sharing under subsection (a), each State and area agency on aging shall develop plans that are designed to ensure that the participation of low-income older individuals (with particular attention to low income older individuals, including low-income minority older individuals, older individuals with limited English proficiency, and older individuals residing in rural areas) receiving services will not decrease with the implementation of the cost sharing under such subsection.

(d) EVALUATION. — Not later than 1 year after the date of the enactment of the Older Americans Act Amendments of 2000, and annually thereafter, the Assistant Secretary shall conduct a comprehensive evaluation of practices for cost sharing to determine its impact on participation rates (with particular attention to low-income older individuals, including low-income minority older individuals, older individuals with limited English proficiency, and older individuals residing in rural areas). If the Assistant Secretary finds that there is a disparate impact upon low-income or minority older individuals or older individuals residing in rural areas in any State or region within the State regarding the provision of services, the Assistant Secretary shall take corrective action to assure that such services are provided to all older individuals without regard to the cost sharing criteria.

(42 U.S.C. 3030c–2)

Section. 316. WAIVERS.

(a) IN GENERAL. — The Assistant Secretary may waive any of the provisions specified in subsection (b) with respect to a State, upon receiving an application by the State agency containing or accompanied by documentation sufficient to establish, to the satisfaction of the Assistant Secretary, that —
(1) approval of the State legislature has been obtained or is not required with respect to the proposal for which waiver is sought;
(2) the State agency has collaborated with the area agencies on aging in the State and other organizations that would be affected with respect to the proposal for which waiver is sought;
(3) the proposal has been made available for public review and comment, including the opportunity for a public hearing upon request, within the State (and a summary of all of the comments received has been included in the application); and

(4) the State agency has given adequate consideration to the probable positive and negative consequences of approval of the waiver application, and the probable benefits for older individuals can reasonably be expected to outweigh any negative consequences, or particular circumstances in the State otherwise justify the waiver.

(b) REQUIREMENTS SUBJECT TO WAIVER. — The provisions of this title that may be waived under this section are —
(1) any provision of sections 305, 306, and 307 requiring statewide uniformity of programs carried out under this title, to the extent necessary to permit demonstrations, in limited areas of a State, of innovative approaches to assist older individuals;
(2) any area plan requirement described in section 306(a) if granting the waiver will promote innovations or improve service delivery and will not diminish services already provided under this Act;
(3) any State plan requirement described in section 307(a) if granting the waiver will promote innovations or improve service delivery and will not diminish services already provided under this Act;
(4) any restriction under paragraph (5) of section 308(b), on the amount that may be transferred between programs carried out under part B and part C; and

(5) the requirement of section 309(c) that certain amounts of a State allotment be used for the provision of services, with respect to a State that reduces expenditures under the State plan of the State (but only to the extent that the non-Federal share of the expenditures is not reduced below any minimum specified in section 304(d) or any other provision of this title).

(c) DURATION OF WAIVER. — The application by a State agency for a waiver under this section shall include a recommendation as to the duration of the waiver (not to exceed the duration of the State plan of the State). The Assistant Secretary, in granting such a waiver, shall specify the duration of the waiver, which may be the duration recommended by the State agency or such shorter time period as the Assistant Secretary finds to be appropriate.

(d) REPORTS TO SECRETARY. — With respect to each waiver granted under this section, not later than 1 year after the expiration of such waiver, and at any time during the waiver period that the Assistant Secretary may require, the State agency shall prepare and submit to the Assistant Secretary a report evaluating the impact of the waiver on the operation and effectiveness of programs and services provided under this title.

(42 U.S.C. 3030c–3)

PART B — SUPPORTIVE SERVICES AND SENIOR CENTERS PROGRAM AUTHORIZED

Section. 321.

(a) The Assistant Secretary shall carry out a program for making grants to States under State plans approved under section 307 for any of the following supportive services:

(1) health (including mental health), education and training, welfare, informational, recreational, homemaker, counseling, or referral services;

(2) transportation services to facilitate access to supportive services or nutrition services, and services provided by an area agency on aging, in conjunction with local transportation service providers, public transportation agencies, and other local government agencies, that result in increased provision of such transportation services for older individuals;

(3) services designed to encourage and assist older individuals to use the facilities and services (including information and assistance services) available to them, including language translation services to assist older individuals with limited English speaking ability to obtain services under this title;

(4) services designed

(A) to assist older individuals to obtain adequate housing, including residential repair and renovation projects designed to enable older individuals to maintain their homes in conformity with minimum housing standards,

(B) to adapt homes to meet the needs of older individuals who have physical disabilities;

(C) to prevent unlawful entry into residences of older individuals, through the installation of security devices and through structural modifications or alterations of such residences; or

(D) to assist older individuals in obtaining housing for which assistance is provided under programs of the Department of Housing and Urban Development;

(5) services designed to assist older individuals in avoiding institutionalization and to assist individuals in long-term care institutions who are able to return to their communities, including —

(A) client assessment, case management services, and development and coordination of community services;

(B) supportive activities to meet the special needs of caregivers, including caretakers who provide in-home services to frail older individuals; and

(C) in-home services and other community services, including home health, homemaker, shopping, escort, reader, and letter writing services, to assist older individuals to live independently in a home environment;

(6) services designed to provide to older individuals legal assistance and other counseling services and assistance, including—

(A) tax counseling and assistance, financial counseling, and counseling regarding appropriate health and life insurance coverage;

(B) representation—

(i) of individuals who are wards (or are allegedly incapacitated); and

(ii) in guardianship proceedings of older individuals who seek to become guardians, if other adequate representation is unavailable in the proceedings; and

(C) provision, to older individuals who provide uncompensated care to their adult children with disabilities, of counseling to assist such older individuals with permanency planning for such children;

(7) services designed to enable older individuals to attain and maintain physical and mental well-being through programs of regular physical activity, exercise, music therapy, art therapy, and dance-movement therapy;

(8) services designed to provide health screening **(including mental health screening)** to detect or prevent illnesses, or both, that occur most frequently in older individuals;

(9) services designed to provide, for older individuals, preretirement counseling and assistance in planning for and assessing future post-retirement needs with regard to public and private insurance, public benefits, lifestyle changes, relocation, legal matters, leisure time, and other appropriate matters;

(10) services of an ombudsman at the State level to receive, investigate, and act on complaints by older individuals who are residents of long-term care facilities and to advocate for the well-being of such individuals;

(11) provision of services and assistive devices (including provision of assistive technology services and assistive technology devices) which are designed to meet the unique needs of older individuals who are disabled, and of older individuals who provide uncompensated care to their adult children with disabilities;

(12) services to encourage the employment of older workers, including job and second career counseling and, where appropriate, job development, referral, and placement, and including the coordination of the services with programs administered by or receiving assistance from the Department of Labor, including programs carried out under the Workforce Investment Act of 1998 (29 U.S.C. 2801 et seq.);

(13) crime prevention services and victim assistance programs for older individuals;

(14) a program, to be known as "Senior Opportunities and Services", designed to identify and meet the needs of low-income older individuals in one or more of the following areas:

(A) development and provision of new volunteer services;

(B) effective referral to existing health (including mental health), employment, housing, legal, consumer, transportation, and other services;

(C) stimulation and creation of additional services and programs to remedy gaps and deficiencies in presently existing services and programs; and

(D) such other services as the Assistant Secretary may determine are necessary or especially appropriate to meet the needs of low-income older individuals and to assure them greater self-sufficiency;

(15) services for the prevention of abuse of older individuals in accordance with chapter 3 of subtitle A of title VII and section 307(a)(12);

(16) inservice training and State leadership for legal assistance activities;

(17) health and nutrition education services, including information concerning prevention, diagnosis, treatment, and rehabilitation of age-related diseases and chronic disabling conditions;

(18) services designed to enable mentally impaired older individuals to attain and maintain emotional well-being and independent living through a coordinated system of support services;

(19) services designed to support family members and other persons providing voluntary care to older individuals that need long-term care services;

(20) services designed to provide information and training for individuals who are or may become guardians or representative payees of older individuals, including information on the powers and duties of guardians and representative payees and on alternatives to guardianships;

(21) services to encourage and facilitate regular interaction between **students** and older individuals, including services for older individuals with limit English proficiency and visits in long-term care facilities, multipurpose senior centers, and other settings;

(22) in-home services for frail older individuals, including individuals with Alzheimer's disease and related disorders with neurological and organic brain dysfunction, and their families, including in-home services defined by a State agency in the State plan submitted under section 307, taking into consideration the age, economic need, and non-economic and non-health factors contributing to the frail condition and need for services of the individuals described in this paragraph, and in-home services defined by an area agency on aging in the area plan submitted under section 306;[12]

(23) services designed to support States, area agencies on aging, and local service providers in carrying out and coordinating activities for older individuals with respect to mental health services, including outreach for, education concerning, and screening for such services, and referral to such services for treatment;

(24) activities to promote and disseminate information about life-long learning programs, including opportunities for distance learning; and

(25) any other services necessary for the general welfare of older individuals, if such services meet standards prescribed by the Assistant Secretary and are necessary for the general welfare of older individuals. For purposes of paragraph (5), the term "client assessment through case management" includes providing information relating to assistive technology.

(b) (1) The Assistant Secretary shall carry out a program for making grants to States under State plans approved under section 307 for the acquisition, alteration, or renovation of existing facilities, including mobile units, and, where appropriate, construction of facilities to serve as multipurpose senior centers.

(2) Funds made available to a State under this part may be used for the purpose of assisting in the operation of multipurpose senior centers and meeting all or part of the costs of compensating professional and technical personnel required for the operation of multipurpose senior centers.

(c) In carrying out the provisions of this part, to more efficiently and effectively deliver services to older individuals, each area agency on aging shall coordinate services described in subsection (a) with other community agencies and voluntary organizations providing the same services. In coordinating the services, the area agency on aging shall make efforts to coordinate the services with agencies and organizations carrying out intergenerational programs or projects.

(d) Funds made available under this part shall supplement, and not supplant, any Federal, State, or local funds expended by a State or unit of general purpose local government (including an area agency on aging) to provide services described in subsection (a).

(42 U.S.C. 3030d)

PART C—NUTRITION SERVICE

Subpart 1—Congregate Nutrition Services

PROGRAM AUTHORIZED

Section. 330. PURPOSES.

The purposes of this part are—
  (1) to reduce hunger and food insecurity;
  (2) to promote socialization of older individuals; and
  (3) to promote the health and well-being of older individuals by assisting such individuals to gain access to nutrition and other disease prevention and health promotion services to delay the onset of adverse health conditions resulting from poor nutritional health or sedentary behavior.

Section. 331.

The Assistant Secretary shall carry out a program for making grants to States under State plans approved under section 307 for the establishment and operation of nutrition projects that—
  (1) 5 or more days a week (except in a rural area where such frequency is not feasible (as defined by the Assistant Secretary by regulation) and a lesser frequency is approved by the State agency), provide at least one hot or other appropriate meal per day and any additional meals which the recipient of a grant or contract under this subpart may elect to provide;
  (2) shall be provided in congregate settings, including adult day care facilities and multigenerational meal sites; and
  (3) provide nutrition education, nutrition counseling, and other nutrition services, as appropriate, based on the needs of meal participants.

(42 U.S.C. 3030e)

Subpart 2—Home Delivered Nutrition Services

PROGRAM AUTHORIZED

Section. 336. PROGRAM AUTHORIZED.

The Assistant Secretary shall establish and carry out a program to make grants to States under State plans approved under section 307 for the establishment and operation of nutrition projects for older individuals that provide—

    (1)   on 5 or more days a week (except in a rural area where such frequency is not feasible (as defined by the Assistant Secretary by rule) and a lesser frequency is approved by the State agency) at least 1 home delivered meal per day, which may consist of hot, cold, frozen, dried, canned, fresh, or supplemental foods and any additional meals that the recipient of a grant or contract under this subpart elects to provide; and

    (2)   nutrition education, nutrition counseling, and other nutrition services, as appropriate, based on the needs of meal recipients.

(42 U.S.C. 3030f)

Section. 337. CRITERIA.

The Assistant Secretary, in consultation with recognized experts in the fields of nutrition science, dietetics, meal planning and food service management, and aging, shall develop minimum criteria of efficiency and quality for the furnishing of home delivered meal services for projects described in section 336.

(42 U.S.C. 3030g)

Subpart 3—General Provisions

Section. 339. NUTRITION.

A State that establishes and operates a nutrition project under this chapter shall—

    (1)   solicit the expertise of a dietitian or other individual with equivalent education and training in nutrition science, or if such an individual is not available, an individual with comparable expertise in the planning of nutritional services, and

    (2)   ensure that the project—

        (A) provides meals that—

            (i) comply with the most recent Dietary Guidelines for Americans, published by the Secretary and the Secretary of Agriculture, and

            (ii) provide to each participating older individual—

                (I) a minimum of 33 1/3 percent of the dietary reference intakes established by the Food and Nutrition Board of the Institute of Medicine of the National Academy of Sciences, if the project provides one meal per day,

                (II) a minimum of 66 2/3 percent of the allowances if the project provides two meals per day, and

                (III) 100 percent of the allowances if the project provides three meals per day, and

(iii) to the maximum extent practicable, are adjusted to meet any special dietary needs of program participants,

(B) provides flexibility to local nutrition providers in designing meals that are appealing to program participants,

(C) encourages providers to enter into contracts that limit the amount of time meals must spend in transit before they are consumed,

(D) where feasible, encourages **joint** arrangements with schools and other facilities serving meals to children in order to promote intergenerational meal programs,

(E) provides that meals, other than in-home meals, are provided in settings in as close proximity to the majority of eligible older individuals' residences as feasible,

(F) comply with applicable provisions of State or local laws regarding the safe and sanitary handling of food, equipment, and supplies used in the storage, preparation, service, and delivery of meals to an older individual,

(G) ensures that meal providers solicit the advice and expertise of—
(i) a dietitian or other individual described in paragraph (1),
(ii) meal participants, and
(iii) other individuals knowledgeable with regard to the needs of older individuals,

(H) ensures that each participating area agency on aging establishes procedures that allow nutrition project administrators the option to offer a meal, on the same basis as meals provided to participating older individuals, to individuals providing volunteer services during the meal hours, and to individuals with disabilities who reside at home with older individuals eligible under this chapter,

(I) ensures that nutrition services will be available to older individuals and to their spouses, and may be made available to individuals with disabilities who are not older individuals but who reside in housing facilities occupied primarily by older individuals at which congregate nutrition services are provided,

(J) provides for nutrition screening and nutrition education, and nutrition assessment and counseling if appropriate, and

(K) encourages individuals who distribute nutrition services under subpart 2 to provide, to homebound older individuals, available medical information approved by health care professionals, such as informational brochures and information on how to get vaccines, including vaccines for influenza, pneumonia, and shingles, in the individuals' communities.

(42 U.S.C. 3030g–21)

Study of Nutrition Projects

(a) STUDY.—

(1) IN GENERAL.—The Assistant Secretary for Aging shall use funds allocated in section 206(g) of the Older Americans Act of 1965 (42 U.S.C. 3017(g)) to enter into a contract with the Food and Nutrition Board of the Institute of Medicine of the National Academy of Sciences, for the purpose of establishing an independent panel of experts that will conduct an evidence-based study of the nutrition projects authorized by such Act.

(2) STUDY.—Such study shall, to the extent data are available, include—

(A) an evaluation of the effect of the nutrition projects authorized by such Act on—

(i)   improvement of the health status, including nutritional status, of participants in the projects;

(ii)   prevention of hunger and food insecurity of the participants; and

(iii) continuation of the ability of the participants to live independently;

(B) a cost-benefit analysis of nutrition projects authorized by such Act, including the potential to affect costs of the Medicaid program under title XIX of the Social Security Act (42 U.S.C. 1396 et seq.); and

(C) an analysis of how and recommendations for how nutrition projects authorized by such Act may be modified to improve the outcomes described in subparagraph (A), including recommendations for improving the nutritional quality of the meals provided through the
projects and undertaking other potential strategies to improve the nutritional status of the participants.

(b) REPORTS. —

(1) REPORT TO THE ASSISTANT SECRETARY. — The panel described in subsection (a)(1) shall submit to the Assistant Secretary a report containing the results of the evidence-based study described   in   subsection   (a),   including   any   recommendations   described in subsection (a)(2)(C).

(2) REPORT TO CONGRESS. — The Assistant Secretary shall submit a report containing the results described in paragraph (1) to the Committee on Education and the Workforce of the House of Representatives and the Committee on Health, Education, Labor, and Pensions of the Senate.

SENSE OF CONGRESS RECOGNIZING THE CONTRIBUTION OF NUTRITION TO THE HEALTH OF OLDER ADULTS

(Note: Section numbering not included in 2006 Amendments)

(b) FINDINGS . — Congress finds that-

(1) good nutrition is vital to good health, and a diet based on the Dietary Guidelines for Americans may reduce the risk of chronic diseases such as cardiovascular disease, osteoporosis, diabetes, macular degeneration, and cancer;

(2) the American Dietetic Association and the American Academy of Family Physicians have estimated that the percentage of older adults who are malnourished is estimated at 20 to 60 percent for those who are in home care and at 40 to 85 percent for those who are in nursing homes;

(3) the Institute of Medicine of the National Academy of Sciences has estimated that approximately 40 percent of community-residing persons age 65 and older have inadequate nutrient intakes;

(4) older adults are susceptible to nutrient deficiencies for a number of reasons, including a reduced capacity to absorb and utilize nutrients, difficulty chewing, and loss of appetite;

(5)   while diet is the preferred source of nutrition, evidence suggests that the use of a single daily multivitamin-mineral supplement may be an effective way to address nutritional gaps that exist among the elderly population, especially the poor; and

(6)   the Dietary Guidelines for Americans state that multivitamin-mineral supplements may be useful when they fill a specific identified nutrient gap that cannot be or is not otherwise being met by the individual's intake of food.

(b)   S ENSE OF CONGRESS . — It is the sense of Congress that—

(1)   meal programs funded by the Older Americans Act of 1965 contribute to the nutritional health of older adults;

(2)   when the nutritional needs of older adults are not fully met by diet, use of a single, daily multivitamin-mineral supplement may help prevent nutrition deficiencies common in many older adults;

(3)   use of a single, daily multivitamin-mineral supplement can be a safe and inexpensive strategy to help ensure the nutritional health of older adults; and

(4)   nutrition service providers under the Older Americans Act of 1965 should consider whether individuals participating in congregate and home-delivered meal programs would benefit from a single, daily multivitamin-mineral supplement that is in compliance with all applicable government quality standards and provides at least 2/ 3 of the essential vitamins and minerals at 100 per cent of the daily value levels as determined by the Commissioner of Food and Drugs.

Section. XXX. STUDY OF NUTRITION.

SENSE OF CONGRESS RECOGNIZING THE CONTRIBUTION OF NUTRITION TO THE HEALTH OF OLDER ADULTS

(Note: Section numbering not included in 2006 Amendments)

(b)   FINDINGS. — Congress finds that-
(1)   good nutrition is vital to good health, and a diet based on the Dietary Guidelines for Americans may reduce the risk of chronic diseases such as cardiovascular disease, osteoporosis, diabetes, macular degeneration, and cancer;
(2)   the American Dietetic Association and the American Academy of Family Physicians have estimated that the percentage of older adults who are malnourished is estimated at 20 to 60 percent for those who are in home care and at 40 to 85 percent for those who are in nursing homes;
(3)   the Institute of Medicine of the National Academy of Sciences has estimated that approximately 40 percent of community-residing persons age 65 and older have inadequate nutrient intakes;
(4)   older adults are susceptible to nutrient deficiencies for a number of reasons, including a reduced capacity to absorb and utilize nutrients, difficulty chewing, and loss of appetite;
(5)   while diet is the preferred source of nutrition, evidence suggests that the use of a single daily multivitamin-mineral supplement may be an effective way to address nutritional gaps that exist among the elderly population, especially the poor; and

(6) the Dietary Guidelines for Americans state that multivitamin-mineral supplements may be useful when they fill a specific identified nutrient gap that cannot be or is not otherwise being met by the individual's intake of food.

Section. XXX. SENSE OF CONGRESS.

(b) SENSE OF CONGRESS.—It is the sense of Congress that—
   (1) meal programs funded by the Older Americans Act of 1965 contribute to the nutritional health of older adults;
   (2) when the nutritional needs of older adults are not fully met by diet, use of a single, daily multivitamin-mineral supplement may help prevent nutrition deficiencies common in many older adults;
   (3) use of a single, daily multivitamin-mineral supplement can be a safe and inexpensive strategy to help ensure the nutritional health of older adults; and
   (4) nutrition service providers under the Older Americans Act of 1965 should consider whether individuals participating in congregate and home-delivered meal programs would benefit from a single, daily multivitamin-mineral supplement that is in compliance with all applicable government quality standards and provides at least 2/3 of the essential vitamins and minerals at 100 percent of the daily value levels as determined by the Commissioner of Food and Drugs.

Section. 339A. PAYMENT REQUIREMENT.

Payments made by a State agency or an area agency on aging for nutrition services (including meals) provided under part A, B, or C may not be reduced to reflect any increase in the level of assistance provided under section 311.

(42 U.S.C. 3030g–22)

PART D—DISEASE PREVENTION AND HEALTH PROMOTION SERVICES PROGRAM AUTHORIZED

Section. 361.

(a) The Assistant Secretary shall carry out a program for making grants to States under State plans approved under section 307 to provide disease prevention and health promotion services and information at multipurpose senior centers, at congregate meal sites, through home delivered meals programs, or at other appropriate sites. In carrying out such program, the Assistant Secretary shall consult with the Directors of the Centers for Disease Control and Prevention and the National Institute on Aging.
(b) The Assistant Secretary shall, to the extent possible, assure that services provided by other community organizations and agencies are used to carry out the provisions of this part.
(c) The Assistant Secretary shall work in consultation with qualified experts to provide information on methods of improving indoor air quality in buildings where older individuals congregate.

(42 U.S.C. 3030m)

The State agency shall give priority, in carrying out this part, to areas of the State —

    (1) which are medically underserved; and

    (2) in which there are a large number of older individuals who have the greatest economic need for such services.

(42 U.S.C. 3030n)

PART E — NATIONAL FAMILY CAREGIVER SUPPORT PROGRAM

Section. 371. SHORT TITLE.

This part may be cited as the "National Family Caregiver Support Act".

(42 U.S.C. 3030s)

Subpart 1 — Caregiver Support Program

Section. 372. DEFINITIONS.

(a) In General. -

In this subpart:

    (1) CHILD. — The term "child" means an individual who is not more than 18 years of age or who is an individual with a disability.

    (2) GRANDPARENT OR OLDER INDIVIDUAL WHO IS A RELATIVE CAREGIVER. — The term "grandparent or older individual who is a relative caregiver" means a grandparent or step-grandparent of a child, or a relative of a child by blood, marriage, or adoption who is 55 years of age or older and —

        (A) lives with the child;

        (B) is the primary caregiver of the child because the biological or adoptive parents are unable or unwilling to serve as the primary caregiver of the child; and

        (C) has a legal relationship to the child, as such legal custody or guardianship, or is raising the child informally.

(b) RULE. — In providing services under this subpart —

    (1) for family caregivers who provide care for individuals with Alzheimer's disease and related disorders with neurological and organic brain dysfunction, the State involved shall give priority to caregivers who provide care for older individuals with such disease or disorder; and

    (2) for grandparents or older individuals who are relative caregivers, the State involved shall give priority to caregivers who provide care for children with severe disabilities.

(42 U.S.C. 3030s)

(ii) IN GENERAL. — The Assistant Secretary shall carry out a program for making grants to States with State plans approved under section 307, to pay for the Federal share of the cost of carrying out State programs, to enable area agencies on aging, or entities that such area agencies on aging contract with, to provide multifaceted systems of support services —

    (1) for family caregivers; and

(2)   for grandparents or older individuals who are relative caregivers.
(iii) SUPPORT SERVICES.—The services provided, in a State program under subsection (a), by an area agency on aging, or entity that such agency has contracted with, shall include—
(1)   information to caregivers about available services;
(2)   assistance to caregivers in gaining access to the services;
(3)   individual counseling, organization of support groups, and caregiver training to assist the caregivers in the areas of health, nutrition, and financial literacy, and in making decisions and solving problems relating to their caregiving roles;
(4)   respite care to enable caregivers to be temporarily relieved from their caregiving responsibilities; and
(5)   supplemental services, on a limited basis, to complement the care provided by caregivers.
(iv) POPULATION SERVED; PRIORITY.—
(1)   POPULATION SERVED.—Services under a State program under this subpart shall be provided to family caregivers, and grandparents and older individuals who are relative caregivers, and who—
(A)   are described in paragraph (1) or (2) of subsection (a); and
(B)   with regard to the services specified in paragraphs (4) and (5) of subsection (b), in the case of a caregiver described in paragraph (1), is providing care to an older individual who meets the condition specified in subparagraph (A)(i) or (B) of section 102(22).
(2)   PRIORITY.—In providing services under this subpart, the State, in addition to giving the priority described in section 372(b), shall give priority—
(A)   to caregivers who are older individuals with greatest social need, and older individuals with greatest economic need (with particular attention to low-income older individuals); and
(B)   to older individuals providing care to individuals with severe disabilities, including children with severe disabilities.
(v)   USE OF VOLUNTEERS.—In carrying out this subpart, each area agency on aging shall make use of trained volunteers to expand the provision of the available services described in subsection (b) and, if possible, work in coordination with organizations that have experience in providing training, placement, and stipends for volunteers or participants (such as organizations carrying out Federal service programs administered by the Corporation for National and Community Service), in community service settings.
(vi) QUALITY STANDARDS AND MECHANISMS AND ACCOUNTABILITY.—
(1)   QUALITY STANDARDS AND MECHANISMS.—The State shall establish standards and mechanisms designed to assure the quality of services provided with assistance made available under this subpart.
(2)   DATA AND RECORDS.—The State shall collect data and maintain records relating to the State program in a standardized format specified by the Assistant Secretary. The State shall furnish the records to the Assistant Secretary, at such time as the Assistant Secretary may require, in order to enable the Assistant Secretary to monitor State program administration and compliance, and to evaluate and compare the effectiveness of the State programs.

(3) REPORTS.—The State shall prepare and submit to the Assistant Secretary reports on the data and records required under paragraph (2), including information on the services funded under this subpart, and standards and mechanisms by which the quality of the services shall be assured. The reports shall describe any mechanisms used in the State to provide to persons who are family caregivers, or grandparents or older individuals who are relative caregivers, information about and access to various services so that the persons can better carry out their care responsibilities.

(vii) CAREGIVER ALLOTMENT.—

(1) IN GENERAL.—

(A) From sums appropriated under section 303(e) for fiscal years 2007, 2008, 2009, 2010, and 2011 the Assistant Secretary shall allot amounts among the States proportionately based on the population of individuals 70 years of age or older in the States.

(B) In determining the amounts allotted to States from the sums appropriated under section 303 for a fiscal year, the Assistant Secretary shall first determine the amount allotted to each State under subparagraph (A) and then proportionately adjust such amounts, if necessary, to meet the requirements of paragraph (2).

(C) The number of individuals 70 years of age or older in any State and in all States shall be determined by the Assistant Secretary on the basis of the most recent data available from the Bureau of the Census and other reliable demographic data satisfactory to the Assistant Secretary.

(2) MINIMUM ALLOTMENT.—

(A) The amounts allotted under paragraph (1) shall be reduced proportionately to the extent necessary to increase other allotments under such paragraph to achieve the amounts described in subparagraph (B).

(B) (i) Each State shall be allotted 1/2 of 1 percent of the amount appropriated for the fiscal year for which the determination is made.

(ii) Guam and the Virgin Islands of the United States shall each be allotted 1/4 of 1 percent of the amount appropriated for the fiscal year for which the determination is made.

(iii) American Samoa and the Commonwealth of the Northern Mariana Islands shall each be allotted 1/16 of 1 percent of the amount appropriated for the fiscal year for which the determination is made.

(C) For the purposes of subparagraph (B)(i), the term "State" does not include Guam, American Samoa, the Virgin Islands of the United States, and the Commonwealth of the Northern Mariana Islands.

(viii) AVAILABILITY OF FUNDS.—

(1) USE OF FUNDS FOR ADMINISTRATION OF AREA PLANS.—Amounts made available to a State to carry out the State program under this subpart may be used, in addition to amounts available in accordance with section 303(c)(1), for costs of administration of area """""plans.

(2) FEDERAL SHARE.—

(A) IN GENERAL.—Notwithstanding section 304(d)(1)(D), the Federal share of the cost of carrying out a State program under this subpart shall be 75 percent.

(B) NON-FEDERAL SHARE.—The non-Federal share of the cost shall be provided from State and local sources.

(C) LIMITATION.—A State may use not more than 10 percent of the total Federal and non-Federal share available to the State to provide support services to grandparents and older individuals who are relative caregivers of a child who is not more than 18 years of age.

(42 U.S.C. 3030s–1)

Section. 374. MAINTENANCE OF EFFORT.

Funds made available under this subpart shall supplement, and not supplant, any Federal, State, or local funds expended by a State or unit of general purpose local government (including an area agency on aging) to provide services described in section 373.

(42 U.S.C. 3030s–2)

TITLE IV – ACTIVITIES FOR HEALTH INDEPENDENCE, AND LONGEVITY

Section. 401. PURPOSES.

The purposes of this title are —
  (1) to expand the Nation's knowledge and understanding of the older population and the aging process;
  (2) to design, test, and promote the use of innovative ideas and best practices in programs and services for older individuals; (3) to help meet the needs for trained personnel in the field of aging; and (4) to increase awareness of citizens of all ages of the need to assume personal responsibility for their own longevity.

(42 U.S.C. 3031)

PART A — GRANT PROGRAMS

Section. 411. PROGRAM AUTHORIZED.

(a) IN GENERAL. — For the purpose of carrying out this section, the Assistant Secretary may make grants to and enter into contracts with States, public agencies, private nonprofit agencies, institutions of higher education, and organizations, including tribal organizations, for —
  (1) education and training to develop an adequately trained workforce to work with and on behalf of older individuals;
  (2) applied social research and analysis to improve access to and delivery of services for older individuals;
  (3) evaluation of the performance of the programs, activities, and services provided under this section;
  (4) the development of methods and practices to improve the quality and effectiveness of the programs, services, and activities provided under this section;
  (5) the demonstration of new approaches to design, deliver, and coordinate programs and services for older individuals;
  (6) technical assistance in planning, developing, implementing, and improving the programs, services, and activities provided under this section;
  (7) coordination with the designated State agency described in section 101(a)(2)(A)(i) of the Rehabilitation Act of 1973 (29 U.S.C. 721(a)(2)(A)(i)) to provide services to older individuals who are blind as described in such Act;
  (8) the training of graduate level professionals specializing in the mental health needs of older individuals;
  (9) planning activities to prepare communities for the aging of the population, which activities may include —
    (A) efforts to assess the aging population;
    (B) activities to coordinate the activities of State and local agencies in order to meet the needs of older individuals; and

(C) training and technical assistance to support States, area agencies on aging, and organizations receiving grants under title VI, in engaging in community planning activities;

(10) the development, implementation, and assessment of technology-based service models and best practices, to support the use of health monitoring and assessment technologies, communication devices, assistive technologies, and other technologies that may remotely connect family and professional caregivers to frail older individuals residing in home and community-based settings or rural areas;

(11) conducting activities of national significance to promote quality and continuous improvement in the support provided to family and other informal caregivers of older individuals through activities that include program evaluation, training, technical assistance, and research, including—

(A) programs addressing unique issues faced by rural caregivers;

(B) programs focusing on the needs of older individuals with cognitive impairment such as Alzheimer's disease and related disorders with neurological and organic brain dysfunction, and their caregivers; and

(C) programs supporting caregivers in the role they play in providing disease prevention and health promotion services;

(12) building public awareness of cognitive impairments such as Alzheimer's disease and related disorders with neurological and organic brain dysfunction, depression, and mental disorders; and

(13) any other activities that the Assistant Secretary determines will achieve the objectives of this section.

(b) AUTHORIZATION OF APPROPRIATIONS.—There are authorized to be appropriated to carry out this section such sums as may be necessary for fiscal years 2007, 2008, 2009, 2010, and 2011.

(42 U.S.C. 3032)

Section. 412. CAREER PREPARATION FOR THE FIELD OF AGING.

(a) GRANTS.—The Assistant Secretary shall make grants to institutions of higher education, including historically Black colleges or universities, Hispanic-serving institutions, and Hispanic Centers of Excellence in Applied Gerontology, to provide education and training that prepares students for careers in the field of aging.

(b) DEFINITIONS.—For purposes of subsection (a):

(1) HISPANIC CENTER OF EXCELLENCE IN APPLIED GERONTOLOGY.—

The term "Hispanic Center of Excellence in Applied Gerontology" means an institution of higher education with a program in applied gerontology that—

(A) has a significant number of Hispanic individuals enrolled in the program, including individuals accepted for enrollment in the program;

(B) has been effective in assisting Hispanic students of the program to complete the program and receive the degree involved;

(C) has been effective in recruiting Hispanic individuals to attend the program, including providing scholarships and other financial assistance to such individuals and encouraging Hispanic students of secondary educational institutions to attend the program; and

(D) has made significant recruitment efforts to increase the number and placement of Hispanic individuals serving in faculty or administrative positions in the program.

(2) HISTORICALLY BLACK COLLEGE OR UNIVERSITY. — The term "historically Black college or university" has the meaning given the term "part B institution" in section 322(2) of the Higher Education Act of 1965 (20 U.S.C. 1061(2)).

(42 U.S.C. 3032a)

Section. 413. OLDER INDIVIDUALS' PROTECTION FROM VIOLENCE PROJECTS.

(a) PROGRAM AUTHORIZED. — The Assistant Secretary shall make grants to States, area agencies on aging, nonprofit organizations, or tribal organizations to carry out the activities described in subsection (b).

(b) ACTIVITIES. — A State, an area agency on aging, a nonprofit organization, or a tribal organization that receives a grant under subsection (a) shall use such grant to—

(1) support projects in local communities, involving diverse sectors of each community, to coordinate activities concerning intervention in and prevention of elder abuse, neglect, and exploitation, including family violence and sexual assault, against older individuals;

(2) develop and implement outreach programs directed toward assisting older individuals who are victims of elder abuse, neglect, and exploitation (including family violence and sexual assault, against older individuals), including programs directed toward assisting the individuals in senior housing complexes, nursing homes, board and care facilities, and senior centers;

(3) expand access to family violence and sexual assault programs (including shelters, rape crisis centers, and support groups), including mental health services, safety planning and legal advocacy for older individuals and encourage the use of senior housing, hotels, or other suitable facilities or services when appropriate as emergency short-term shelters for older individuals who are the victims of elder abuse, including family violence and sexual assault; or

(4) promote research on legal, organizational, or training impediments to providing services to older individuals through shelters and other programs, such as impediments to provision of services in coordination with delivery of health care or services delivered under this Act.

(c) PREFERENCE. — In awarding grants under subsection (a), the Assistant Secretary shall give preference to a State, an area agency on aging, a nonprofit organization, or a tribal organization that has the ability to carry out the activities described in this section and title VII of this Act.

(d) COORDINATION. — The Assistant Secretary shall encourage each State, area agency on aging, nonprofit organization, and tribal organization that receives a grant under subsection (a) to coordinate activities provided under this section with activities provided by other area agencies on aging, tribal organizations, State adult protective service programs, private nonprofit organizations, and by other entities receiving funds under title VII of this Act.

(42 U.S.C. 3032b)

Section. 414. HEALTH CARE SERVICE DEMONSTRATION PROJECTS IN RURAL AREAS.

(b) AUTHORITY.—The Assistant Secretary, after consultation with the State agency of the State involved, shall make grants to eligible public agencies and nonprofit private organizations to pay part or all of the cost of developing or operating model health care, mental health services, projects (including related home health care services, adult day health care, outreach, and transportation) through multipurpose senior centers that are located in rural areas and that provide nutrition services under section 331, to meet the health care needs of medically underserved older individuals residing in such areas.

(c) ELIGIBILITY.—To be eligible to receive a grant under subsection (a), a public agency or nonprofit private organization shall submit to the Assistant Secretary an application containing such information and assurances as the Secretary may require, including—
  (1) information describing the nature and extent of the applicant's—
    (A) experience in providing medical services of the type to be provided in the project for which a grant is requested; and
    (B) coordination and cooperation with—
      (i) institutions of higher education having graduate programs with capability in public health, mental health, the medical sciences, psychology, pharmacology, nursing, social work, health education, nutrition, or gerontology, for the purpose of designing and developing such project; and
      (ii) critical access hospitals (as defined in section 1861(mm)(1) of the Social Security Act (42 U.S.C. 1395x(mm)(1)) and rural health clinics (as defined in section 1861(aa)(2) of the Social Security Act (42 U.S.C. 1395x(aa)(2)));
  (2) assurances that the applicant will carry out the project for which a grant is requested, through a multipurpose senior center located—
    (A) (i) in a rural area that has a population of less than 5,000; or
        (ii) in a county that has fewer than seven individuals per square mile; and
    (B) in a State in which—
      (i) not less than 331/3 of the population resides in rural areas; and
      (ii) not less than 5 percent of the population resides in counties with fewer than seven individuals per square mile, as defined by and determined in accordance with the most recent data available from the Bureau of the Census; and
  (3) assurances that the applicant will submit to the Assistant Secretary such evaluations and reports as the Assistant Secretary may require.

(d) REPORTS.—The Assistant Secretary shall prepare and submit to the appropriate committees of Congress a report that includes summaries of the evaluations and reports required under subsection (b).

(42 U.S.C. 3032c)

Section. 415. COMPUTER TRAINING.

(a) PROGRAM AUTHORIZED.—The Assistant Secretary, in consultation with the Assistant Secretary of Commerce for Communications and Information, may award grants or contracts to entities to provide computer training and enhanced Internet access for older individuals.

(b) PRIORITY.—If the Assistant Secretary awards grants under subsection (a), the Assistant Secretary shall give priority to an entity that—
(1) will provide services to older individuals living in rural areas;
(2) has demonstrated expertise in providing computer training to older individuals; or
(3) has demonstrated that it has a variety of training delivery methods, including facility-based, computer-based, and Internet-based training, that may facilitate a determination of the best method of training older individuals.
(c) SPECIAL CONSIDERATION.—In awarding grants under this section, the Assistant Secretary shall give special consideration to applicants that have entered into a partnership with one or more private entities providing such applicants with donated information technologies including software, hardware, or training.
(d) USE OF FUNDS.—An entity that receives a grant or contract under subsection (a) shall use funds received under such grant or contract to provide training for older individuals that—
(1) relates to the use of computers and related equipment, in order to improve the self-employment and employment-related technology skills of older individuals, as well as their ability to use the Internet; and
(2) is provided at senior centers, housing facilities for older individuals, elementary schools, secondary schools, and institutions of higher education.

(42 U.S.C. 3032d)

Section. 416. TECHNICAL ASSISTANCE AND INNOVATION TO IMPROVE TRANSPORTATION FOR OLDER INDIVIDUALS.

(a) IN GENERAL.—The Secretary may award grants or contracts to nonprofit organizations to improve transportation services for older individuals.
(b) USE OF FUNDS.—
(1) IN GENERAL.—A nonprofit organization receiving a grant or contract under subsection (a) shall use the funds received through such grant or contract to carry out a demonstration project, or to provide technical assistance to assist local transit providers, area agencies on aging, senior centers, and local senior support groups, to encourage and facilitate coordination of Federal, State, and local transportation services and resources for older individuals. The organization may use the funds to develop and carry out an innovative transportation demonstration project to create transportation services for older individuals.
(2) SPECIFIC ACTIVITIES.—In carrying out a demonstration project or providing technical assistance under paragraph (1) the organization may carry out activities that include—
(A) developing innovative approaches for improving access by older individuals to transportation services, including volunteer driver programs, economically sustainable transportation programs, and programs that allow older individuals to transfer their automobiles to a provider of transportation services in exchange for the services;
(B) preparing information on transportation options and resources for older individuals and organizations serving such individuals, and disseminating the information by establishing and operating a toll-free telephone number;

(C) developing models and best practices for providing comprehensive integrated transportation services for older individuals, including services administered by the Secretary of Transportation, by providing ongoing technical assistance to agencies providing services under title III and by assisting in coordination of public and community transportation services; and

(D) providing special services to link older individuals to transportation services not provided under title III.

(c) ECONOMICALLY SUSTAINABLE TRANSPORTATION.—In this section, the term 'economically sustainable transportation' means demand responsive transportation for older individuals—

(1) that may be provided through volunteers; and

(2) that the provider will provide without receiving Federal or other public financial assistance, after a period of not more than 5 years of providing the services under this section.

(42 U.S.C. 3032e)

SECTION.417. DEMONSTRATION, SUPPORT, AND RESEARCH PROJECTS FOR MULTIGENERATIONAL AND CIVIC ENGAGEMENT ACTIVITIES.

(a) GRANTS AND CONTRACTS.—The Assistant Secretary shall award grants and enter into contracts with eligible organizations to carry out projects to—

(1) provide opportunities for older individuals to participate in multigenerational activities and civic engagement activities designed to meet critical community needs, and use the full range of time, skills, and experience of older individuals, including demonstration and support projects that—

(A) provide support for grandparents and other older individuals who are relative caregivers raising children (such as kinship navigator programs); or

(B) involve volunteers who are older individuals who provide support and information to families who have a child with a disability or chronic illness, or other families in need of such family support; and

(2) coordinate multigenerational activities and civic engagement activities, promote volunteerism, and facilitate development of and participation in multigenerational activities and civic engagement activities.

(b) USE OF FUNDS.—An eligible organization shall use funds made available under a grant awarded, or a contract entered into, under this section to—

(1) carry out a project described in subsection (a); and

(2) evaluate the project in accordance with subsection (f).

(c) PREFERENCE.—In awarding grants and entering into contracts to carry out a project described in subsection (a), the Assistant Secretary shall give preference to—

(1) eligible organizations with a demonstrated record of carrying out multigenerational activities or civic engagement activities;

(2) eligible organizations proposing multigenerational activity projects that will serve older individuals and communities with the greatest need (with particular attention to low income minority individuals, older individuals with limited English proficiency, older individuals residing in rural areas, and low-income minority communities);

(3) eligible organizations proposing civic engagement projects that will serve communities with the greatest need; and

(4) eligible organizations with the capacity to develop meaningful roles and assignments that use the time, skills, and experience of older individuals to serve public and nonprofit organizations.

(d) APPLICATION.—To be eligible to receive a grant or enter into a contract under subsection (a), an organization shall submit an application to the Assistant Secretary at such time, in such manner, and accompanied by such information as the Assistant Secretary may reasonably require.

(e) ELIGIBLE ORGANIZATIONS.—Organizations eligible to receive a grant or enter into a contract under subsection (a)—

    (1) to carry out activities described in subsection (a)(1), shall be organizations that provide opportunities for older individuals to participate in activities described in subsection (a)(1); and

    (2) to carry out activities described in subsection (a)(2), shall be organizations with the capacity to conduct the coordination, promotion, and facilitation described in subsection (a)(2), through the use of multigenerational coordinators.

(f) LOCAL EVALUATION AND REPORT.—

    (1) EVALUATION.—Each organization receiving a grant or a contract under subsection (a) to carry out a project described in subsection (a) shall evaluate the multigenerational activities or civic engagement activities carried out under the project to determine—

        (A) the effectiveness of the activities involved;

        (B) the impact of such activities on the community being served and the organization providing the activities; and

        (C) the impact of such activities on older individuals involved in such project.

    (2) REPORT.—The organization shall submit a report to the Assistant Secretary containing the evaluation not later than 6 months after the expiration of the period for which the grant or contract is in effect.

(g) REPORT TO CONGRESS.—Not later than 6 months after the Assistant Secretary receives the reports described in subsection (f)(2), the Assistant Secretary shall prepare and submit to the Speaker of the House of Representatives and the President pro-tempore of the Senate a report that assesses the evaluations and includes, at a minimum—

    (1) the names or descriptive titles of the projects funded under subsection (a);

    (2) a description of the nature and operation of the projects;

    (3) the names and addresses of organizations that conducted the projects;

    (4) in the case of projects carried out under subsection (a)(1), a description of the methods and success of the projects in recruiting older individuals as employees and as volunteers to participate in the projects;

    (5) in the case of projects carried out under subsection (a)(1), a description of the success of the projects in retaining older individuals participating in the projects as employees and as volunteers;

    (6) in the case of projects carried out under subsection (a)(1), the rate of turnover of older individual employees and volunteers in the projects;

    (7) a strategy for disseminating the findings resulting from the projects described in paragraph (1); and

    (8) any policy change recommendations relating to the projects.

(h) DEFINITIONS.—As used in this section:

(1) MULTIGENERATIONAL ACTIVITY.—The term 'multigenerational activity' means an activity that provides an opportunity for interaction between 2 or more individuals of different generations, including activities connecting older individuals and youth in a child care program, a youth day care program, an educational assistance program, an at-risk youth intervention program, a juvenile delinquency treatment program, a before- or after-school program, a library program, or a family support program.

(2) MULTIGENERATIONAL COORDINATOR.—The term 'multigenerational coordinator' means a person who—

    (A) builds the capacity of public and nonprofit organizations to develop meaningful roles and assignments, that use the time, skill, and experience of older individuals to serve those organizations; and

    (B) nurtures productive, sustainable working relationships between—

        (i) individuals from the generations with older individuals; and

        (ii) individuals in younger generations.

(42 U.S.C. 3032f)

Section. 418. NATIVE AMERICAN PROGRAMS.

(a) ESTABLISHMENT.—

(1) IN GENERAL.—The Assistant Secretary shall make grants or enter into contracts with not fewer than two and not more than four eligible entities to establish and operate Resource Centers on Native American Elders (referred to in this section as "Resource Centers"). The Assistant Secretary shall make such grants or enter into such contracts for periods of not less than 3 years.

(2) FUNCTIONS.—

    (A) IN GENERAL.—Each Resource Center that receives funds under this section shall—

        (i) gather information;

        (ii) perform research;

        (iii) provide for the dissemination of results of the research; and

        (iv) provide technical assistance and training to entities that provide services to Native Americans who are older individuals.

    (B) AREAS OF CONCERN.—In conducting the functions described in subparagraph (A), a Resource Center shall focus on priority areas of concern for the Resource Centers regarding Native Americans who are older individuals, which areas shall be—

        (i) health (including mental health) problems;

        (ii) long-term care, including in-home care;

        (iii) elder abuse; and

        (iv) other problems and issues that the Assistant Secretary determines are of particular importance to Native Americans who are older individuals.

(3) PREFERENCE.—In awarding grants and entering into contracts under paragraph (1), the Assistant Secretary shall give preference to institutions of higher education that have conducted research on, and assessments of, the characteristics and needs of Native Americans who are older individuals.

(4) CONSULTATION.—In determining the type of information to be sought from, and activities to be performed by, Resource Centers, the Assistant Secretary shall consult with the Director of the Office for American Indian, Alaskan Native, and Native Hawaiian Aging and with national organizations with special expertise in serving Native Americans who are older individuals.

(5) ELIGIBLE ENTITIES.—To be eligible to receive a grant or enter into a contract under paragraph (1), an entity shall be an institution of higher education with experience conducting research and assessment on the needs of older individuals.

(6) REPORT TO CONGRESS.—The Assistant Secretary, with assistance from each Resource Center, shall prepare and submit to the Speaker of the House of Representatives and the President pro tempore of the Senate an annual report on the status and needs, including the priority areas of concern, of Native Americans who are older individuals.

(b) TRAINING GRANTS.—The Assistant Secretary shall make grants and enter into contracts to provide in-service training opportunities and courses of instruction on aging to Indian tribes through public or nonprofit Indian aging organizations and to provide annually a national meeting to train directors of programs under this title.

(42 U.S.C. 3032g)

Section.419. MULTIDISCIPLINARY CENTERS AND MULTIDISCIPLINARY SYSTEMS.

(a) MULTIDISCIPLINARY CENTERS.-

(1) PROGRAM AUTHORIZED. - The Assistant Secretary may make grants to public and private nonprofit agencies, organizations, and institutions for the purpose of establishing or supporting multidisciplinary centers of gerontology, and gerontology centers of special emphasis (including emphasis on nutrition, employment, health (including mental health), disabilities (including severe disabilities), income maintenance, counseling services, supportive services, minority populations, diverse populations of older individuals residing in urban communities, and older individuals residing in rural areas).

(2) USE OF FUNDS.

(A) IN GENERAL.—The centers described in paragraph (1) shall conduct research and policy analysis and function as a technical resource for the Assistant Secretary, policymakers, service providers, and Congress.

(B) MULTIDISCIPLINARY CENTERS.—The multidisciplinary centers of gerontology described in paragraph (1) shall—

(i) recruit and train personnel;

(ii) conduct basic and applied research toward the development of information related to aging;

(iii) stimulate the incorporation of information on aging into the teaching of biological, behavioral, and social sciences at colleges and universities;

(iv) help to develop training programs in the field of aging at schools of public health, education, social work, and psychology, and other appropriate schools within colleges and universities;

(v) serve as a repository of information and knowledge on aging, including information about best practices in long-term care service delivery, housing, and transportation;

(vi) provide information and other technical assistance to public and voluntary organizations, including State agencies and area agencies on aging, which serve the needs of older individuals in planning and developing services provided under other provisions of this Act;

(vii) if appropriate, provide information relating to assistive technology; and

(viii) provide training and technical assistance to support the provision of community-based mental health services for older individuals.

(3) DATA

    (A) IN GENERAL.—Each center that receives a grant under paragraph (1) shall provide data to the Assistant Secretary on the projects and activities carried out with funds received under such paragraph.

    (B) INFORMATION INCLUDED.—Such data described in subparagraph (A) shall include—

        (i) information on the number of personnel trained;

        (ii) information on the number of older individuals served;

        (iii) information on the number of schools assisted; and

        (iv) other information that will facilitate achieving the objectives of this subsection.

(b) MULTIDISCIPLINARY HEALTH SERVICES IN COMMUNITIES.—

(1) PROGRAM AUTHORIZED.—The Assistant Secretary shall make grants to States, on a competitive basis, for the development and operation of—

    (A) systems for the delivery of mental health screening and treatment services for older individuals who lack access to such services; and

    (B) programs to—

        (i) increase public awareness regarding the benefits of prevention and treatment of mental disorders in older individuals;

        (ii) reduce the stigma associated with mental disorders in older individuals and other barriers to the diagnosis and treatment of the disorders; and

        (iii) reduce age-related prejudice and discrimination regarding mental disorders in older individuals.

(2) APPLICATION.—To be eligible to receive a grant under this subsection for a State, a State agency shall submit an application to the Assistant Secretary at such time, in such manner, and containing such information as the Assistant Secretary may require.

(3) STATE ALLOCATION AND PRIORITIES.—A State agency that receives funds through a grant made under this subsection shall allocate the funds to area agencies on aging to carry out this subsection in planning and service areas in the State. In allocating the funds, the State agency shall give priority to planning and service areas in the State—

    (A) that are medically underserved; and

    (B) in which there are large numbers of older individuals.

(4) AREA COORDINATION OF SERVICES WITH OTHER PROVIDERS.— In carrying out this subsection, to more efficiently and effectively deliver services to older individuals, each area agency on aging shall—

    (A) coordinate services described in subparagraphs (A) and (B) of paragraph (1) with such services or similar or related services of other community agencies, and voluntary organizations; and

(B) to the greatest extent practicable, integrate outreach and educational activities with such activities of existing (as of the date of the integration) social service and health care (including mental health) providers serving older individuals in the planning and service area involved.

(5) RELATIONSHIP TO OTHER FUNDING SOURCES.—Funds made available under this subsection shall supplement, and not supplant, any Federal, State, and local funds expended by a State or unit of general purpose local government (including an area agency on aging) to provide the services described in subparagraphs (A) and (B) of paragraph (1).

(6) DEFINITION.—In this subsection, the term 'mental health screening and treatment services' means patient screening, diagnostic services, care planning and oversight, therapeutic interventions, and referrals, that are—

(A) provided pursuant to evidence-based intervention and treatment protocols (to the extent such protocols are available) for mental disorders prevalent in older individuals; and

(B) coordinated and integrated with the services of social service and health care (including mental health) providers in an area in order to—

(i) improve patient outcomes; and

(ii) ensure, to the maximum extent feasible, the continuing independence of older individuals who are residing in the area.

(42 U.S.C. 3032h)

Section. 420. DEMONSTRATION AND SUPPORT PROJECTS FOR LEGAL ASSISTANCE FOR OLDER INDIVIDUALS.

(a) PROGRAM AUTHORIZED.—The Assistant Secretary shall make grants and enter into contracts, in order to—

(1) provide a national legal assistance support system (operated by one or more grantees or contractors) of activities to State and area agencies on aging for providing, developing, or supporting legal assistance for older individuals, including—

(A) case consultations;

(B) training;

(C) provision of substantive legal advice and assistance; and

(D) assistance in the design, implementation, and administration of legal assistance delivery systems to local providers of legal assistance for older individuals; and

(2) support demonstration projects to expand or improve the delivery of legal assistance to older individuals with social or economic needs.

(b) ASSURANCES.—Any grants or contracts made under subsection (a)(2) shall contain assurances that the requirements of section 307(a)(11) are met.

(c) ASSISTANCE.—To carry out subsection (a)(1), the Assistant Secretary shall make grants to or enter into contracts with national nonprofit organizations experienced in providing support and technical assistance on a nationwide basis to States, area agencies on aging, legal assistance providers, ombudsmen, elder abuse prevention programs, and other organizations interested in the legal rights of older individuals.

(42 U.S.C. 3032i)

Section. 421. OMBUDSMAN AND ADVOCACY DEMONSTRATION PROJECTS.

(a) PROGRAM AUTHORIZED. — The Assistant Secretary shall award grants to not fewer than three and not more than 10 States to conduct demonstrations and evaluate cooperative projects between the State long-term care ombudsman program, legal assistance agencies, and the State protection and advocacy systems for individuals with developmental disabilities and individuals with mental illness, established under part C of the Developmental Disabilities Assistance and Bill of Rights Act (42 U.S.C. 6041 et seq.) and under the Protection and Advocacy for Mentally Ill Individuals Act of 1986 (42 U.S.C. 10801 et seq.).

(b) REPORT. — The Assistant Secretary shall prepare and submit to Congress a report containing the results of the evaluation required by subsection (a). Such report shall contain such recommendations as the Assistant Secretary determines to be appropriate.

(42 U.S.C. 3032j)

Section. 422. COMMUNITY INNOVATIONS FOR AGING IN PLACE.

(a) DEFINITIONS. — In this section:
  (1) ELIGIBLE ENTITY. — The term 'eligible entity' —
    (A) means a nonprofit health or social service organization, a community-based nonprofit organization, an area agency on aging or other local government agency, a tribal organization, or another entity that —
      (i)   the Assistant Secretary determines to be appropriate to carry out a project under this part; and
      (ii) demonstrates a record of, and experience in, providing or administering group and individual health and social services for older individuals; and
    (B) does not include an entity providing housing under the congregate housing services program carried out under section 802 of the Cranston-Gonzalez National Affordable Housing Act (42 U.S.C. 8011) or the multifamily service coordinator program carried out under section 202(g) of the Housing Act of 1959 (12 U.S.C. 1701q(g)).
  (2) NATURALLY OCCURRING RETIREMENT COMMUNITY. — The term 'Naturally Occurring Retirement Community' means a community with a concentrated population of older individuals, which may include a residential building, a housing complex, an area (including a rural area) of single family residences, or a neighborhood composed of age-integrated housing —
    (A) where —
      (i)   40 percent of the heads of households are older individuals; or
      (ii) a critical mass of older individuals exists, based on local factors that, taken in total, allow an organization to achieve efficiencies in the provision of health and social services to older individuals living in the community; and
    (B) that is not an institutional care or assisted living setting.
(b) GRANTS. —

(1) IN GENERAL.—The Assistant Secretary shall make grants, on a competitive basis, to eligible entities to develop and carry out model aging in place projects. The projects shall promote aging in place for older individuals (including such individuals who reside in Naturally Occurring Retirement Communities), in order to sustain the independence of older individuals. A recipient of a grant under this subsection shall identify innovative strategies for providing, and linking older individuals to programs and services that provide, comprehensive and coordinated health and social services to sustain the quality of life of older individuals and support aging in place.

(2) GRANT PERIODS.—The Assistant Secretary shall make the grants for periods of 3 years.

(c) APPLICATIONS.—

(1) IN GENERAL.—To be eligible to receive a grant under subsection (b) for a project, an entity shall submit an application to the Assistant Secretary at such time, in such manner, and containing such information as the Assistant Secretary may require.

(2) CONTENTS.—The application shall include—

(A) a detailed description of the entity's experience in providing services to older individuals in age-integrated settings;

(B) a definition of the contiguous service area and a description of the project area in which the older individuals reside or carry out activities to sustain their wellbeing;

(C) the results of a needs assessment that identifies—

(i) existing (as of the date of the assessment) community-based health and social services available to individuals residing in the project area;

(ii) the strengths and gaps of such existing services in the project area;

(iii) the needs of older individuals who reside in the project area; and

(iv) services not being delivered that would promote aging in place and contribute to the well-being of older individuals residing in the project area;

(D) a plan for the development and implementation of an innovative model for service coordination and delivery within the project area;

(E) a description of how the plan described in subparagraph (D) will enhance existing services described in subparagraph (C)(i) and support the goal of this section to promote aging in place;

(F) a description of proposed actions by the entity to prevent the duplication of services funded under a provision of this Act, other than this section, and a description of how the entity will cooperate, and coordinate planning and services (including any formal agreements), with agencies and organizations that provide publicly supported services for older individuals in the project area, including the State agency and area agencies on aging with planning and service areas in the project area;

(G) an assurance that the entity will seek to establish cooperative relationships with interested local entities, including private agencies and businesses that provide health and social services, housing entities, community development organizations, philanthropic organizations, foundations, and other non-Federal entities;

(H) a description of the entity's protocol for referral of residents who may require long-term care services, including coordination with local agencies, including area agencies on aging and Aging and Disability Resource Centers that serve as single points of entry to public services;

(I) a description of how the entity will offer opportunities for older individuals to be involved in the governance, oversight, and operation of the project;

        (J)   an assurance that the entity will submit to the Assistant Secretary such evaluations and reports as the Assistant Secretary may require; and

        (K) a plan for long-term sustainability of the project.

(d) USE OF FUNDS.—

    (1) IN GENERAL.—An eligible entity that receives a grant under subsection (b) shall use the funds made available through the grant to—

        (A) ensure access by older individuals in the project area to community-based health and social services consisting of—

           (i)   case management, case assistance, and social work services;

           (ii) health care management and health care assistance, including disease prevention and health promotion services;

           (iii) education, socialization, and recreational activities; and

           (iv) volunteer opportunities for project participants;

        (B) conduct outreach to older individuals within the project area; and

        (C) develop and implement innovative, comprehensive, and cost-effective approaches for the delivery and coordination of community-based health and social services, including those identified in subparagraph (A)(iv), which may include mental health services, for eligible older individuals.

    (2) COORDINATION.—An eligible entity receiving a grant under subsection (b) for a project shall coordinate activities with organizations providing services funded under title III to support such services for or facilitate the delivery of such services to eligible older individuals served by the project.

    (3) PREFERENCE.—In carrying out an aging in place project, an eligible entity shall, to the extent practicable, serve a community of low-income individuals and operate or locate the project and services in or in close proximity to a location where a large concentration of older individuals has aged in place and resided, such as a Naturally Occurring Retirement Community.

    (4) SUPPLEMENT NOT SUPPLANT.—Funds made available to an eligible entity under subsection (b) shall be used to supplement, not supplant, any Federal, State, or other funds otherwise available to the entity to provide health and social services to eligible older individuals.

(e) COMPETITIVE GRANTS FOR TECHNICAL ASSISTANCE.—

    (1) GRANTS.—The Assistant Secretary shall (or shall make a grant, on a competitive basis, to an eligible nonprofit organization, to enable the organization to)—

        (A) provide technical assistance to recipients of grants under subsection (b); and

        (B) carry out other duties, as determined by the Assistant Secretary.

    (2) ELIGIBLE ORGANIZATION.—To be eligible to receive a grant under this subsection, an organization shall be a nonprofit organization (including a partnership of nonprofit organizations), that—

        (A) has experience and expertise in providing technical assistance to a range of entities serving older individuals and experience evaluating and reporting on programs; and

        (B) has demonstrated knowledge of and expertise in community-based health and social services.

(3) APPLICATION.—To be eligible to receive a grant under this subsection, an organization (including a partnership of nonprofit organizations) shall submit an application to the Assistant Secretary at such time, in such manner, and containing such information as the Assistant Secretary may require, including an assurance that the organization will submit to the Assistant Secretary such evaluations and reports as the Assistant Secretary may require.

(f) REPORT.—The Assistant Secretary shall annually prepare and submit a report to Congress that shall include—

(1) the findings resulting from the evaluations of the model projects conducted under this section;

(2) a description of recommended best practices regarding carrying out health and social service projects for older individuals aging in place; and

(3) recommendations for legislative or administrative action, as the Assistant Secretary determines appropriate.

PART B—GENERAL PROVISIONS

Section. 431. PAYMENT OF GRANTS.

(a) CONTRIBUTIONS.—To the extent the Assistant Secretary determines a contribution to be appropriate, the Assistant Secretary shall require the recipient of any grant or contract under this title to contribute money, facilities, or services for carrying out the project for which such grant or contract was made.

(b) PAYMENTS.—Payments under this title pursuant to a grant or contract may be made (after necessary adjustment, in the case of grants, on account of previously made overpayments or underpayments) in advance or by way of reimbursement, and in such installments and on such conditions, as the Assistant Secretary may determine.

(c) CONSULTATION.—The Assistant Secretary shall make no grant or contract under this title in any State that has established or designated a State agency for purposes of title III unless the Assistant Secretary—

(1) consults with the State agency prior to issuing the grant or contract; and

(2) informs the State agency of the purposes of the grant or contract when the grant or contract is issued.

(42 U.S.C. 3033)

Section. 432. RESPONSIBILITIES OF ASSISTANT SECRETARY.

(a) IN GENERAL.—The Assistant Secretary shall be responsible for the administration, implementation, and making of grants and contracts under this title and shall not delegate authority under this title to any other individual, agency, or organization.

(b) REPORT.—

(1) IN GENERAL.—Not later than January 1 following each fiscal year, the Assistant Secretary shall submit, to the Speaker of the House of Representatives and the President pro-tempore of the Senate, a report for such fiscal year that describes each project and each program—

(A) for which funds were provided under this title; and

(B) that was completed in the fiscal year for which such report is prepared.

(2) CONTENTS.—Such report shall contain—

(A) the name or descriptive title of each project or program;

(B) the name and address of the individual or governmental entity that conducted such project or program;

(C) a specification of the period throughout which such project or program was conducted;

(D) the identity of each source of funds expended to carry out such project or program and the amount of funds provided by each such source;

(E) an abstract describing the nature and operation of such project or program; and

(F) a bibliography identifying all published information relating to such project or program.

(c) EVALUATIONS. —

(1) IN GENERAL. — The Assistant Secretary shall establish by regulation and implement a process to evaluate the results of projects and programs carried out under this title.

(2) RESULTS. — The Assistant Secretary shall —

(A) make available to the public the results of each evaluation carried out under paragraph (1); and

(B) use such evaluation to improve services delivered, or the operation of projects and programs carried out, under this Act, including preparing an analysis of such services, projects, and programs, and of how the evaluation relates to improvements in such services, projects, and program and in the strategic plan of the Administration.

(42 U.S.C. 3033a)

TITLE V—COMMUNITY SERVICE SENIOR OPPORTUNITIES ACT

Section. 501. SHORT TITLE.

This title may be cited as the 'Community Service Senior Opportunities Act'.

Section. 502. OLDER AMERICAN COMMUNITY SERVICE EMPLOYMENT PROGRAM.

(a) IN GENERAL.—
  (1) ESTABLISHMENT OF PROGRAM.—To foster individual economic self-sufficiency and promote useful opportunities in community service activities (which shall include community service employment) for unemployed low-income persons who are age 55 or older, particularly persons who have poor employment prospects, and to increase the number of persons who may enjoy the benefits of unsubsidized employment in both the public and private sectors, the Secretary of Labor (referred to in this title as the 'Secretary') may establish an older American community service employment program.
  (2) USE OF APPROPRIATED AMOUNTS.—Amounts appropriated to carry out this title shall be used only to carry out the provisions contained in this title.
(b) GRANT AUTHORITY.—
  (1) PROJECTS.—To carry out this title, the Secretary may make grants to public and nonprofit private agencies and organizations, agencies of a State, and tribal organizations to carry out the program established under subsection (a). Such grants may provide for the payment of costs, as provided in subsection (c), of projects developed by such organizations and agencies in cooperation with the Secretary in order to make such program effective or to supplement such program. The Secretary shall make the grants from allotments made under section 506, and in accordance with section 514. No payment shall be made by the Secretary toward the cost of any project established or administered by such an organization or agency unless the Secretary determines that such project—
  (A) will provide community service employment only for eligible individuals except for necessary technical, administrative, and supervisory personnel, and such personnel will, to the fullest extent possible, be recruited from among eligible individuals;
  (B)
    (i) will provide community service employment and other authorized activities for eligible individuals in the community in which such individuals reside, or in nearby communities; or
    (ii) if such project is carried out by a tribal organization that receives a grant under this subsection or receives assistance from a State that receives a grant under this subsection, will provide community service employment and other authorized activities for such individuals, including those who are Indians residing on an Indian reservation, as defined in section 2601 of the Energy Policy Act of 1992 (25 U.S.C. 3501);
  (C) will comply with an average participation cap for eligible individuals (in the aggregate) of—

(i) 27 months; or

(ii) pursuant to the request of a grantee, an extended period of participation established by the Secretary for a specific project area for such grantee, up to a period of not more than 36 months, if the Secretary determines that extenuating circumstances exist relating to the factors identified in section 513(a)(2)(D) that justify such an extended period for the program year involved;

(D) will employ eligible individuals in service related to publicly owned and operated facilities and projects, or projects sponsored by nonprofit organizations (excluding political parties exempt from taxation under section 501(c)(3) of the Internal Revenue Code of 1986), but excluding projects involving the construction, operation, or maintenance of any facility used or to be used as a place for sectarian religious instruction or worship;

(E) will contribute to the general welfare of the community, which may include support for children, youth, and families;

(F) will provide community service employment and other authorized activities for eligible individuals;

(G) (G)(i) will not reduce the number of employment opportunities or vacancies that would otherwise be available to individuals not participating in the program;

(ii) will not displace currently employed workers (including partial displacement, such as a reduction in the hours of non-overtime work, wages, or employment benefits);

(iii) will not impair existing contracts or result in the substitution of Federal funds for other funds in connection with work that would otherwise be performed; and

(iv) will not employ or continue to employ any eligible individual to perform the same work or substantially the same work as that performed by any other individual who is on layoff;

(H) will coordinate activities with training and other services provided under title I of the Workforce Investment Act of 1998 (29 U.S.C. 2801 et seq.), including utilizing the one-stop delivery system of the local workforce investment areas involved to recruit eligible individuals to ensure that the maximum number of eligible individuals will have an opportunity to participate in the project;

(I) will include such training (such as work experience, on-the-job training, and classroom training) as may be necessary to make the most effective use of the skills and talents of those individuals who are participating, and will provide for the payment of the reasonable expenses of individuals being trained, including a reasonable subsistence allowance equivalent to the wage described in subparagraph (J);

(J) will ensure that safe and healthy employment conditions will be provided, and will ensure that participants employed in community service and other jobs assisted under this title will be paid wages that shall not be lower than whichever is the highest of —

(i) the minimum wage that would be applicable to such a participant under the Fair Labor Standards Act of 1938 (29 U.S.C. 201 et seq.), if section 6(a)(1) of such Act (29 U.S.C. 206(a)(1)) applied to the participant and if the participant were not exempt under section 13 of such Act (29 U.S.C. 213);

(ii) the State or local minimum wage for the most nearly comparable covered employment; or

(iii) the prevailing rates of pay for individuals employed in similar public occupations by the same employer;

(K) will be established or administered with the advice of persons competent in the field of service in which community service employment or other authorized activities are being provided, and of persons who are knowledgeable about the needs of older individuals;

(L) will authorize payment for necessary supportive services costs (including transportation costs) of eligible individuals that may be incurred in training in any project funded under this title, in accordance with rules issued by the Secretary;

(M) will ensure that, to the extent feasible, such project will serve the needs of minority and Indian eligible individuals, eligible individuals with limited English proficiency, and eligible individuals with greatest economic need, at least in proportion to their numbers in the area served and take into consideration their rates of poverty and unemployment;

(N) (i) will prepare an assessment of the participants' skills and talents and their needs for services, except to the extent such project has, for the participant involved, recently prepared an assessment of such skills and talents, and such needs, pursuant to another employment or training program (such as a program under the Workforce Investment Act of 1998 (29 U.S.C. 2801 et seq.), the Carl D. Perkins Career and Technical Education Act of 2006 (20 U.S.C. 2301 et seq.), or part A of title IV of the Social Security Act (42 U.S.C. 601 et seq.)) and will prepare a related service strategy;

(ii) will provide training and employment counseling to eligible individuals based on strategies that identify appropriate employment objectives and the need for supportive services, developed as a result of the assessment and service strategy provided for in clause (i), and provide other appropriate information regarding such project; and

(iii) will provide counseling to participants on their progress in meeting such objectives and satisfying their need for supportive services;

(O) will provide appropriate services for participants, or refer the participants to appropriate services, through the one-stop delivery system of the local workforce investment areas involved as established under section 134(c) of the Workforce Investment Act of 1998 (29 U.S.C. 2864(c)), and will be involved in the planning and operations of such system pursuant to a memorandum of understanding with the local workforce investment board in accordance with section 121(c) of such Act (29 U.S.C. 2841(c));

(P) will post in such project workplace a notice, and will make available to each person associated with such project a written explanation—

(i) clarifying the law with respect to political activities allowable and unallowable under chapter 15 of title 5, United States Code, applicable to the project and to each category of individuals associated with such project; and

(ii) containing the address and telephone number of the Inspector General of the Department of Labor, to whom questions regarding the application of such chapter may be addressed;

(Q) will provide to the Secretary the description and information described in—

(i) paragraph (8), relating to coordination with other Federal programs, of section 112(b) of the Workforce Investment Act of 1998 (29 U.S.C. 2822(b)); and

(ii) paragraph (14), relating to implementation of one-stop delivery systems, of section 112(b) of the Workforce Investment Act of 1998; and

(R) will ensure that entities that carry out activities under the project (including State agencies, local entities, subgrantees, and subcontractors) and affiliates of such entities receive an amount of the administrative cost allocation determined by the Secretary, in consultation with grantees, to be sufficient.

(2) REGULATIONS. — The Secretary may establish, issue, and amend such regulations as may be necessary to effectively carry out this title.

(3) ASSESSMENT AND SERVICE STRATEGIES. —

(A) PREPARED UNDER THIS ACT. — An assessment and service strategy required by paragraph (1)(N) to be prepared for an eligible individual shall satisfy any condition for an assessment and service strategy or individual employment plan for an adult participant under subtitle B of title I of the Workforce Investment Act of 1998 (29 U.S.C. 2811 et seq.), in order to determine whether such eligible individual also qualifies for intensive or training services described in section 134(d) of such Act (29 U.S.C. 2864(d)).

(B) PREPARED UNDER WORKFORCE INVESTMENT ACT OF 1998. — An assessment and service strategy or individual employment plan prepared under subtitle B of title I of the Workforce Investment Act of 1998 (29 U.S.C. 2811 et seq.) for an eligible individual may be used to comply with the requirement specified in subparagraph (A).

(c) FEDERAL SHARE AND USE OF FUNDS. —

(1) FEDERAL SHARE. — The Secretary may pay a Federal share not to exceed 90 percent of the cost of any project for which a grant is made under subsection (b), except that the Secretary may pay all of such cost if such project is —

(A) an emergency or disaster project; or

(B) a project located in an economically depressed area, as determined by the Secretary in consultation with the Secretary of Commerce and the Secretary of Health and Human Services.

(2) NON-FEDERAL SHARE. — The non-Federal share shall be in cash or in kind. In determining the amount of the non- Federal share, the Secretary may attribute fair market value to services and facilities contributed from non-Federal sources.

(3) USE OF FUNDS FOR ADMINISTRATIVE COSTS. — Of the grant amount to be paid under this subsection by the Secretary for a project, not to exceed 13.5 percent shall be available for any fiscal year to pay the administrative costs of such project, except that —

(A) the Secretary may increase the amount available to pay the administrative costs to an amount not to exceed 15 percent of the grant amount if the Secretary determines, based on information submitted by the grantee under subsection (b), that such increase is necessary to carry out such project; and

(B) if the grantee under subsection (b) demonstrates to the Secretary that —

(i) major administrative cost increases are being incurred in necessary program components, including liability insurance, payments for workers' compensation, costs associated with achieving unsubsidized placement goals, and costs associated with other operation requirements imposed by the Secretary;

(ii) the number of community service employment positions in the project or the number of minority eligible individuals participating in the project will decline if the amount available to pay the administrative costs is not increased; or

     (iii) the size of the project is so small that the amount of administrative costs incurred to carry out the project necessarily exceeds 13.5 percent of the grant amount; the Secretary shall increase the amount available for such fiscal year to pay the administrative costs to an amount not to exceed 15 percent of the grant amount.

(4) ADMINISTRATIVE COSTS.—For purposes of this title, administrative costs are the costs, both personnel-related and nonpersonnel-related and both direct and indirect, associated

  (A) The costs of performing general administrative functions and of providing for the coordination of functions, such as the costs of—
    (i)   accounting, budgeting, and financial and cash management;
    (ii)   procurement and purchasing;
    (iii) property management;
    (iv) personnel management;
    (v)   payroll functions;
    (vi) coordinating the resolution of findings arising from audits, reviews, investigations, and incident reports;
    (vii) audits;
    (viii) general legal services;
    (ix) developing systems and procedures, including information systems, required for administrative functions;
    (x)   preparing administrative reports; and
    (xi) other activities necessary for the general administration of government funds and associated programs.

  (B) The costs of performing oversight and monitoring responsibilities related to administrative functions.

  (C) The costs of goods and services required for administrative functions of the project involved, including goods and services such as rental or purchase of equipment, utilities, office supplies, postage, and rental and maintenance of office space.

  (D) The travel costs incurred for official business in carrying out administrative activities or overall management.

  (E) The costs of information systems related to administrative functions (such as personnel, procurement, purchasing, property management, accounting, and payroll systems), including the purchase, systems development, and operating costs of such systems.

  (F) The costs of technical assistance, professional organization membership dues, and evaluating results obtained by the project involved against stated objectives.

(5) NON-FEDERAL SHARE OF ADMINISTRATIVE COSTS.—To the extent practicable, an entity that carries out a project under this title shall provide for the payment of the expenses described in paragraph (4) from non-Federal sources.

(6) USE OF FUNDS FOR WAGES AND BENEFITS AND PROGRAMMATIC ACTIVITY COSTS.—

  (A) IN GENERAL.—Amounts made available for a project under this title that are not used to pay for the administrative costs shall be used to pay for the costs of programmatic activities, including the costs of—

(i) participant wages, such benefits as are required by law (such as workers' compensation or unemployment compensation), the costs of physical examinations, compensation for scheduled work hours during which an employer's business is closed for a Federal holiday, and necessary sick leave that is not part of an accumulated sick leave program, except that no amounts provided under this title may be used to pay the cost of pension benefits, annual leave, accumulated sick leave, or bonuses;

(ii) participant training (including the payment of reasonable costs of instructors, classroom rental, training supplies, materials, equipment, and tuition), which may be provided prior to or subsequent to placement and which may be provided on the job, in a classroom setting, or pursuant to other appropriate arrangements;

(iii) job placement assistance, including job development and job search assistance;

(iv) participant supportive services to enable a participant to successfully participate in a project under this title, which may include the payment of reasonable costs of transportation, health and medical services, special job-related or personal counseling, incidentals (such as work shoes, badges, uniforms, eyeglasses, and tools), child and adult care, temporary shelter, and follow-up services; and

(v) outreach, recruitment and selection, intake, orientation, and assessments.

(B) USE OF FUNDS FOR WAGES AND BENEFITS.—From the funds made available through a grant made under subsection (b), a grantee under this title—

(i) except as provided in clause (ii), shall use not less than 75 percent of the grant funds to pay the wages, benefits, and other costs described in subparagraph (A)(i) for eligible individuals who are employed under projects carried out under this title; or

(ii) that obtains approval for a request described in subparagraph (C) may use not less than 65 percent of the grant funds to pay the wages, benefits, and other costs described in subparagraph (A)(i).

(C) REQUEST TO USE ADDITIONAL FUNDS FOR PROGRAMMATIC ACTIVITY COSTS.—

(i) IN GENERAL.—A grantee may submit to the Secretary a request for approval—

(I) to use not less than 65 percent of the grant funds to pay the wages, benefits, and other costs described in subparagraph (A)(i);

(II) to use the percentage of grant funds described in paragraph (3) to pay for administrative costs, as specified in that paragraph;

(III) to use not more than 10 percent of the grant funds for individual participants to provide activities described in clauses (ii) and (iv) of subparagraph (A), in which case the grantee shall provide (from the funds described in this subclause) the subsistence allowance described in subsection (b)(1)(I) for those individual participants who are receiving training described in that subsection from the funds described in this subclause, but may not use the funds described in this subclause to pay for any administrative costs; and

(IV) to use the remaining grant funds to provide activities described in clauses (ii) through (v) of subparagraph (A).

(ii) CONTENTS.—In submitting the request the grantee shall include in the request—

(I) a description of the activities for which the grantee will spend the grant funds described in subclauses (III) and (IV) of clause (i), consistent with those subclauses;

(II) an explanation documenting how the provision of such activities will improve the effectiveness of the project, including an explanation concerning whether any displacement of eligible individuals or elimination of positions for such individuals will occur, information on the number of such individuals to be displaced and of such positions to be eliminated, and an explanation concerning how the activities will improve employment outcomes for individuals served, based on the assessment conducted under subsection (b)(1)(N); and

(III) a proposed budget and work plan for the activities, including a detailed description of the funds to be spent on the activities described in subclauses (III) and (IV) of clause (i).

(iii) SUBMISSION.—The grantee shall submit a request described in clause (i) not later than 90 days before the proposed date of implementation contained in the request. Not later than 30 days before the proposed date of implementation, the Secretary shall approve, approve as modified, or reject the request, on the basis of the information included in the request as described in clause (ii).

(D) REPORT.—Each grantee under subsection (b) shall annually prepare and submit to the Secretary a report documenting the grantee's use of funds for activities described in clauses (i) through (v) of subparagraph (A).

(d) PROJECT DESCRIPTION.—Whenever a grantee conducts a project within a planning and service area in a State, such grantee shall conduct such project in consultation with the area agency on aging of the planning and service area and shall submit to the State agency and the area agency on aging a description of such project to be conducted in the State, including the location of the project, 90 days prior to undertaking the project, for review and public comment according to guidelines the Secretary shall issue to assure efficient and effective coordination of projects under this title.

(e) PILOT, DEMONSTRATION, AND EVALUATION PROJECTS.—

(1) IN GENERAL.—The Secretary, in addition to exercising any other authority contained in this title, shall use funds reserved under section 506(a)(1) to carry out demonstration projects, pilot projects, and evaluation projects, for the purpose of developing and implementing techniques and approaches, and demonstrating the effectiveness of the techniques and approaches, in addressing the employment and training needs of eligible individuals. The Secretary shall enter into such agreements with States, public agencies, nonprofit private organizations, or private business concerns, as may be necessary, to conduct the projects authorized by this subsection. To the extent practicable, the Secretary shall provide an opportunity, prior to the development of a demonstration or pilot project, for the appropriate area agency on aging to submit comments on such a project in order to ensure coordination of activities under this title.

(2) PROJECTS.—Such projects may include—

(A) activities linking businesses and eligible individuals, including activities providing assistance to participants transitioning from subsidized activities to private sector employment;

(B) demonstration projects and pilot projects designed to—

(i) attract more eligible individuals into the labor force;

(ii) improve the provision of services to eligible individuals under one-stop delivery systems established under title I of the Workforce Investment Act of 1998 (29 U.S.C. 2801 et seq.);

(iii) enhance the technological skills of eligible individuals; and

(iv) provide incentives to grantees under this title for exemplary performance and incentives to businesses to promote their participation in the program under this title;

(C) demonstration projects and pilot projects, as described in subparagraph (B), for workers who are older individuals (but targeted to eligible individuals) only if such demonstration projects and pilot projects are designed to assist in developing and implementing techniques and approaches in addressing the employment and training needs of eligible individuals;

(D) provision of training and technical assistance to support any project funded under this title;

(E) dissemination of best practices relating to employment of eligible individuals; and

(F) evaluation of the activities authorized under this title.

(3) CONSULTATION.—To the extent practicable, entities carrying out projects under this subsection shall consult with appropriate area agencies on aging and with other appropriate agencies and entities to promote coordination of activities under this title.

Section. 503. ADMINISTRATION.

(ii) STATE PLAN.—

(1) GOVERNOR.—For a State to be eligible to receive an allotment under section 506, the Governor of the State shall submit to the Secretary for consideration and approval, a single State plan (referred to in this title as the 'State plan') that outlines a 4-year strategy for the statewide provision of community service employment and other authorized activities for eligible individuals under this title. The plan shall contain such provisions as the Secretary may require, consistent with this title, including a description of the process used to ensure the participation of individuals described in paragraph (2). Not less often than every 2 years, the Governor shall review the State plan and submit an update to the State plan to the Secretary for consideration and approval.

(2) RECOMMENDATIONS.—In developing the State plan prior to its submission to the Secretary, the Governor shall seek the advice and recommendations of—

(A) individuals representing the State agency and the area agencies on aging in the State, and the State and local workforce investment boards established under title I of the Workforce Investment Act of 1998 (29 U.S.C. 2801 et seq.);

(B) individuals representing public and nonprofit private agencies and organizations providing employment services, including each grantee operating a project under this title in the State; and

(C) individuals representing social service organizations providing services to older individuals, grantees under title III of this Act, affected communities, unemployed older individuals, community-based organizations serving the needs of older individuals, business organizations, and labor organizations.

(3) COMMENTS. — Any State plan submitted by the Governor in accordance with paragraph (1) shall be accompanied by copies of public comments relating to the plan received pursuant to paragraph (7), and a summary of the comments.

(4) PLAN PROVISIONS. — The State plan shall identify and address —

(A) the relationship that the number of eligible individuals in each area bears to the total number of eligible individuals, respectively, in the State;

(B) the relative distribution of eligible individuals residing in rural and urban areas in the State; and

(C) the relative distribution of —

(i) eligible individuals who are individuals with greatest economic need;

(ii) eligible individuals who are minority individuals;

(iii) eligible individuals who are limited English proficient; and

(iv) eligible individuals who are individuals with greatest social need;

(D) the current and projected employment opportunities in the State (such as by providing information available under section 15 of the Wagner-Peyser Act (29 U.S.C. 491- 2) by occupation), and the type of skills possessed by local eligible individuals;

(E) the localities and populations for which projects of the type authorized by this title are most needed; and

(F) plans for facilitating the coordination of activities of grantees in the State under this title with activities carried out in the State under title I of the Workforce Investment Act of 1998 (29 U.S.C. 2801 et seq.).

(5) GOVERNOR'S RECOMMENDATIONS. — Before a proposal for a grant under this title for any fiscal year is submitted to the Secretary, the Governor of the State in which projects are proposed to be conducted under such grant shall be afforded a reasonable opportunity to submit to the Secretary —

(A) recommendations regarding the anticipated effect of each such proposal upon the overall distribution of enrollment positions under this title in the State (including such distribution among urban and rural areas), taking into account the total number of positions to be provided by all grantees in the State;

(B) any recommendations for redistribution of positions to underserved areas as vacancies occur in previously encumbered positions in other areas; and

(C) in the case of any increase in funding that may be available for use in the State under this title for the fiscal year, any recommendations for distribution of newly available positions in excess of those available during the preceding year to underserved areas.

(6) DISRUPTIONS. — In developing a plan or considering a recommendation under this subsection, the Governor shall avoid disruptions in the provision of services for participants to the greatest possible extent.

(7) DETERMINATION; REVIEW. —

(A) DETERMINATION. — In order to effectively carry out this title, each State shall make the State plan available for public comment. The Secretary, in consultation with the Assistant Secretary, shall review the plan and make a written determination with findings and a decision regarding the plan.

(B) REVIEW.—The Secretary may review, on the Secretary's own initiative or at the request of any public or private agency or organization or of any agency of the State, the distribution of projects and services under this title in the State, including the distribution between urban and rural areas in the State. For each proposed reallocation of projects or services in a State, the Secretary shall give notice and opportunity for public comment.

(8) EXEMPTION.—The grantees that serve eligible individuals who are older Indians or Pacific Island and Asian Americans with funds reserved under section 506(a)(3) may not be required to participate in the State planning processes described in this section but shall collaborate with the Secretary to develop a plan for projects and services to eligible individuals who are Indians or Pacific Island and Asian Americans, respectively.

(iii) COORDINATION WITH OTHER FEDERAL PROGRAMS.—

(1) IN GENERAL.—The Secretary and the Assistant Secretary shall coordinate the program carried out under this title with programs carried out under other titles of this Act, to increase employment opportunities available to older individuals.

(2) PROGRAMS.—

(A) IN GENERAL.—The Secretary shall coordinate programs carried out under this title with the program carried out under the Workforce Investment Act of 1998 (29 U.S.C. 2801 et seq.), the Community Services Block Grant Act (42 U.S.C. 9901 et seq.), the Rehabilitation Act of 1973 (29 U.S.C. 701 et seq.), the Carl D. Perkins Career and Technical Education Act of 2006 (20 U.S.C. 2301 et seq.), the National and Community Service Act of 1990 (42 U.S.C. 12501 et seq.), and the Domestic Volunteer Service Act of 1973 (42 U.S.C. 4950 et seq.). The Secretary shall coordinate the administration of this title with the administration of other titles of this Act by the Assistant Secretary to increase the likelihood that eligible individuals for whom employment opportunities under this title are available and who need services under such titles receive such services.

(B) USE OF FUNDS.—

(i) PROHIBITION.—Funds appropriated to carry out this title may not be used to carry out any program under the Workforce Investment Act of 1998, the Community Services Block Grant Act, the Rehabilitation Act of 1973, the Carl D. Perkins Career and Technical Education Act of 2006, the National and Community Service Act of 1990, or the Domestic Volunteer Service Act of 1973.

(ii) JOINT ACTIVITIES.—Clause (i) shall not be construed to prohibit carrying out projects under this title jointly with programs, projects, or activities under any Act specified in clause (i), or from carrying out section 511.

(3) INFORMATIONAL MATERIALS ON AGE DISCRIMINATION.— The Secretary shall distribute to grantees under this title, for distribution to program participants, and at no cost to grantees or participants, informational materials developed and supplied by the Equal Employment Opportunity Commission and other appropriate Federal agencies that the Secretary determines are designed to help participants identify age discrimination and to understand their rights under the Age Discrimination in Employment Act of 1967 (29 U.S.C. 621 et seq.).

(iv) USE OF SERVICES, EQUIPMENT, PERSONNEL, AND FACILITIES.— In carrying out this title, the Secretary may use the services, equipment, personnel, and facilities of Federal and other agencies, with their consent, with or without reimbursement, and on a similar basis cooperate with other public and nonprofit private agencies and organizations in the use of services, equipment, and facilities.

(v) PAYMENTS.—Payments under this title may be made in advance or by way of reimbursement and in such installments as the Secretary may determine.

(vi) NO DELEGATION OF FUNCTIONS.—The Secretary shall not delegate any function of the Secretary under this title to any other Federal officer or entity.

(vii) COMPLIANCE.—

    (1) MONITORING.—The Secretary shall monitor projects for which grants are made under this title to determine whether the grantees are complying with rules and regulations issued to carry out this title (including the statewide planning, consultation, and coordination requirements of this title).

    (2) COMPLIANCE WITH UNIFORM COST PRINCIPLES AND ADMINISTRATIVE REQUIREMENTS.—Each grantee that receives funds under this title shall comply with the applicable uniform cost principles and appropriate administrative requirements for grants and contracts that are applicable to the type of entity that receives funds, as issued as circulars or rules of the Office of Management and Budget.

    (3) REPORTS.—Each grantee described in paragraph (2) shall prepare and submit a report in such manner and containing such information as the Secretary may require regarding activities carried out under this title.

    (4) RECORDS.—Each grantee described in paragraph (2) shall keep records that—

        (A) are sufficient to permit the preparation of reports required by this title;

        (B) are sufficient to permit the tracing of funds to a level of expenditure adequate to ensure that the funds have not been spent unlawfully; and

        (C) contain any other information that the Secretary determines to be appropriate.

(viii) EVALUATIONS.—The Secretary shall establish by rule and implement a process to evaluate, in accordance with section 513, the performance of projects carried out and services provided under this title. The Secretary shall report to Congress, and make available to the public, the results of each such evaluation and shall use such evaluation to improve services delivered by, or the operation of, projects carried out under this title.

Section. 504. PARTICIPANTS NOT FEDERAL EMPLOYEES.

(a) INAPPLICABILITY OF CERTAIN PROVISIONS COVERING FEDERAL EMPLOYEES.—Eligible individuals who are participants in any project funded under this title shall not be considered to be Federal employees as a result of such participation and shall not be subject to part III of title 5, United States Code.

(b) WORKERS' COMPENSATION.—No grant or subgrant shall be made and no contract or subcontract shall be entered into under this title with an entity who is, or whose employees are, under State law, exempted from operation of the State workers' compensation law, generally applicable to employees, unless the entity shall undertake to provide either through insurance by a recognized carrier or by self-insurance, as authorized by State law, that the persons employed under the grant, subgrant, contract, or subcontract shall enjoy workers' compensation coverage equal to that provided by law for covered employment.

Section. 505. INTERAGENCY COOPERATION.

(a) CONSULTATION WITH THE ASSISTANT SECRETARY.—The Secretary shall consult with and obtain the written views of the Assistant Secretary before issuing rules and before establishing general policy in the administration of this title.

(b) CONSULTATION WITH HEADS OF OTHER AGENCIES.—The Secretary shall consult and cooperate with the Secretary of Health and Human Services (acting through officers including the Director of the Office of Community Services), and the heads of other Federal agencies that carry out programs related to the program carried out under this title, in order to achieve optimal coordination of the program carried out under this title with such related programs. Each head of a Federal agency shall cooperate with the Secretary in disseminating information relating to the availability of assistance under this title and in promoting the identification and interests of individuals eligible for employment in projects assisted under this title.

(c) COORDINATION.—

  (1) IN GENERAL.—The Secretary shall promote and coordinate efforts to carry out projects under this title jointly with programs, projects, or activities carried out under other Acts, especially activities provided under the Workforce Investment Act of 1998 (29 U.S.C. 2801 et seq.), including activities provided through one-stop delivery systems established under section 134(c)) of such Act (29 U.S.C. 2864(c)), that provide training and employment opportunities to eligible individuals.

  (2) COORDINATION WITH CERTAIN ACTIVITIES.—The Secretary shall consult with the Secretary of Education to promote and coordinate efforts to carry out projects under this title jointly with activities in which eligible individuals may participate that are carried out under the Carl D. Perkins Career and Technical Education Act of 2006 (20 U.S.C. 2301 et seq.).

Section. 506. DISTRIBUTION OF ASSISTANCE.

(ii) RESERVATIONS.—

  (1) RESERVATION FOR PILOT DEMONSTRATION AND EVALUATION PROJECTS.—Of the funds appropriated to carry out this title for each fiscal year, the Secretary may first reserve not more than 1.5 percent to carry out demonstration projects, pilot projects, and evaluation projects under section 502(e).

  (2) RESERVATION FOR TERRITORIES.—Of the funds appropriated to carry out this title for each fiscal year, the Secretary shall reserve 0.75 percent, of which—

    (A) Guam, American Samoa, and the United States Virgin Islands shall each receive 30 percent of the funds so reserved; and

    (B) the Commonwealth of the Northern Mariana Islands shall receive 10 percent of the funds so reserved.

  (3) RESERVATION FOR ORGANIZATIONS.—Of the funds appropriated to carry out this title for each fiscal year, the Secretary shall reserve such amount as may be necessary to make national grants to public or nonprofit national Indian aging organizations with the ability to provide community service employment and other authorized activities for eligible individuals who are Indians and to national public or nonprofit Pacific Island and Asian American aging organizations with the ability to provide community service employment and other authorized activities for eligible individuals who are Pacific Island and Asian Americans.

(iii) STATE ALLOTMENTS.—The allotment for each State shall be the sum of the amounts allotted for national grants in such State under subsection (d) and for the grant to such State under subsection (e).

(iv) DIVISION BETWEEN NATIONAL GRANTS AND GRANTS TO STATES.—The funds appropriated to carry out this title for any fiscal year that remain after amounts are reserved under paragraphs (1), (2), and (3) of subsection (a) shall be divided by the Secretary between national grants and grants to States as follows:

(1) RESERVATION OF FUNDS FOR FISCAL YEAR 2000 LEVEL OF ACTIVITIES. —

(A) IN GENERAL.—The Secretary shall reserve the amount of funds necessary to maintain the fiscal year 2000 level of activities supported by grantees that operate under this title under national grants from the Secretary, and the fiscal year 2000 level of activities supported by State grantees under this title, in proportion to their respective fiscal year 2000 levels of activities.

(B) INSUFFICIENT APPROPRIATIONS.—If in any fiscal year the funds appropriated to carry out this title are insufficient to satisfy the requirement specified in subparagraph (A), then the amount described in subparagraph (A) shall be reduced proportionally.

(2) FUNDING IN EXCESS OF FISCAL YEAR 2000 LEVEL OF ACTIVITIES.—

(A) UP TO $35,000,000.—The amount of funds remaining (if any) after the application of paragraph (1), but not to exceed $35,000,000, shall be divided so that 75 percent shall be provided to State grantees and 25 percent shall be provided to grantees that operate under this title under national grants from the Secretary.

(B) OVER $35,000,000.—The amount of funds remaining (if any) after the application of subparagraph (A) shall be divided so that 50 percent shall be provided to State grantees and 50 percent shall be provided to grantees that operate under this title under national grants from the Secretary.

(v) ALLOTMENTS FOR NATIONAL GRANTS.—From funds available under subsection (c) for national grants, the Secretary shall allot for public and nonprofit private agency and organization grantees that operate under this title under national grants from the Secretary in each State, an amount that bears the same ratio to such funds as the product of the number of individuals age 55 or older in the State and the allotment percentage of such State bears to the sum of the corresponding products for all States, except as follows:

(1) MINIMUM ALLOTMENT.—No State shall be provided an amount under this subsection that is less than 1/2 of 1 percent of the amount provided under subsection (c) for public and nonprofit private agency and organization grantees that operate under this title under national grants from the Secretary in all of the States.

(2) HOLD HARMLESS.—If such amount provided under subsection (c) is—

(A) equal to or less than the amount necessary to maintain the fiscal year 2000 level of activities, allotments for grantees that operate under this title under national grants from the Secretary in each State shall be proportional to the amount necessary to maintain their fiscal year 2000 level of activities; or

(B) greater than the amount necessary to maintain the fiscal year 2000 level of activities, no State shall be provided a percentage increase above the amount necessary to maintain the fiscal year 2000 level of activities for grantees that operate under this title under national grants from the Secretary in the State that is less than 30 percent of the percentage increase above the amount necessary to maintain the fiscal year 2000 level of activities for public and private nonprofit agency and organization grantees that operate under this title under national grants from the Secretary in all of the States.

(3) REDUCTION.—Allotments for States not affected by paragraphs (1) and (2)(B) shall be reduced proportionally to satisfy the conditions in such paragraphs.

(vi) ALLOTMENTS FOR GRANTS TO STATES.—From the amount provided for grants to States under subsection (c), the Secretary shall allot for the State grantee in each State an amount that bears the same ratio to such amount as the product of the number of individuals age 55 or older in the State and the allotment percentage of such State bears to the sum of the corresponding products for all States, except as follows:

(1) MINIMUM ALLOTMENT.—No State shall be provided an amount under this subsection that is less than 1/2 of 1 percent of the amount provided under subsection (c) for State grantees in all of the States.

(2) HOLD HARMLESS.—If such amount provided under subsection (c) is—

(A) equal to or less than the amount necessary to maintain the fiscal year 2000 level of activities, allotments for State grantees in each State shall be proportional to the amount necessary to maintain their fiscal year 2000 level of activities; or

(B) greater than the amount necessary to maintain the fiscal year 2000 level of activities, no State shall be provided a percentage increase above the amount necessary to maintain the fiscal year 2000 level of activities for State grantees in the State that is less than 30 percent of the percentage increase above the amount necessary to maintain the fiscal year 2000 level of activities for State grantees in all of the States.

(3) REDUCTION.—Allotments for States not affected by paragraphs (1) and (2)(B) shall be reduced proportionally to satisfy the conditions in such paragraphs.

(vii) ALLOTMENT PERCENTAGE.—For purposes of subsections (d) and (e) and this subsection—

(1) the allotment percentage of each State shall be 100 percent less that percentage that bears the same ratio to 50 percent as the per capita income of such State bears to the per capita income of the United States, except that—

(A) the allotment percentage shall be not more than 75 percent and not less than 33 percent; and

(B) the allotment percentage for the District of Columbia and the Commonwealth of Puerto Rico shall be 75 percent;

(2) the number of individuals age 55 or older in any State and in all States, and the per capita income in any State and in all States, shall be determined by the Secretary on the basis of the most satisfactory data available to the Secretary; and

(3) for the purpose of determining the allotment percentage, the term 'United States' means the 50 States, and the District of Columbia.

(viii) DEFINITIONS.—In this section:

(1) COST PER AUTHORIZED POSITION.—The term 'cost per authorized position' means the sum of—

(A) the hourly minimum wage rate specified in section 6(a)(1) of the Fair Labor Standards Act of 1938 (29 U.S.C. 206(a)(1)), multiplied by the number of hours equal to the product of 21 hours and 52 weeks;

(B) an amount equal to 11 percent of the amount specified under subparagraph (A), for the purpose of covering Federal payments for fringe benefits; and

(C) an amount determined by the Secretary, for the purpose of covering Federal payments for the remainder of all other program and administrative costs.

(2) FISCAL YEAR 2000 LEVEL OF ACTIVITIES.—The term 'fiscal year 2000 level of activities' means—

(A) with respect to public and nonprofit private agency and organization grantees that operate under this title under national grants from the Secretary, their level of activities for fiscal year 2000; and

(B) with respect to State grantees, their level of activities for fiscal year 2000.

(3) GRANTS TO STATES.—The term 'grants to States' means grants made under this title by the Secretary to the States.

(4) LEVEL OF ACTIVITIES.—The term 'level of activities' means the number of authorized positions multiplied by the cost per authorized position.

(5) NATIONAL GRANTS.—The term 'national grants' means grants made under this title by the Secretary to public and nonprofit private agency and organization grantees that operate under this title.

(6) STATE.—The term 'State' does not include Guam, American Samoa, the Commonwealth of the Northern Mariana Islands, and the United States Virgin Islands.

Section. 507. EQUITABLE DISTRIBUTION.

(a) INTERSTATE ALLOCATION.—In making grants under section 502(b) from allotments made under section 506, the Secretary shall ensure, to the extent feasible, an equitable distribution of activities under such grants, in the aggregate, among the States, taking into account the needs of underserved States.

(b) INTRASTATE ALLOCATION.—The amount allocated for projects within each State under section 506 shall be allocated among areas in the State in an equitable manner, taking into consideration the State priorities set out in the State plan in effect under section 503(a).

Section. 508. REPORT.

To carry out the Secretary's responsibilities for reporting in section 503(g), the Secretary shall require the State agency for each State that receives funds under this title to prepare and submit a report at the beginning of each fiscal year on such State's compliance with section 507(b). Such report shall include the names and geographic location of all projects assisted under this title and carried out in the State and the amount allocated to each such project under section 506.

Section. 509. EMPLOYMENT ASSISTANCE AND FEDERAL HOUSING AND FOOD STAMP PROGRAMS.

Funds received by eligible individuals from projects carried out under the program established under this title shall not be considered to be income of such individuals for purposes of determining the eligibility of such individuals, or of any other individuals, to participate in any housing program for which Federal funds may be available or for any income determination under the Food Stamp Act of 1977 (7 U.S.C. 2011 et seq.).

Section. 510. ELIGIBILITY FOR WORKFORCE INVESTMENT ACTIVITIES.

Eligible individuals under this title may be considered by local workforce investment boards and one-stop operators established under title I of the Workforce Investment Act of 1998 (29 U.S.C. 2801 et seq.) to satisfy the requirements for receiving services under such title I that are applicable to adults.

Section. 511. COORDINATION WITH THE WORKFORCE INVESTMENT ACT OF 1998.

(a) PARTNERS.—Grantees under this title shall be one-stop partners as described in subparagraphs (A) and (B)(vi) of section 121(b)(1) of the Workforce Investment Act of 1998 (29 U.S.C. 2841(b)(1)) in the one-stop delivery system established under section 134(c) of such Act (29 U.S.C. 2864(c)) for the appropriate local workforce investment areas, and shall carry out the responsibilities relating to such partners.

(b) COORDINATION.—In local workforce investment areas where more than 1 grantee under this title provides services, the grantees shall—
  (1) coordinate their activities related to the one-stop delivery systems; and
  (2) be signatories of the memorandum of understanding established under section 121(c) of the Workforce Investment Act of 1998 (29 U.S.C. 2841(c)).

Section. 512. TREATMENT OF ASSISTANCE.

Assistance provided under this title shall not be considered to be financial assistance described in section 245A(h)(1)(A) of the Immigration and Nationality Act (8 U.S.C. 1255a(h)(1)(A)).

Section. 513. PERFORMANCE.

(a) MEASURES AND INDICATORS.—
  (1) ESTABLISHMENT AND IMPLEMENTATION OF MEASURES AND INDICATORS.—The Secretary shall establish and implement, after consultation with grantees, sub-grantees, and host agencies under this title, States, older individuals, area agencies on aging, and other organizations serving older individuals, core measures of performance and additional indicators of performance for each grantee for projects and services carried out under this title. The core measures of performance and additional indicators of performance shall be applicable to each grantee under this title without regard to whether such grantee operates the program directly or through subcontracts, sub-grants, or agreements with other entities.
  (2) CONTENT.—
    (A) COMPOSITION OF MEASURES AND INDICATORS.—

(i) MEASURES.—The core measures of performance established by the Secretary in accordance with paragraph (1) shall consist of core indicators of performance specified in subsection (b)(1) and the expected levels of performance applicable to each core indicator of performance.

(ii) ADDITIONAL INDICATORS.—The additional indicators of performance established by the Secretary in accordance with paragraph (1) shall be the additional indicators of performance specified in subsection (b)(2).

(B) CONTINUOUS IMPROVEMENT.—The measures described in subparagraph (A)(i) shall be designed to promote continuous improvement in performance.

(C) EXPECTED LEVELS OF PERFORMANCE.—The Secretary and each grantee shall reach agreement on the expected levels of performance for each program year for each of the core indicators of performance specified in subparagraph (A)(i). The agreement shall take into account the requirement of subparagraph (B) and the factors described in subparagraph (D), and other appropriate factors as determined by the Secretary, and shall be consistent with the requirements of subparagraph (E). Funds may not be awarded under the grant until such agreement is reached. At the conclusion of negotiations concerning the levels with all grantees, the Secretary shall make available for public review the final negotiated expected levels of performance for each grantee, including any comments submitted by the grantee regarding the grantee's satisfaction with the negotiated levels.

(D) ADJUSTMENT.—The expected levels of performance described in subparagraph (C) applicable to a grantee shall be adjusted after the agreement under subparagraph (C) has been reached only with respect to the following factors:

(i) High rates of unemployment or of poverty or participation in the program of block grants to States for temporary assistance for needy families established under part A of title IV of the Social Security Act (42 U.S.C. 601 et seq.), in the areas served by a grantee, relative to other areas of the State involved or Nation.

(ii) Significant downturns in the areas served by the grantee or in the national economy.

(iii) Significant numbers or proportions of participants with 1 or more barriers to employment, including individuals described in subsection (a)(3)(B)(ii) or (b)(2) of section 518, served by a grantee relative to such numbers or proportions for grantees serving other areas of the State or Nation.

(iv) Changes in Federal, State, or local minimum wage requirements.

(v) Limited economies of scale for the provision of community service employment and other authorized activities in the areas served by the grantee.

(E) PLACEMENT.—

(i) LEVEL OF PERFORMANCE.—For all grantees, the Secretary shall establish an expected level of performance of not less than the percentage specified in clause (ii) (adjusted in accordance with subparagraph (D)) for the entry into unsubsidized employment core indicator of performance described in subsection (b)(1)(B).

(ii) REQUIRED PLACEMENT PERCENTAGES.—The minimum percentage for the expected level of performance for the entry into unsubsidized employment core indicator of performance described in subsection (b)(1)(B) is—

(I) 21 percent for fiscal year 2007;

(II) 22 percent for fiscal year 2008;

(III) 23 percent for fiscal year 2009;

(IV) 24 percent for fiscal year 2010; and

(V) 25 percent for fiscal year 2011.

(3) LIMITATION. — An agreement to be evaluated on the core measures of performance and to report information on the additional indicators of performance shall be a requirement for application for, and a condition of, all grants authorized by this title.

(b) INDICATORS OF PERFORMANCE. —

(1) CORE INDICATORS. — The core indicators of performance described in subsection (a)(2)(A)(i) shall consist of —

(A) hours (in the aggregate) of community service employment;

(B) entry into unsubsidized employment;

(C) retention in unsubsidized employment for 6 months;

(D) earnings; and

(E) the number of eligible individuals served, including the number of participating individuals described in subsection (a)(3)(B)(ii) or (b)(2) of section 518.

(2) ADDITIONAL INDICATORS. — The additional indicators of performance described in subsection (a)(2)(A)(ii) shall consist of —

(A) retention in unsubsidized employment for 1 year;

(B) satisfaction of the participants, employers, and their host agencies with their experiences and the services provided;

(C) any other indicators of performance that the Secretary determines to be appropriate to evaluate services and performance.

(3) DEFINITIONS OF INDICATORS. — The Secretary, after consultation with national and State grantees, representatives of business and labor organizations, and providers of services, shall, by regulation, issue definitions of the indicators of performance described in paragraphs (1) and (2).

(c) EVALUATION. — The Secretary shall —

(1) annually evaluate, and publish and make available for public review information on, the actual performance of each grantee with respect to the levels achieved for each of the core indicators of performance, compared to the expected levels of performance established under subsection (a)(2)(C) (including any adjustments to such levels made in accordance with subsection (a)(2)(D)); and

(2) annually publish and make available for public review information on the actual performance of each grantee with respect to the levels achieved for each of the additional indicators of performance.

(d) TECHNICAL ASSISTANCE AND CORRECTIVE EFFORTS —

(1) INITIAL DETERMINATIONS. —

(A) IN GENERAL. — As soon as practicable after July 1, 2007, the Secretary shall determine if a grantee under this title has, for program year 2006 —

(i) met the expected levels of performance established under subsection (a)(2)(C) (including any adjustments to such levels made in accordance with subsection (a)(2)(D)) for the core indicators of performance described in subparagraphs (A), (C), (D), and (E) of subsection (b)(1); and

(ii) achieved the applicable percentage specified in subsection (a)(2)(E)(ii) for the core indicator of performance described in subsection (b)(1)(B).

(B) TECHNICAL ASSISTANCE.—If the Secretary determines that the grantee, for program year 2006—

    (i) failed to meet the expected levels of performance described in subparagraph (A)(i); or

    (ii) failed to achieve the applicable percentage described in subparagraph (A)(ii), the Secretary shall provide technical assistance to assist the grantee to meet the expected levels of performance and achieve the applicable percentage.

(2) NATIONAL GRANTEES.—

(A) IN GENERAL.—Not later than 120 days after the end of each program year, the Secretary shall determine if a national grantee awarded a grant under section 502(b) in accordance with section 514 has met the expected levels of performance established under subsection (a)(2)(C) (including any adjustments to such levels made in accordance with subsection (a)(2)(D)) for the core indicators of performance described in subsection (b)(1).

(B) TECHNICAL ASSISTANCE AND CORRECTIVE ACTION PLAN.—

    (i) IN GENERAL.—If the Secretary determines that a national grantee fails to meet the expected levels of performance described in subparagraph (A), the Secretary after each year of such failure, shall provide technical assistance and require such grantee to submit a corrective action plan not later than 160 days after the end of the program year.

    (ii) CONTENT.—The plan submitted under clause (i) shall detail the steps the grantee will take to meet the expected levels of performance in the next program year.

    (iii) RECOMPETITION.—Any grantee who has failed to meet the expected levels of performance for 4 consecutive years (beginning with program year 2007) shall not be allowed to compete in the subsequent grant competition under section 514 following the fourth consecutive year of failure but may compete in the next such grant competition after that subsequent competition.

(3) STATE GRANTEES.—

(A) IN GENERAL.—Not later than 120 days after the end of each program year, the Secretary shall determine if a State grantee allotted funds under section 506(e) has met the expected levels of performance established under subsection (a)(2)(C) (including any adjustments to such levels made in accordance with subsection (a)(2)(D)) for the core indicators of performance described in subsection (b)(1).

(B) TECHNICAL ASSISTANCE AND CORRECTIVE ACTION PLAN.—

    (i) IN GENERAL.—If the Secretary determines that a State fails to meet the expected levels of performance described in subparagraph (A), the Secretary, after each year of such failure, shall provide technical assistance and require the State to submit a corrective action plan not later than 160 days after the end of the program year.

    (ii) CONTENT.—The plan submitted under clause (i) shall detail the steps the State will take to meet the expected levels of performance in the next program year.

    (iii) COMPETITION.—If the Secretary determines that the State fails to meet the expected levels of performance described in subparagraph (A) for 3 consecutive program years (beginning with program year 2007), the Secretary shall provide for the conduct by the State of a competition to award the funds allotted to the State under section 506(e) for the first full program year following the Secretary's determination.

(4) SPECIAL RULE FOR ESTABLISHMENT AND IMPLEMENTATION.— The Secretary shall establish and implement the core measures of performance and additional indicators of performance described in this section, including all required indicators described in subsection (b), not later than July 1, 2007.

(e) IMPACT ON GRANT COMPETITION.—The Secretary may not publish a notice announcing a grant competition under this title, and solicit proposals for grants, until the day that is the later of—

(1) the date on which the Secretary implements the core measures of performance and additional indicators of performance described in this section; and

(2) January 1, 2010.

Section. 514. COMPETITIVE REQUIREMENTS RELATING TO GRANT AWARDS.

(a) PROGRAM AUTHORIZED.—

(1) INITIAL APPROVAL OF GRANT APPLICATIONS.—From the funds available for national grants under section 506(d), the Secretary shall award grants under section 502(b) to eligible applicants, through a competitive process that emphasizes meeting performance requirements, to carry out projects under this title for a period of 4 years, except as provided in paragraph (2). The Secretary may not conduct a grant competition under this title until the day described in section 513(e).

(2) CONTINUATION OF APPROVAL BASED ON PERFORMANCE.— If the recipient of a grant made under paragraph (1) meets the expected levels of performance described in section 513(d)(2)(A) for each year of such 4-year period with respect to a project, the Secretary may award a grant under section 502(b) to such recipient to continue such project beyond such 4-year period for 1 additional year without regard to such process.

(b) ELIGIBLE APPLICANTS.—An applicant shall be eligible to receive a grant under section 502(b) in accordance with subsections (a), (c), and (d).

(c) CRITERIA.—For purposes of subsection (a)(1), the Secretary shall select the eligible applicants to receive grants based on the following:

(1) The applicant's ability to administer a project that serves the greatest number of eligible individuals, giving particular consideration to individuals with greatest economic need, individuals with greatest social need, and individuals described in subsection (a)(3)(B)(ii) or (b)(2) of section 518.

(2) The applicant's ability to administer a project that provides employment for eligible individuals in the communities in which such individuals reside, or in nearby communities, that will contribute to the general welfare of the communities involved.

(3) The applicant's ability to administer a project that moves eligible individuals into unsubsidized employment.

(4) The applicant's prior performance, if any, in meeting core measures of performance and addressing additional indicators of performance under this title and the applicant's ability to address core indicators of performance and additional indicators of performance under this title and under other Federal or State programs in the case of an applicant that has not previously received a grant under this title.

(5) The applicant's ability to move individuals with multiple barriers to employment, including individuals described in subsection (a)(3)(B)(ii) or (b)(2) of section 518, into unsubsidized employment.

(6) The applicant's ability to coordinate activities with other organizations at the State and local level.

(7) The applicant's plan for fiscal management of the project to be administered with funds received in accordance with this section.

(8) The applicant's ability to administer a project that provides community service.

(9) The applicant's ability to minimize disruption in services for participants and in community services provided.

(10) Any additional criteria that the Secretary considers to be appropriate in order to minimize disruption in services for participants.

(d) RESPONSIBILITY TESTS. —

(1) IN GENERAL. — Before final selection of a grantee, the Secretary shall conduct a review of available records to assess the applicant's overall responsibility to administer Federal funds.

(2) REVIEW. — As part of the review described in paragraph (1), the Secretary may consider any information, including the applicant's history with regard to the management of other grants.

(3) FAILURE TO SATISFY TEST. — The failure to satisfy a responsibility test with respect to any 1 factor that is listed in paragraph (4), excluding those listed in subparagraphs (A) and (B) of such paragraph, does not establish that the applicant is not responsible unless such failure is substantial or persists for 2 or more consecutive years.

(4) TEST. — The responsibility tests include review of the following factors:

(A) Unsuccessful efforts by the applicant to recover debts, after 3 demand letters have been sent, that are established by final agency action, or a failure to comply with an approved repayment plan.

(B) Established fraud or criminal activity of a significant nature within the organization or agency involved.

(C) Serious administrative deficiencies identified by the Secretary, such as failure to maintain a financial management system as required by Federal rules or regulations.

(D) Willful obstruction of the audit process.

(E) Failure to provide services to participants for a current or recent grant or to meet applicable core measures of performance or address applicable indicators of performance.

(F) Failure to correct deficiencies brought to the grantee's attention in writing as a result of monitoring activities, reviews, assessments, or other activities.

(G) Failure to return a grant closeout package or outstanding advances within 90 days of the grant expiration date or receipt of the closeout package, whichever is later, unless an extension has been requested and granted.

(H) Failure to submit required reports.

(I) Failure to properly report and dispose of Government property as instructed by the Secretary.

(J) Failure to have maintained effective cash management or cost controls resulting in excess cash on hand.

(K) Failure to ensure that a subrecipient complies with its Office of Management and Budget Circular A– 133 audit requirements specified at section 667.200(b) of title 20, Code of Federal Regulations.

(L) Failure to audit a subrecipient within the required period.

(M) Final disallowed costs in excess of 5 percent of the grant or contract award if, in the judgment of the grant officer, the disallowances are egregious.

(N) Failure to establish a mechanism to resolve a subrecipient's audit in a timely fashion.

(5) DETERMINATION.—Applicants that are determined to be not responsible shall not be selected as grantees.

(6) DISALLOWED COSTS.—Interest on disallowed costs shall accrue in accordance with the Debt Collection Improvement Act of 1996, including the amendments made by that Act.

(e) GRANTEES SERVING INDIVIDUALS WITH BARRIERS TO EMPLOYMENT.—

(1) DEFINITION.—In this subsection, the term 'individuals with barriers to employment' means minority individuals, Indian individuals, individuals with greatest economic need, and individuals described in subsection (a)(3)(B)(ii) or (b)(2) of section 518.

(2) SPECIAL CONSIDERATION.—In areas where a substantial population of individuals with barriers to employment exists, a grantee that receives a national grant in accordance with this section shall, in selecting subgrantees, give special consideration to organizations (including former recipients of such national grants) with demonstrated expertise in serving individuals with barriers to employment.

(f) MINORITY-SERVING GRANTEES.—The Secretary may not promulgate rules or regulations affecting grantees in areas where a substantial population of minority individuals exists, that would significantly compromise the ability of the grantees to serve their targeted population of minority older individuals.

Section. 515. REPORT ON SERVICE TO MINORITY INDIVIDUALS.

(a) IN GENERAL.—The Secretary shall annually prepare a report on the levels of participation and performance outcomes of minority individuals served by the program carried out under this title.

(b) CONTENTS.—

(1) ORGANIZATION AND DATA.—Such report shall present information on the levels of participation and the outcomes achieved by such minority individuals with respect to each grantee under this title, by service area, and in the aggregate, beginning with data that applies to program year 2005.

(2) EFFORTS.—The report shall also include a description of each grantee's efforts to serve minority individuals, based on information submitted to the Secretary by each grantee at such time and in such manner as the Secretary determines to be appropriate.

(3) RELATED MATTERS.—The report shall also include—

(A) an assessment of individual grantees based on the criteria established under subsection (c);

(B) an analysis of whether any changes in grantees have affected participation rates of such minority individuals;

(C) information on factors affecting participation rates among such minority individuals; and

(D) recommendations for increasing participation of minority individuals in the program.

(c) CRITERIA.—The Secretary shall establish criteria for determining the effectiveness of grantees in serving minority individuals in accordance with the goals set forth in section 502(a)(1).

(d) SUBMISSION.—The Secretary shall annually submit such a report to the appropriate committees of Congress.

Section. 516. SENSE OF CONGRESS.

It is the sense of Congress that—

    (1)   the older American community service employment program described in this title was established with the intent of placing older individuals in community service positions and providing job training; and

    (2)   placing older individuals in community service positions strengthens the ability of the individuals to become self-sufficient, provides much-needed support to organizations that benefit from increased civic engagement, and strengthens the communities that are served by such organizations.

Section. 517. AUTHORIZATION OF APPROPRIATIONS.

(a)   IN GENERAL.—There are authorized to be appropriated to carry out this title such sums as may be necessary for fiscal years 2007, 2008, 2009, 2010, and 2011.

(b)   OBLIGATION.—Amounts appropriated under this section for any fiscal year shall be available for obligation during the annual period that begins on July 1 of the calendar year immediately following the beginning of such fiscal year and that ends on June 30 of the following calendar year. The Secretary may extend the period during which such amounts may be obligated or expended in the case of a particular organization or agency that receives funds under this title if the Secretary determines that such extension is necessary to ensure the effective use of such funds by such organization or agency.

(c)   RECAPTURING FUNDS.—At the end of the program year, the Secretary may recapture any unexpended funds for the program year, and reobligate such funds within the 2 succeeding program years for—

    (1)   incentive grants to entities that are State grantees or national grantees under section 502(b);

    (2)   technical assistance; or

    (3)   grants or contracts for any other activity under this title.

Section. 518. DEFINITIONS AND RULE.

(a)   DEFINITIONS.—For purposes of this title:

    (1)   COMMUNITY SERVICE.—The term 'community service' means—

        (A)   social, health, welfare, and educational services (including literacy tutoring), legal and other counseling services and assistance, including tax counseling and assistance and financial counseling, and library, recreational, and other similar services;

        (B)   conservation, maintenance, or restoration of natural resources;

        (C)   community betterment or beautification;

        (D)   antipollution and environmental quality efforts;

        (E)   weatherization activities;

        (F)   economic development; and

        (G)   such other services essential and necessary to the community as the Secretary determines by rule to be appropriate.

(2) COMMUNITY SERVICE EMPLOYMENT.—The term 'community service employment' means part-time, temporary employment paid with grant funds in projects described in section 502(b)(1)(D), through which eligible individuals are engaged in community service and receive work experience and job skills that can lead to unsubsidized employment.

(3) ELIGIBLE INDIVIDUAL.—

(A) IN GENERAL.—The term 'eligible individual' means an individual who is age 55 or older and who has a low income (including any such individual whose income is not more than 125 percent of the poverty line), excluding any income that is unemployment compensation, a benefit received under title XVI of the Social Security Act (42 U.S.C. 1381 et seq.), a payment made to or on behalf of veterans or former members of the Armed Forces under the laws administered by the Secretary of Veterans Affairs, or 25 percent of a benefit received under title II of the Social Security Act (42 U.S.C. 401 et seq.), subject to subsection (b).

(B) PARTICIPATION.—

(i) EXCLUSION.—Notwithstanding any other provision of this paragraph, the term 'eligible individual' does not include an individual who has participated in projects under this title for a period of 48 months in the aggregate (whether or not consecutive) after July 1, 2007, unless the period was increased as described in clause (ii).

(ii) INCREASED PERIODS OF PARTICIPATION.—The Secretary shall authorize a grantee for a project to increase the period of participation described in clause (i), pursuant to a request submitted by the grantee, for individuals who—

(I)   have a severe disability;

(II)   are frail or are age 75 or older;

(III) meet the eligibility requirements related to age for, but do not receive, benefits under title II of the Social Security Act (42 U.S.C. 401 et seq.);

(IV) live in an area with persistent unemployment and are individuals with severely limited employment prospects; or

(V)   have limited English proficiency or low literacy skills.

(4) INCOME.—In this section, the term 'income' means income received during the 12-month period (or, at the option of the grantee involved, the annualized income for the 6-month period) ending on the date an eligible individual submits an application to participate in a project carried out under this title by such grantee.

(5) PACIFIC ISLAND AND ASIAN AMERICANS.—The term 'Pacific Island and Asian Americans' means Americans having origins in any of the original peoples of the Far East, Southeast Asia, the Indian Subcontinent, or the Pacific Islands

(6) PROGRAM.—The term 'program' means the older American community service employment program established under this title.

(7) SUPPORTIVE SERVICES.—The term 'supportive services' means services, such as transportation, child care, dependent care, housing, and needs-related payments, that are necessary to enable an individual to participate in activities authorized under this title, consistent with the provisions of this title.

(8) UNEMPLOYED.—The term 'unemployed', used with respect to a person or individual, means an individual who is without a job and who wants and is available for work, including an individual who may have occasional employment that does not result in a constant source of income.

(b) RULE.—Pursuant to regulations prescribed by the Secretary, an eligible individual shall have priority for the community service employment and other authorized activities provided under this title if the individual—

  (1) is 65 years of age or older; or

  (2) (A) has a disability;

      (B) has limited English proficiency or low literacy skills;

      (C) resides in a rural area;

      (D) is a veteran;

      (E) has low employment prospects;

      (F) has failed to find employment after utilizing services provided under title I of the Workforce Investment Act of 1998 (29 U.S.C. 2801 et seq.); or

      (G) is homeless or at risk for homelessness.

(42 U.S.C. 3056n)

TITLE VI—GRANTS FOR NATIVE AMERICANS

Section. 601. STATEMENT OF PURPOSE

It is the purpose of this title to promote the delivery of supportive services, including nutrition services to American Indians, Alaskan Natives, and Native Hawaiians that are comparable to services provided under title III.

(42 U.S.C. 3057)

Section. 602. SENSE OF CONGRESS

It is the sense of the Congress that older individuals who are Indians, older individuals who are Alaskan Natives, and older individuals who are Native Hawaiians are a vital resource entitled to all benefits and services available and that such services and benefits should be provided in a manner that preserves and restores their respective dignity, self-respect, and cultural identities.

(42 U.S.C. 3057a)

PART A—INDIAN PROGRAM FINDINGS

Section. 611.

(a) [13] The Congress finds that the older individuals who are Indians of the United States—
    (1)   are a rapidly increasing population;
    (2)   suffer from high unemployment;
    (3)   live in poverty at a rate estimated to be as high as 61 percent;
    (4)   have a life expectancy between 3 and 4 years less than the general population;
    (5)   lack sufficient nursing homes, other long-term care facilities, and other health care facilities;
    (6)   lack sufficient Indian area agencies on aging;
    (7)   frequently live in substandard and over-crowded housing;
    (8)   receive less than adequate health care;
    (9)   are served under this title at a rate of less than 19 percent of the total national population of older individuals who are Indians living on Indian reservations; and
    (10) are served under title III at a rate of less than 1 percent of the total participants under that title.

(42 U.S.C. 3057b)

Section. 612. ELIGIBILITY

(b) A tribal organization of an Indian tribe is eligible for assistance under this part only if—
    (1)   the tribal organization represents at least 50 individuals who are 60 years of age or older; and
    (2)   the tribal organization demonstrates the ability to deliver supportive services, including nutritional services.

(c) An Indian tribe represented by an organization specified in subsection (a) shall be eligible for only one grant under this part for any fiscal year. Nothing in this subsection shall preclude an Indian tribe represented by an organization specified in subsection (a) from receiving a grant under section 631.

(d) For the purposes of this part the terms "Indian tribe" and "tribal organization" have the same meaning as in section 4 of the Indian Self-Determination and Education Assistance Act (25 U.S.C. 450b).

(42 U.S.C. 3057c)

Section. 613. GRANTS AUTHORIZED

The Assistant Secretary may make grants to eligible tribal organizations to pay all of the costs for delivery of supportive services and nutrition services for older individuals who are Indians.

(42 U.S.C. 3057d)

Section. 614. APPLICATIONS

(a) No grant may be made under this part unless the eligible tribal organization submits an application to the Assistant Secretary which meets such criteria as the Assistant Secretary may by regulation prescribe. Each such application shall—

(1) provide that the eligible tribal organization will evaluate the need for supportive and nutrition services among older individuals who are Indians to be represented by the tribal organizations;

(2) provide for the use of such methods of administration as are necessary for the proper and efficient administration of the program to be assisted;

(3) provide that the tribal organization will make such reports in such form and containing such information, as the Assistant Secretary may reasonably require, and comply with such requirements as the Assistant Secretary may impose to assure the correctness of such reports;

(4) provide for periodic evaluation of activities and projects carried out under the application;

(5) establish objectives consistent with the purposes of this part toward which activities under the application will be directed, identify obstacles to the attainment of such objectives, and indicate the manner in which the tribal organization proposes to overcome such obstacles;

(6) provide for establishing and maintaining information and assistance services to assure that older individuals who are Indians to be served by the assistance made available under this part will have reasonably convenient access to such services;

(7) provide a preference for older individuals who are Indians for full or part-time staff positions whenever feasible;

(8) provide assistance that either directly or by way of grant or contract with appropriate entities nutrition services will be delivered to older individuals who are Indians represented by the tribal organization substantially in compliance with the provisions of part C of title III, except that in any case in which the need for nutritional services for older individuals who are Indians represented by the tribal organization is already met from other sources, the tribal organization may use the funds otherwise required to be expended under this paragraph for supportive services;

(9) provide that any legal or ombudsman services made available to older individuals who are Indians represented by the tribal organization will be substantially in compliance with the provisions of title III relating to the furnishing of similar services;

(10) provide satisfactory assurance that fiscal control and fund accounting procedures will be adopted as may be necessary to assure proper disbursement of, and accounting for, Federal funds paid under this part to the tribal organization, including any funds paid by the tribal organization to a recipient of a grant or contract; and

(11) contain assurances that the tribal organization will coordinate services provided under this part with services provided under title III in the same geographical area.

(b) For the purpose of any application submitted under this part, the tribal organization may develop its own population statistics, with approval from the Bureau of Indian Affairs, in order to establish eligibility.

(c) (1) The Assistant Secretary shall approve any application which complies with the provisions of subsection (a).

(2) The Assistant Secretary shall provide waivers and exemptions of the reporting requirements of subsection (a)(3) for applicants that serve Indian populations in geographically isolated areas, or applicants that serve small Indian populations, where the small scale of the project, the nature of the applicant, or other factors make the reporting requirements unreasonable under the circumstances. The Assistant Secretary shall consult with such applicants in establishing appropriate waivers and exemptions.

(3) The Assistant Secretary shall approve any application that complies with the provisions of subsection (a), except that in determining whether an application complies with the requirements of subsection (a)(8), the Assistant Secretary shall provide maximum flexibility to an applicant that seeks to take into account subsistence needs, local customs, and other characteristics that are appropriate to the unique cultural, regional, and geographic needs of the Indian populations to be served.

(4) In determining whether an application complies with the requirements of subsection (a)(12), the Assistant Secretary shall require only that an applicant provide an appropriate narrative description of the geographic area to be served and an assurance that procedures will be adopted to ensure against duplicate services being provided to the same recipients.

(d) Whenever the Assistant Secretary determines not to approve an application submitted under subsection (a) the Assistant Secretary shall —

(1) state objections in writing to the tribal organization within 60 days after such decision;

(2) provide to the extent practicable technical assistance to the tribal organization to overcome such stated objections; and

(3) provide the tribal organization with a hearing, under such rules and regulations as the Assistant Secretary may prescribe.

(e) Whenever the Assistant Secretary approves an application of a tribal organization under this part, funds shall be awarded for not less than 12 months.

(42 U.S.C. 3057e)

Section. 614A. DISTRIBUTION OF FUNDS AMONG TRIBAL ORGANIZATIONS.

(a) MAINTENANCE of 1991 AMOUNTS.—Subject to the availability of appropriations to carry out this part, the amount of the grant (if any) made under this part to a tribal organization for fiscal year 1992 and for each subsequent fiscal year shall be not less than the amount of the grant made under this part to the tribal organization for fiscal year 1991.

(b) USE OF ADDITIONAL AMOUNTS APPROPRIATED.—If the funds appropriated to carry out this part in a fiscal year subsequent to fiscal year 1991 exceed the funds appropriated to carry out this part in fiscal year 1991, then the amount of the grant (if any) made under this part to a tribal organization for the subsequent fiscal year shall be—

(1) increased by such amount as the Assistant Secretary considers to be appropriate, in addition to the amount of any increase required by subsection (a), so that the grant equals or more closely approaches the amount of the grant made under this part to the tribal organization for fiscal year 1980; or

(2) an amount the Assistant Secretary considers to be sufficient if the tribal organization did not receive a grant under this part for either fiscal year 1980 or fiscal year 1991.

(c) CLARIFICATION.—

(1) DEFINITION.—In this subsection, the term 'covered year' means fiscal year 2006 or a subsequent fiscal year.

(2) CONSORTIA OF TRIBAL ORGANIZATIONS.—If a tribal organization received a grant under this part for fiscal year 1991 as part of a consortium, the Assistant Secretary shall consider the tribal organization to have received a grant under this part for fiscal year 1991 for purposes of subsections (a) and (b), and shall apply the provisions of subsections (a) and (b)(1) (under the conditions described in subsection (b)) to the tribal organization for each covered year for which the tribal organization submits an application under this part, even if the tribal organization submits—

(A) a separate application from the remaining members of the consortium; or

(B) an application as 1 of the remaining members of the consortium.

(42 U.S.C. 3057e-1)

Section. 615. SURPLUS EDUCATIONAL FACILITIES

(a) Notwithstanding any other provision of law, the Secretary of the Interior through the Bureau of Indian Affairs shall make available surplus Indian educational facilities to tribal organizations, and nonprofit organizations with tribal approval, for use as multipurpose senior centers. Such centers may be altered so as to provide extended care facilities, community center facilities, nutrition services, child care services, and other supportive services.

(b) Each eligible tribal organization desiring to take advantage of such surplus facilities shall submit an application to the Secretary of the Interior at such time and such manner, and containing or accompanied by such information, as the Secretary of the Interior determines to be necessary to carry out the provisions of this section.

(42 U.S.C. 3057f)

PART B — NATIVE HAWAIIAN PROGRAM FINDINGS

Section. 621.

The Congress finds the older Native Hawaiians —

    (1) have a life expectancy 10 years less than any other ethnic group in the State of Hawaii;

    (2) rank lowest on 9 of 11 standard health indices for all ethnic groups in Hawaii;

    (3) are often unaware of social services and do not know how to go about seeking such assistance; and

    (4) live in poverty at a rate of 34 percent.

(42 U.S.C. 3057g)

Section. 622. ELIGIBILITY

A public or nonprofit private organization having the capacity to provide services under this part for Native Hawaiians is eligible for assistance under this part only if —

    (1) the organization will serve at least 50 individuals who have attained 60 years of age or older; and

    (2) the organization demonstrates the ability to deliver supportive services, including nutrition services.

(42 U.S.C. 3057h)

Section. 623. GRANTS AUTHORIZED

The Assistant Secretary may make grants to public and nonprofit private organizations to pay all of the costs for the delivery of supportive services and nutrition services to older Native Hawaiians.

(42 U.S.C. 3057i)

Section. 624. APPLICATION

(a) No grant may be made under this part unless the public or nonprofit private organization submits an application to the Assistant Secretary which meets such criteria as the Assistant Secretary may by regulation prescribe. Each such application shall —

    (1) provide that the organization will evaluate the need for supportive and nutrition services among older Native Hawaiians to be represented by the organization;

    (2) provide for the use of such methods of administration as are necessary for the proper and efficient administration of the program to be assisted;

    (3) provide assurances that the organization will coordinate its activities with the State agency on aging and with the activities carried out under title III in the same geographical area;

    (4) provide that the organization will make such reports in such form and containing such information as the Assistant Secretary may reasonably require, and comply with such requirements as the Assistant Secretary may impose to ensure the correctness of such reports;

    (5) provide for periodic evaluation of activities and projects carried out under the application;

(6) establish objectives, consistent with the purpose of this title, toward which activities described in the application will be directed, identify obstacles to the attainment of such objectives, and indicate the manner in which the organization proposes to overcome such obstacles;

(7) provide for establishing and maintaining information and assistance services to assure that older Native Hawaiians to be served by the assistance made available under this part will have reasonably convenient access to such services;

(8) provide a preference for Native Hawaiians 60 years of age and older for full or part-time staff positions wherever feasible;

(9) provide that any legal or ombudsman services made available to older Native Hawaiians represented by the nonprofit private organization will be substantially in compliance with the provisions of title III relating to the furnishing and similar services; and

(10) provide satisfactory assurance that the fiscal control and fund accounting procedures will be adopted as may be necessary to assure proper disbursement of, and accounting for, Federal funds paid under this part to the nonprofit private organization, including any funds paid by the organization to a recipient of a grant or contract.

(b) The Assistant Secretary shall approve any application which complies with the provisions of subsection (a).

(c) Whenever the Assistant Secretary determines not to approve an application submitted under subsection (a) the Assistant Secretary shall—

(1) state objections in writing to the nonprofit private organization within 60 days after such decision;

(2) provide to the extent practicable technical assistance to the nonprofit private organization to overcome such stated objections; and

(3) provide the organization with a hearing under such rules and regulations as the Assistant Secretary may prescribe.

(d) Whenever the Assistant Secretary approves an application of a nonprofit private or public organization under this part funds shall be awarded for not less than 12 months.

(42 U.S.C. 3057j)

Section. 624A. DISTRIBUTION OF FUNDS AMONG ORGANIZATIONS.

Subject to the availability of appropriations to carry out this part, the amount of the grant (if any) made under this part to an organization for fiscal year 1992 and for each subsequent fiscal year shall be not less than the amount of the grant made under this part to the organization for fiscal year 1991.

(42 U.S.C. 3057j–1)

Section. 625. DEFINITION

For the purpose of this part, the term "Native Hawaiian" means any individual any of whose ancestors were natives of the area which consists of the Hawaiian Islands prior to 1778.

(42 U.S.C. 3057k)

PART C—NATIVE AMERICAN CAREGIVER SUPPORT PROGRAM

Section. 631. PROGRAM.

(a)   IN GENERAL.—The Assistant Secretary shall carry out a program for making grants to tribal organizations with applications approved under parts A and B, to pay for the Federal share of carrying out tribal programs, to enable the tribal organizations to provide multifaceted systems of the support services described in section 373 for caregivers described in section 373.

(b)   REQUIREMENTS.—In providing services under subsection (a), a tribal organization shall meet the requirements specified for an area agency on aging and for a State in the provisions of subsections (c), (d), and (e) of section 373 and of section 374. For purposes of this subsection, references in such provisions to a State program shall be considered to be references to a tribal program under this part.

(42 U.S.C. 3057k-11)

PART D—GENERAL PROVISIONS ADMINISTRATION

Section. 641.

In establishing regulations for the purpose of part A the Assistant Secretary shall consult with the Secretary of the Interior.

(42 U.S.C. 3057l)

Section. 642. PAYMENTS

Payments may be made under this title (after necessary adjustments, in the case of grants, on account of previously made overpayments or underpayments) in advance or by way of reimbursement in such installments and on such conditions as the Assistant Secretary may determine.

(42 U.S.C. 3057m)

Section. 643. AUTHORIZATION OF APPROPRIATIONS.

There are authorized to be appropriated to carry out this title—

    (1)   for parts A and B, such sums as may be necessary for fiscal year 2007, and such sums as may be necessary for subsequent fiscal years; and

    (2)   for part C, $6,500,000 for fiscal year 2007, $6,800,000 for fiscal year 2008, $7,200,000 for fiscal year 2009, $7,500,000 for fiscal year 2010, and $7,900,000 for fiscal year 2011.

(42 U.S.C. 3057n)

TITLE VII—ALLOTMENTS FOR VULNERABLE ELDER RIGHTS PROTECTION ACTIVITIES

Subtitle A—State Provision

CHAPTER 1—GENERAL STATE PROVISIONS

Section. 701. ESTABLISHMENT.

The Assistant Secretary, acting through the Administration, shall establish and carry out a program for making allotments to States to pay for the cost of carrying out vulnerable elder rights protection activities.

(42 U.S.C. 3058)

Section. 702. AUTHORIZATION OF APPROPRIATIONS.

(a) OMBUDSMAN PROGRAM.—There are authorized to be appropriated to carry out chapter 2, such sums as may be necessary for fiscal year 2007, and such sums as may be necessary for subsequent fiscal years.

(b) PREVENTION OF ELDER ABUSE, NEGLECT, AND EXPLOITATION.—

There are authorized to be appropriated to carry out chapter 3, such sums as may be necessary for fiscal year 2007, and such sums as may be necessary for subsequent fiscal years.

(c) LEGAL ASSISTANCE DEVELOPMENT PROGRAM.—There are authorized to be appropriated to carry out chapter 4, such sums as may be necessary for fiscal year 2007, and such sums as may be necessary for subsequent fiscal years.

(42 U.S.C. 3058a)

Section. 703. ALLOTMENT.

(a) IN GENERAL.—

    (1) POPULATION.—In carrying out the program described in section 701, the Assistant Secretary shall initially allot to each State, from the funds appropriated under section 702 for each fiscal year, an amount that bears the same ratio to the funds as the population of older individuals in the State bears to the population of older individuals in all States.

    (2) MINIMUM ALLOTMENTS.—

        (A) IN GENERAL.—After making the initial allotments described in paragraph (1), the Assistant Secretary shall adjust the allotments on a pro rata basis in accordance with subparagraphs (B) and (C).

        (B) GENERAL MINIMUM ALLOTMENTS.—

            (i) MINIMUM ALLOTMENT FOR STATES.—No State shall be allotted less than one-half of 1 percent of the funds appropriated under section 702 for the fiscal year for which the determination is made.

     (ii) MINIMUM ALLOTMENT FOR TERRITORIES.—Guam, the United States Virgin Islands, and the Trust Territory of the Pacific Islands, shall each be allotted not less than one-fourth of 1 percent of the funds appropriated under section 702 for the fiscal year for which the determination is made. American Samoa and the Commonwealth of the Northern Mariana Islands shall each be allotted not less than one-sixteenth of 1 percent of the sum appropriated under section 702 for the fiscal year for which the determination is made.

   (C) MINIMUM ALLOTMENTS FOR OMBUDSMAN AND ELDER ABUSE PROGRAMS.—

     (i) OMBUDSMAN PROGRAM.—No State shall be allotted for a fiscal year, from the funds appropriated under section 702 and made available to carry out chapter 2, less than the amount allotted to the State under section 304 in fiscal year 2000 to carry out the State Long-Term Care Ombudsman program under title III.

     (ii) ELDER ABUSE PROGRAMS.—No State shall be allotted for a fiscal year, from the funds appropriated under section 702 and made available to carry out chapter 3, less than the amount allotted to the State under section 304 in fiscal year 2000 to carry out programs with respect to the prevention of elder abuse, neglect, and exploitation under title III.

   (D) DEFINITION.—For the purposes of this paragraph, the term "State" does not include Guam, American Samoa, the United States Virgin Islands, the Trust Territory of the Pacific Islands, and the Commonwealth of the Northern Mariana Islands.

(b) REALLOTMENT.—

   (1) IN GENERAL.—If the Assistant Secretary determines that any amount allotted to a State for a fiscal year under this section will not be used by the State for carrying out the purpose for which the allotment was made, the Assistant Secretary shall make the amount available to a State that the Assistant Secretary determines will be able to use the amount for carrying out the purpose.

   (2) AVAILABILITY.—Any amount made available to a State from an appropriation for a fiscal year in accordance with paragraph (1) shall, for purposes of this subtitle, be regarded as part of the allotment of the State (as determined under subsection (a)) for the year, but shall remain available until the end of the succeeding fiscal year.

(c) WITHHOLDING.—If the Assistant Secretary finds that any State has failed to carry out this title in accordance with the assurances made and description provided under section 705, the Assistant Secretary shall withhold the allotment of funds to the State. The Assistant Secretary shall disburse the funds withheld directly to any public or nonprofit private institution or organization, agency, or political subdivision of the State submitting an approved plan containing the assurances and description.

(42 U.S.C. 3058h)

Section. 704. ORGANIZATION.

In order for a State to be eligible to receive allotments under this subtitle—

   (1) the State shall demonstrate eligibility under section 305;

   (2) the State agency designated by the State shall demonstrate compliance with the applicable requirements of section 305; and

   (3) each area agency on aging designated by the State agency and participating in such a program shall demonstrate compliance with the applicable requirements of section 305.

(42 U.S.C. 3058c)

Section. 705. ADDITIONAL STATE PLAN REQUIREMENTS.

(5) ELIGIBILITY.—In order to be eligible to receive an allotment under this subtitle, a State shall include in the State plan submitted under section 307—

(1) an assurance that the State, in carrying out any chapter of this subtitle for which the State receives funding under this subtitle, will establish programs in accordance with the requirements of the chapter and this chapter;

(2) an assurance that the State will hold public hearings, and use other means, to obtain the views of older individuals, area agencies on aging, recipients of grants under title VI, and other interested persons and entities regarding programs carried out under this subtitle;

(3) an assurance that the State, in consultation with area agencies on aging, will identify and prioritize statewide activities aimed at ensuring that older individuals have access to, and assistance in securing and maintaining, benefits and rights;

(4) an assurance that the State will use funds made available under this subtitle for a chapter in addition to, and will not supplant, any funds that are expended under any Federal or State law in existence on the day before the date of the enactment of this subtitle, to carry out each of the vulnerable elder rights protection activities described in the chapter;

(5) an assurance that the State will place no restrictions, other than the requirements referred to in clauses (i) through (iv) of section 712(a)(5)(C), on the eligibility of entities for designation as local Ombudsman entities under section 712(a)(5);

(6) an assurance that, with respect to programs for the prevention of elder abuse, neglect, and exploitation under chapter 3—

    (A) in carrying out such programs the State agency will conduct a program of services consistent with relevant State law and coordinated with existing State adult protective service activities for—

        (i) public education to identify and prevent elder abuse;

        (ii) receipt of reports of elder abuse;

        (iii) active participation of older individuals participating in programs under this Act through outreach, conferences, and referral of such individuals to other social service agencies or sources of assistance if appropriate and if the individuals to be referred consent; and

        (iv) referral of complaints to law enforcement or public protective service agencies if appropriate;

    (B) the State will not permit involuntary or coerced participation in the program of services described in subparagraph by alleged victims, abusers, or their households; and

    (C) all information gathered in the course of receiving reports and making referrals shall remain confidential except—

        (i) if all parties to such complaint consent in writing to the release of such information;

        (ii) if the release of such information is to a law enforcement agency, public protective service agency, licensing or certification agency, ombudsman program, or protection or advocacy system; or

        (iii) upon court order; and

  a. a description of the manner in which the State agency will carry out this title in accordance with the assurances described in paragraphs (1) through (6).

(7) PRIVILEGE.—Neither a State, nor a State agency, may require any provider of legal assistance under this subtitle to reveal any information that is protected by the attorney-client privilege.

(42 U.S.C. 3058d)

Section. 706. DEMONSTRATION PROJECTS.

(a) ESTABLISHMENT.—From amounts made available under section 304(d)(1)(C) after September 30, 1992, each State may provide for the establishment of at least one demonstration project, to be conducted by one or more area agencies on aging within the State, for outreach to older individuals with greatest economic need with respect to—
   (1) benefits available under title XVI of the Social Security Act (42 U.S.C. 1381 et seq.) (or assistance under a State program established in accordance with such title);
   (2) medical assistance available under title XIX of such Act (42 U.S.C. 1396 et seq.); and
   (3) benefits available under the Food Stamp Act of 1977 (7 U.S.C. 2011 et seq.).
(b) BENEFITS.—Each outreach project carried out under subsection (a) shall—
   (1) provide to older individuals with greatest economic need information and assistance regarding their eligibility to receive the benefits and assistance described in paragraphs (1) through (3) of subsection (a);
   (2) be carried out in a planning and service area that has a high proportion of older individuals with greatest economic need, relative to the aggregate number of older individuals in such area; and
   (3) be coordinated with State and local entities that administer benefits under such titles.

(42 U.S.C. 3058e)

CHAPTER 2—OMBUDSMAN PROGRAMS

Section. 711. DEFINITIONS.

As used in this chapter:
   (1) OFFICE.—The term "Office" means the office established in section 712(a)(1)(A).
   (2) OMBUDSMAN.—The term "Ombudsman" means the individual described in section 712(a)(2).
   (3) LOCAL OMBUDSMAN ENTITY.—The term "local Ombudsman entity" means an entity designated under section 712(a)(5)(A) to carry out the duties described in section 712(a)(5)(B) with respect to a planning and service area or other substate area.
   (4) PROGRAM.—The term "program" means the State Long-Term Care Ombudsman program established in section 712(a)(1)(B).
   (5) REPRESENTATIVE.—The term "representative" includes an employee or volunteer who represents an entity designated under section 712(a)(5)(A) and who is individually designated by the Ombudsman.
   (6) RESIDENT.—The term "resident" means an older individual who resides in a long-term care facility.

(42 U.S.C. 3058f)

Section. 712. STATE LONG-TERM CARE OMBUDSMAN PROGRAM.

(ii) ESTABLISHMENT.—
  (1) IN GENERAL.—In order to be eligible to receive an allotment under section 703 from funds appropriated under section 702 and made available to carry out this chapter, a State agency shall, in accordance with this section—
    (A) establish and operate an Office of the State Long-Term Care Ombudsman; and
    (B) carry out through the Office a State Long-Term Care Ombudsman program.
  (2) OMBUDSMAN.—The Office shall be headed by an individual, to be known as the State Long-Term Care Ombudsman, who shall be selected from among individuals with expertise and experience in the fields of long-term care and advocacy.
  (3) FUNCTIONS.—The Ombudsman shall serve on a fulltime basis, and shall, personally or through representatives of the Office—
    (B) identify, investigate, and resolve complaints that—
      (i)   are made by, or on behalf of, residents; and
      (ii) relate to action, inaction, or decisions, that may adversely affect the health, safety, welfare, or rights of the residents (including the welfare and rights of the residents with respect to the appointment and activities of guardians and representative payees), of—
        (I)   providers, or representatives of providers, of long-term care services;
        (II)   public agencies; or
        (III) health and social service agencies;
    (B) provide services to assist the residents in protecting the health, safety, welfare, and rights of the residents;
    (C) inform the residents about means of obtaining services provided by providers or agencies described in subparagraph (A)(ii) or services described in subparagraph (B);
    (D) ensure that the residents have regular and timely access to the services provided through the Office and that the residents and complainants receive timely responses from representatives of the Office to complaints;
    (E) represent the interests of the residents before governmental agencies and seek administrative, legal, and other remedies to protect the health, safety, welfare, and rights of the residents;
    (F) provide administrative and technical assistance to entities designated under paragraph (5) to assist the entities in participating in the program;
    (G)
      (i)   analyze, comment on, and monitor the development and implementation of Federal, State, and local laws, regulations, and other governmental policies and actions, that pertain to the health, safety, welfare, and rights of the residents, with respect to the adequacy of long-term care facilities and services in the State;
      (ii) recommend any changes in such laws, regulations, policies, and actions as the Office determines to be appropriate; and
      (iii) facilitate public comment on the laws, regulations, policies, and actions;
    (H)
      (i)   provide for training representatives of the Office;

     (ii) promote the development of citizen organizations, to participate in the program; and

     (iii) provide technical support for the development of resident and family councils to protect the well-being and rights of residents; and

  (I) carry out such other activities as the Assistant Secretary determines to be appropriate.

(4) CONTRACTS AND ARRANGEMENTS. —

  (A) IN GENERAL. — Except as provided in subparagraph (B) the State agency may establish and operate the Office, and carry out the program, directly, or by contract or other arrangement with any public agency or nonprofit private organization.

  (B) LICENSING AND CERTIFICATION ORGANIZATIONS; ASSOCIATIONS. — The State agency may not enter into the contract or other arrangement described in subparagraph (A) with —

     (i) an agency or organization that is responsible for licensing or certifying long-term care services in the State; or

     (ii) an association (or an affiliate of such an association) of long-term care facilities, or of any other residential facilities for older individuals.

(5) DESIGNATION OF LOCAL OMBUDSMAN ENTITIES AND REPRESENTATIVES. —

  (A) DESIGNATION. — In carrying out the duties of the Office, the Ombudsman may designate an entity as a local Ombudsman entity, and may designate an employee or volunteer to represent the entity.

  (B) DUTIES. — An individual so designated shall, in accordance with the policies and procedures established by the Office and the State agency —

     (i) provide services to protect the health, safety, welfare[14] and rights of residents;

     (ii) ensure that residents in the service area of the entity have regular, timely access to representatives of the program and timely responses to complaints and requests for assistance;

     (iii) identify, investigate, and resolve complaints made by or on behalf of residents that relate to action, inaction, or decisions, that may adversely affect the health, safety, welfare, or rights of the residents;

     (iv) represent the interests of residents before government agencies and seek administrative, legal, and other remedies to protect the health, safety, welfare, and rights of the residents;

     (v)

        (I) review, and if necessary, comment on any existing and proposed laws, regulations, and other government policies and actions, that pertain to the rights and well-being of residents, and

        (II) facilitate the ability of the public to comment on the laws, regulations, policies, and actions;

     (vi) support the development of resident and family councils; and

     (vii) carry out other activities that the Ombudsman determines to be appropriate.

  (C) ELIGIBILITY FOR DESIGNATION. — Entities eligible to be designated as local Ombudsman entities, and individuals eligible to be designated as representatives of such entities, shall —

     (i) have demonstrated capability to carry out the responsibilities of the Office;

(ii) be free of conflicts of interest and not stand to gain financially through an action or potential action brought on behalf of individuals the Ombudsman serves;

(iii) in the case of the entities, be public or nonprofit private entities; and

(iv) meet such additional requirements as the Ombudsman may specify.

(D) POLICIES AND PROCEDURES. —

(i) IN GENERAL. — The State agency shall establish, in accordance with the Office, policies and procedures for monitoring local Ombudsman entities designated to carry out the duties of the Office.

(ii) POLICIES. — In a case in which the entities are grantees, or the representatives are employees, of area agencies on aging, the State agency shall develop the policies in consultation with the area agencies on aging. The policies shall provide for participation and comment by the agencies and for resolution of concerns with respect to case activity.

(iii) CONFIDENTIALITY AND DISCLOSURE. — The State agency shall develop the policies and procedures in accordance with all provisions of this subtitle regarding confidentiality and conflict of interest.

(iii) PROCEDURES FOR ACCESS. —

(1) IN GENERAL. — The State shall ensure that representatives of the Office shall have —

(A) access to long-term care facilities and residents;

(B) (i) appropriate access to review the medical and social records of a resident, if —

(I) the representative has the permission of the resident, or the legal representative of the resident; or

(II) the resident is unable to consent to the review and has no legal representative; or

(ii) access to the records as is necessary to investigate a complaint if —

(I) a legal guardian of the resident refuses to give the permission;

(II) a representative of the Office has reasonable cause to believe that the guardian is not acting in the best interests of the resident; and

(III) the representative obtains the approval of the Ombudsman;

(C) access to the administrative records, policies, and documents, to which the residents have, or the general public has access, of long-term care facilities; and

(D) access to and, on request, copies of all licensing and certification records maintained by the State with respect to long-term care facilities.

(2) PROCEDURES. — The State agency shall establish procedures to ensure the access described in paragraph (1).

(iv) REPORTING SYSTEM. — The State agency shall establish a statewide uniform reporting system to —

(1) collect and analyze data relating to complaints and conditions in long-term care facilities and to residents for the purpose of identifying and resolving significant problems; and

(2) submit the data, on a regular basis, to —

(A) the agency of the State responsible for licensing or certifying long-term care facilities in the State;

(B) other State and Federal entities that the Ombudsman determines to be appropriate;

(C) the Assistant Secretary; and

(D) the National Ombudsman Resource Center established in section 202(a)(21).

(v) DISCLOSURE. —

(1) IN GENERAL.—The State agency shall establish procedures for the disclosure by the Ombudsman or local Ombudsman entities of files maintained by the program, including records described in subsection (b)(1) or (c).

(2) IDENTITY OF COMPLAINANT OR RESIDENT.—The procedures described in paragraph (1) shall—

(A) provide that, subject to subparagraph (B), the files and records described in paragraph (1) may be disclosed only at the discretion of the Ombudsman (or the person designated by the Ombudsman to disclose the files and records); and

(B) prohibit the disclosure of the identity of any complainant or resident with respect to whom the Office maintains such files or records unless—

   (i) the complainant or resident, or the legal representative of the complainant or resident, consents to the disclosure and the consent is given in writing;

   (ii) (I) the complainant or resident gives consent orally; and

   (II) the consent is documented contemporaneously in a writing made by a representative of the Office in accordance with such requirements as the State agency shall establish; or

   (iii) the disclosure is required by court order.

(vi) CONSULTATION.—In planning and operating the program, the State agency shall consider the views of area agencies on aging, older individuals, and providers of long-term care.

(vii) CONFLICT OF INTEREST.—The State agency shall—

(1) ensure that no individual, or member of the immediate family of an individual, involved in the designation of the Ombudsman (whether by appointment or otherwise) or the designation of an entity designated under subsection (a)(5), is subject to a conflict of interest;

(2) ensure that no officer or employee of the Office, representative of a local Ombudsman entity, or member of the immediate family of the officer, employee, or representative, is subject to a conflict of interest;

(3) ensure that the Ombudsman—

(A) does not have a direct involvement in the licensing or certification of a long-term care facility or of a provider of a long-term care service;

(B) does not have an ownership or investment interest (represented by equity, debt, or other financial relationship) in a long-term care facility or a long-term care service;

(C) is not employed by, or participating in the management of, a long-term care facility; and

(E) does not receive, or have the right to receive, directly or indirectly, remuneration (in cash or in kind) under a compensation arrangement with an owner or operator of a long-term care facility; and

(4) establish, and specify in writing, mechanisms to identify and remove conflicts of interest referred to in paragraphs (1) and (2), and to identify and eliminate the relationships described in subparagraphs (A) through (D) of paragraph (3), including such mechanisms as—

(A) the methods by which the State agency will examine individuals, and immediate family members, to identify the conflicts; and

(B) the actions that the State agency will require the individuals and such family members to take to remove such conflicts.

(viii) LEGAL COUNSEL.—The State agency shall ensure that—

(1) (A) adequate legal counsel is available, and is able, without conflict of interest, to—

        (i)   provide advice and consultation needed to protect the health, safety, welfare, and rights of residents; and

        (ii) assist the Ombudsman and representatives of the Office in the performance of the official duties of the Ombudsman and representatives; and

    (B) legal representation is provided to any representative of the Office against whom suit or other legal action is brought or threatened to be brought in connection with the performance of the official duties of the Ombudsman or such a representative; and

(2) the Office pursues administrative, legal, and other appropriate remedies on behalf of residents.

(a) ADMINISTRATION. — The State agency shall require the Office to —

(1) prepare an annual report —

    (A) describing the activities carried out by the Office in the year for which the report is prepared;

    (B) containing and analyzing the data collected under subsection (c);

    (C) evaluating the problems experienced by, and the complaints made by or on behalf of, residents;

    (D) containing recommendations for —

        (i)   improving quality of the care and life of the residents; and

        (ii) protecting the health, safety, welfare, and rights of the residents;

    (E) (i) analyzing the success of the program including success in providing services to residents of board and care facilities and other similar adult care facilities; and

        (ii) identifying barriers that prevent the optimal operation of the program; and

    (F) providing policy, regulatory, and legislative recommendations to solve identified problems, to resolve the complaints, to improve the quality of care and life of residents, to protect the health, safety, welfare, and rights of residents, and to remove the barriers;

(2) analyze, comment on, and monitor the development and implementation of Federal, State, and local laws, regulations, and other government policies and actions that pertain to long-term care facilities and services, and to the health, safety, welfare, and rights of residents, in the State, and recommend any changes in such laws, regulations, and policies as the Office determines to be appropriate;

(3) (A) provide such information as the Office determines to be necessary to public and private agencies, legislators, and other persons, regarding —

        (i)   the problems and concerns of older individuals residing in long-term care facilities; and

        (ii) recommendations related to the problems and concerns; and

    (F) make available to the public, and submit to the Assistant Secretary, the chief executive officer of the State, the State legislature, the State agency responsible for licensing or certifying long-term care facilities, and other appropriate governmental entities, each report prepared under paragraph (1);

(4) (A) not later than 1 year after the date of the enactment of this title, establish[15] procedures for the training of the representatives of the Office, including unpaid volunteers, based on model standards established by the Director of the Office of Long-Term Care Ombudsman Programs, in consultation with representatives of citizen groups, long-term care providers, and the Office, that —

    (A) specify a minimum number of hours of initial training;

    (B) specify the content of the training, including training relating to —

(i) Federal, State, and local laws, regulations, and policies, with respect to long-term care facilities in the State;

(ii) investigative techniques; and

(iii) such other matters as the State determines to be appropriate; and

(C) specify an annual number of hours of in-service training for all designated representatives;

(5) prohibit any representative of the Office (other than the Ombudsman) from carrying out any activity described in subparagraphs (A) through (G) of subsection (a)(3) unless the representative —

(A) has received the training required under paragraph (4); and

(B) has been approved by the Ombudsman as qualified to carry out the activity on behalf of the Office;

(6) coordinate ombudsman services with the protection and advocacy systems for individuals with developmental disabilities and mental illnesses established under —

(A) subtitle C of the Developmental Disabilities Assistance and Bill of Rights Act of 2000[16]; and

(B) the Protection and Advocacy for Mentally Ill Individuals Act of 1986 (42 U.S.C. 10801 et seq.);

(7) coordinate, to the greatest extent possible, ombudsman services with legal assistance provided under section 306(a)(2)(C), through adoption of memoranda of understanding and other means;

(8) coordinate services with State and local law enforcement agencies and courts of competent jurisdiction; and

(9) permit any local Ombudsman entity to carry out the responsibilities described in paragraph (1), (2), (3), (6), or (7).

(i) LIABILITY. — The State shall ensure that no representative of the Office will be liable under State law for the good faith performance of official duties.

(j) NONINTERFERENCE. — The State shall —

(1) ensure that willful interference with representatives of the Office in the performance of the official duties of the representatives (as defined by the Assistant Secretary) shall be unlawful;

(2) prohibit retaliation and reprisals by a long-term care facility or other entity with respect to any resident, employee, or other person for filing a complaint with, providing information to, or otherwise cooperating with any representative of, the Office; and

(3) provide for appropriate sanctions with respect to the interference, retaliation, and reprisals.

(42 U.S.C. 3058g)

Section. 713. REGULATIONS.

The Assistant Secretary shall issue and periodically update regulations respecting —

(1) conflicts of interest by persons described in paragraphs (1) and (2) of section 712(f); and

(2) the relationships described in subparagraphs (A) through (D) of section 712(f)(3).

(42 U.S.C. 3058h)

CHAPTER 3—PROGRAMS FOR PREVENTION OF ELDER ABUSE, NEGLECT, AND EXPLOITATION

Section. 721. PREVENTION OF ELDER ABUSE, NEGLECT, AND EXPLOITATION.

(b) ESTABLISHMENT.—In order to be eligible to receive an allotment under section 703 from funds appropriated under section 702 and made available to carry out this chapter, a State agency shall, in accordance with this section, and in consultation with area agencies on aging, develop and enhance **programs to address** elder abuse, neglect, and exploitation.

(c) USE OF ALLOTMENTS.—The State agency shall use an allotment made under subsection (a) to carry out, through the programs described in subsection (a), activities to develop, strengthen, and carry out programs for the prevention, detection, assessment, and treatment of, intervention in, investigation of, and response to elder abuse, neglect, and exploitation (including financial exploitation), including—

(1) providing for public education and outreach to identify and prevent elder abuse, neglect, and exploitation;

(2) providing for public education and outreach to promote financial literacy and prevent identity theft and financial exploitation of older individuals;

(3) ensuring the coordination of services provided by area agencies on aging with services instituted under the State adult protection service program, State and local law enforcement systems, and courts of competent jurisdiction;

(4) promoting the development of information and data systems, including elder abuse reporting systems, to quantify the extent of elder abuse, neglect, and exploitation in the State;

(5) conducting analyses of State information concerning elder abuse, neglect, and exploitation and identifying unmet service, enforcement, or intervention needs;

(6) conducting training for individuals, including caregivers described in part E of title III, professionals, and paraprofessionals, in relevant fields on the identification, prevention, and treatment of elder abuse, neglect, and exploitation, with particular focus on prevention and enhancement of self-determination and autonomy;

(7) providing technical assistance to programs that provide or have the potential to provide services for victims of elder abuse, neglect, and exploitation and for family members of the victims;

(8) conducting special and on-going training, for individuals involved in serving victims of elder abuse, neglect, and exploitation, on the topics of self-determination, individual rights, State and Federal requirements concerning confidentiality, and other topics determined by a State agency to be appropriate;

(9) promoting the development of an elder abuse, neglect, and exploitation system-

(A) that includes a State elder abuse, neglect, and exploitation law that includes provisions for immunity, for persons reporting instances of elder abuse, neglect, and exploitation, from prosecution arising out of such reporting, under any State or local law;

(B) under which a State agency—

(i) on receipt of a report of known or suspected instances of elder abuse, neglect, or exploitation, shall promptly initiate an investigation to substantiate the accuracy of the report; and

(ii) on a finding of elder abuse, neglect, or exploitation, shall take steps, including appropriate referral, to protect the health and welfare of the abused, neglected, or exploited older individual;

(C) that includes, throughout the State, in connection with the enforcement of elder abuse, neglect, and exploitation laws and with the reporting of suspected instances of elder abuse, neglect, and exploitation—

(i) such administrative procedures;

(ii) such personnel trained in the special problems of elder abuse, neglect, and exploitation prevention and treatment;

(iii) such training procedures;

(iv) such institutional and other facilities (public and private); and

(v) such related multidisciplinary programs and services, as may be necessary or appropriate to ensure that the State will deal effectively with elder abuse, neglect, and exploitation cases in the State;

(D) that preserves the confidentiality of records in order to protect the rights of older individuals;

(E) that provides for the cooperation of law enforcement officials, courts of competent jurisdiction, and State agencies providing human services with respect to special problems of elder abuse, neglect, and exploitation;

(F) that enables an older individual to participate in decisions regarding the welfare of the older individual, and makes the least restrictive alternatives available to an older individual who is abused, neglected, or exploited; and

(G) that includes a State clearinghouse for dissemination of information to the general public with respect to—

(i) the problems of elder abuse, neglect, and exploitation;

(ii) the facilities described in subparagraph (C)(iv); and

(iii) prevention and treatment methods available to combat instances of elder abuse, neglect, and exploitation;

(10) examining various types of shelters serving older individuals (in this paragraph referred to as 'safe havens'), and testing various safe haven models for establishing safe havens (at home or elsewhere), that recognize autonomy and self-determination, and fully protect the due process rights of older individuals;

(11) supporting multidisciplinary elder justice activities, such as—

(A) supporting and studying team approaches for bringing a coordinated multidisciplinary or interdisciplinary response to elder abuse, neglect, and exploitation, including a response from individuals in social service, health care, public safety, and legal disciplines;

(B) establishing a State coordinating council, which shall identify the individual State's needs and provide the Assistant Secretary with information and recommendations relating to efforts by the State to combat elder abuse, neglect, and exploitation;

(C) providing training, technical assistance, and other methods of support to groups carrying out multidisciplinary efforts at the State (referred to in some States as 'State Working Groups');

(D) broadening and studying various models for elder fatality and serious injury review teams, to make recommendations about their composition, protocols, functions, timing, roles, and responsibilities, with a goal of producing models and information that will allow for replication based on the needs of States and communities (other than the ones in which the review teams were used); and

(E) developing best practices, for use in long-term care facilities, that reduce the risk of elder abuse for residents, including the risk of resident-to-resident abuse; and

(12) addressing underserved populations of older individuals, such as—

(A) older individuals living in rural locations;

(B) older individuals in minority populations; or

(C) low-income older individuals.

(d) APPROACH.—In developing and enhancing programs under subsection (a), the State agency shall use a comprehensive approach, in consultation with area agencies on aging, to identify and assist older individuals who are subject to abuse, neglect, and exploitation, including older individuals who live in State licensed facilities, unlicensed facilities, or domestic or community-based settings.

(e) COORDINATION.—In developing and enhancing programs under subsection (a), the State agency shall coordinate the programs with other State and local programs and services for the protection of vulnerable adults, particularly vulnerable older individuals, including programs and services such as—

(1) area agency on aging programs;

(2) adult protective service programs;

(3) the State Long-Term Care Ombudsman program established in chapter 2;

(4) protection and advocacy programs;

(5) facility and long-term care provider licensure and certification programs;

(6) medicaid fraud and abuse services, including services provided by a State medicaid fraud control unit, as defined in section 1903(q) of the Social Security Act (42 U.S.C. 1396b(q));

(7) victim assistance programs; and

(8) consumer protection and State and local law enforcement programs, as well as other State and local programs that identify and assist vulnerable older individuals, and services provided by agencies and courts of competent jurisdiction.

(f) REQUIREMENTS.—In developing and enhancing programs under subsection (a), the State agency shall—

(1) not permit involuntary or coerced participation in such programs by alleged victims, abusers, or members of their households;

(2) require that all information gathered in the course of receiving a report described in subsection (b)(9)(B)(i), and making a referral described in subsection (b)(9)(B)(ii), shall remain confidential except—

(A) if all parties to such complaint or report consent in writing to the release of such information;

(B) if the release of such information is to a law enforcement agency, public protective service agency, licensing or certification agency, ombudsman program, or protection or advocacy system; or

(C) upon court order; and

(3) make all reasonable efforts to resolve any conflicts with other public agencies with respect to confidentiality of the information described in paragraph (2) by entering into memoranda of understanding that narrowly limit disclosure of information, consistent with the requirement described in paragraph (2).

(g) DESIGNATION.—The State agency may designate a State entity to carry out the programs and activities described in this chapter.

(h) STUDY AND REPORT.—

    (1) STUDY.—The Secretary, in consultation with the Department of the Treasury and the Attorney General of the United States, State attorneys general, and tribal and local prosecutors, shall conduct a study of the nature and extent of financial exploitation of older individuals. The purpose of this study would be to define and describe the scope of the problem of financial exploitation of the elderly and to provide an estimate of the number and type of financial transactions considered to constitute financial exploitation faced by older individuals. The study shall also examine the adequacy of current Federal and State legal protections to prevent such exploitation.

    (2) REPORT.—Not later than 18 months after the date of the enactment of the Older Americans Act Amendments of 2000, the Secretary shall submit to Congress a report, which shall include—

        (A) the results of the study conducted under this subsection; and

        (B) recommendations for future actions to combat the financial exploitation of older individuals.

(i) ACCOUNTABILITY MEASURES.—The Assistant Secretary shall develop accountability measures to ensure the effectiveness of the activities carried out under this section.

(j) EVALUATING PROGRAMS.—The Assistant Secretary shall evaluate the activities carried out under this section, using funds made available under section 206(g).

(k) COMPLIANCE WITH APPLICABLE LAWS.—In order to receive funds made available to carry out this section, an entity shall comply with all applicable laws, regulations, and guidelines.

(42 U.S.C. 3058i)

CHAPTER 4—STATE LEGAL ASSISTANCE DEVELOPMENT PROGRAM

Section. 731. STATE LEGAL ASSISTANCE DEVELOPMENT.

A State agency shall provide the services of an individual who shall be known as a State legal assistance developer, and the services of other personnel, sufficient to ensure—

(1) State leadership in securing and maintaining the legal rights of older individuals;

(2) State capacity for coordinating the provision of legal assistance;

(3) State capacity to provide technical assistance, training, and other supportive functions to area agencies on aging, legal assistance providers, ombudsmen, and other persons, as appropriate;

(4) State capacity to promote financial management services to older individuals at risk of conservatorship;

(5) State capacity to assist older individuals in understanding their rights, exercising choices, benefiting from services and opportunities authorized by law, and maintaining the rights of older individuals at risk of guardianship; and

(6) State capacity to improve the quality and quantity of legal services provided to older individuals.

(42 U.S.C. 3058j)

Subtitle B — Native American Organization and Elder Justice Provisions

Section. 751. NATIVE AMERICAN PROGRAM.

(b) ESTABLISHMENT.—The Assistant Secretary, acting through the Director of the Office for American Indian, Alaskan Native, and Native Hawaiian Aging, shall establish and carry out a program for—

(1) assisting eligible entities in prioritizing, on a continuing basis, the needs of the service population of the entities relating to elder rights;

(2) making grants to eligible entities to carry out vulnerable elder rights protection activities that the entities determine to be priorities; and

(3) enabling the eligible entities to support multidisciplinary elder justice activities, such as—

    (A) establishing a coordinating council, which shall identify the needs of an individual Indian tribe or other Native American group and provide the Assistant Secretary with information and recommendations relating to efforts by the Indian tribe or the governing entity of the Native American group to combat elder abuse, neglect, and exploitation;

    (B) providing training, technical assistance, and other methods of support to groups carrying out multidisciplinary efforts for an Indian tribe or other Native American group; and

    (C) broadening and studying various models for elder fatality and serious injury review teams, to make recommendations about their composition, protocols, functions, timing, roles, and responsibilities, with a goal of producing models and information that will allow for replication based on the needs of Indian tribes and other Native American groups (other than the ones in which the review teams were used).

(c) APPLICATION.—In order to be eligible to receive assistance under **this section,** an entity shall submit an application to the Assistant Secretary, at such time, in such manner, and containing such information as the Assistant Secretary may require.

(d) ELIGIBLE ENTITY.—An entity eligible to receive assistance under this section shall be—

(1) an Indian tribe; or

(2) a public agency, or a nonprofit organization, serving older individuals who are Native Americans.

(e) AUTHORIZATION OF APPROPRIATIONS.—There are authorized to be appropriated to carry out this subtitle such sums as may be necessary for fiscal year 2007, and such sums as may be necessary for subsequent fiscal years.

Section. 752. GRANTS TO PROMOTE COMPREHENSIVE STATE ELDER JUSTICE SYSTEMS.

(a) PURPOSE AND AUTHORITY.—For each fiscal year, the Assistant Secretary may make grants to States, on a competitive basis, in accordance with this section, to promote the development and implementation, within each such State, of a comprehensive elder justice system, as defined in subsection (b).

(b) COMPREHENSIVE ELDER JUSTICE SYSTEM DEFINED.—In this section, the term 'comprehensive elder justice system' means an integrated, multidisciplinary, and collaborative system for preventing, detecting, and addressing elder abuse, neglect, and exploitation in a manner that—

(1) provides for widespread, convenient public access to the range of available elder justice information, programs, and services;

(2) coordinates the efforts of public health, social service, and law enforcement authorities, as well as other appropriate public and private entities, to identify and diminish duplication and gaps in the system;

(3) provides a uniform method for the standardization, collection, management, analysis, and reporting of data; and

(4) provides such other elements as the Assistant Secretary determines appropriate.

(c) APPLICATIONS.—To be eligible to receive a grant under this section for a fiscal year, a State shall submit an application to the Assistant Secretary, at such time, in such manner, and containing such information and assurances as the Assistant Secretary determines appropriate.

(d) AMOUNT OF GRANTS.—The amount of a grant to a State with an application approved under this section for a fiscal year shall be such amount as the Assistant Secretary determines appropriate.

(e) USE OF FUNDS.—

(1) IN GENERAL.—A State that receives a grant under this section shall use funds made available through such grant to promote the development and implementation of a comprehensive elder justice system by—

(A) establishing formal working relationships among public and private providers of elder justice programs, service providers, and stakeholders in order to create a unified elder justice network across such State to coordinate programmatic efforts;

(B) facilitating and supporting the development of a management information system and standard data elements;

(C) providing for appropriate education (including educating the public about the range of available elder justice information, programs, and services), training, and technical assistance; and

(D) taking such other steps as the Assistant Secretary determines appropriate.

(2) MAINTENANCE OF EFFORT.—Funds made available to States pursuant to this section shall be used to supplement and not supplant other Federal, State, and local funds expended to support activities described in paragraph (1).

(42 U.S.C. 3058aa)

Subtitle C—General Provisions

Section. 761. DEFINITIONS.

As used in this title:
  (1) ELDER RIGHT.—The term "elder right" means a right of an older individual.
  (2) VULNERABLE ELDER RIGHTS PROTECTION ACTIVITY.—The term "vulnerable elder rights protection activity" means an activity funded under subtitle A.

(42 U.S.C. 3058bb)

Section. 762. ADMINISTRATION.

A State agency may carry out vulnerable elder rights protection activities either directly or through contracts or agreements with public or nonprofit private agencies or organizations, such as—
  (1) other State agencies;
  (2) area agencies on aging;
  (3) county governments;
  (4) institutions of higher education;
  (5) Indian tribes; or
  (6) nonprofit service providers or volunteer organizations.

(42 U.S.C. 3058cc)

Section. 763. TECHNICAL ASSISTANCE.

(a) OTHER AGENCIES.—In carrying out the provisions of this title, the Assistant Secretary may request the technical assistance and cooperation of such Federal entities as may be appropriate.
(b) ASSISTANT SECRETARY.—The Assistant Secretary shall provide technical assistance and training (by contract, grant, or otherwise) to persons and entities that administer programs established under this title.

(42 U.S.C. 3058dd)

Section. 764. AUDITS.

(a) ACCESS.—The Assistant Secretary, the Comptroller General of the United States, and any duly authorized representative of the Assistant Secretary or the Comptroller shall have access, for the purpose of conducting an audit or examination, to any books, documents, papers, and records that are pertinent to financial assistance received under this title.
(b) LIMITATION.—State agencies and area agencies on aging shall not request information or data from providers that is not pertinent to services furnished under this title or to a payment made for the services.

(42 U.S.C. 3058ee)

Section. 765. RULE OF CONSTRUCTION.

Nothing in this title shall be construed to interfere with or abridge the right of an older individual to practice the individual's religion through reliance on prayer alone for healing, in a case in which a decision to so practice the religion—

    (1) is contemporaneously expressed by the older individual—
        (A) either orally or in writing;
        (B) with respect to a specific illness or injury that the older individual has at the time of the decision; and
        (C) when the older individual is competent to make the decision;
    (2) is set forth prior to the occurrence of the illness or injury in a living will, health care proxy, or other advance directive document that is validly executed and applied under State law; or
    (3) may be unambiguously deduced from the older individual's life history.

---

[1] Section 801(a) of the Older Americans Act Amendments of 2000 (P.L. 106–501; 114 Stat. 2291) amends paragraph (34)(C), by striking "307(a)(12)" and inserting "307(a)(9)". The amendment could not be executed due to an earlier amendment made by section 101(5) (114 Stat. 2229) which redesignates paragraph (34) as paragraph (32).

[2] Section 801(b)(2)(A)(i) of the Older Americans Act Amendments of 2000 (P.L. 106–501; 114 Stat. 2292) amends paragraph (19)(C) by striking "paragraphs (2) and (5)(A) of section 306(a)" and inserting "paragraphs (2) and (4)(A) of section 306(a)". The amendment could not be executed due to an earlier amendment made by section 201(1)(B) which redesignated paragraph (19) as paragraph (16).

[3] Section 801(b)(2)(A)(ii) of the Older Americans Act Amendments of 2000 (P.L. 106–501; 114 Stat. 2292) amends paragraph (26), by striking "sections 307(a)(18) and 731(b)(2)" and inserting "section 307(a)(13) and section 731". The amendment could not be executed due to an earlier amendment made by section 201(1)(B) which redesignated paragraph (26) as paragraph (23).

[4] Margin error in the amendment made by section 801(b)(2)(C)(i) of the Older Americans Act Amendments of 2000 (P.L. 106–501; 114 Stat. 2292).

[5] Effective July 1, 2000, strike "the Job Training Partnership Act and".

[6] Effective July 1, 2000, amend paragraph (1) to read as follows: "(1) title I of the Workforce Investment Act of 1998".

[7] Error in amendment made by section 103(c) of Public Law 101–175. Should strike "Finance" and insert "Financing".

[8] Error in amendment made by section 303(a) of the Older Americans Act Amendments of 2000 (P.L. 106-501; 114 Stat. 2239) which included double quotation marks around the word "State".

[9] Section 304(2)(C) of the Older Americans Act Amendments of 2000 (P.L. 106-5011; 114 Stat. 2292) amends this clause by inserting "and older individuals residing in rural areas" after "low-income minority individuals". The amendment could not be executed because of an incorrect reference to text.

[10] Error in amendment made by section 305(b) of Public Law 102-375. Should strike "services" and insert "service".

[11] Section 307(1)(A)(i) of the Older Americans Act Amendments of 2000 (P.L. 106-501; 114 Stat. 2245) amends this subparagraph by striking "in its plan under section 307(a)(13) regarding Part C of this title," The amendment can not be executed because of an incorrect reference to text.

[12] Error in the amendment made by section 311(1)(F) of the Older Americans Act Amendments of 2000 (P.L. 106-501; 114 Stat 2251).

[13] Error in amendment made by section 171 of Public Law 100-175. Should strike "(a)".

[14] Error in amendment made by section 701 of Public Law 102-375. Should insert a comma.

[15] Error in the amendment made by section 704(2)(A)(i) of the Older Americans Act Amendment of 2000 (P.O. 106-501; 114 Stat. 2289) by striking "(A) not later than 1 year after the date of enactment of this title, establish" and inserting "strengthen and update". The amendment could not be executed because of an incorrect reference to text.

[16] So in law. Probably should read "subtitle C of title I of the Developmental Disabilities Assistance and Bill of Rights Act of 2000". See the amendment made by section 401(b)(9)(D) of the Developmental Disabilities Assistance and Bill of Rights Act of 2000 (Public Law 106-402; 114 Stat. 1739).

9 781987 462142